The Pathology of
Public Policy

The Pathology of
Public Policy

BRIAN W. HOGWOOD
and
B. GUY PETERS

CLARENDON PRESS · OXFORD
1985

Oxford University Press, Walton Street, Oxford OX2 6DP
London New York Toronto
Delhi Bombay Calcutta Madras Karachi
Kuala Lumpur Singapore Hong Kong Tokyo
Nairobi Dar es Salaam Cape Town
Melbourne Auckland
and associated companies in
Beirut Berlin Ibadan Mexico City Nicosia

Oxford is a trade mark of Oxford University Press

Published in the United States
by Oxford University Press, New York

British Library Cataloguing in Publication Data

Hogwood, Brian W.
    The pathology of public policy.
    1. Policy sciences
    I. Title II. Peters, B. Guy
    351.007'2 H97

    ISBN 0-19-878011-7
    ISBN 0-19-878010-9 Pbk

Library of Congress Cataloging in Publication Data

Hogwood, Brian W.
    The pathology of public policy.
    Bibliography: p.
    Includes index.
    1. Policy sciences. I. Peters, B. Guy. II. Title.
    H97.H624 1985 361.6'1 85-2971

    ISBN 0-19-878011-7
    ISBN 0-19-878010-9 (pbk.)

Set by Colset Ltd, Singapore
Printed in Great Britain by
St Edmundsbury Press, Bury St Edmunds

Acknowledgements

This book was made possible by the 'Manchester Connection'. In successive academic years Guy Peters (1982/3) and Brian Hogwood (1983/4) held Hallsworth Fellowships in the Department of Government at the University of Manchester. As well as enabling each of us to pursue our specific fellowship projects, it enabled us to work on this book with the additional advantage of being on the same side of the Atlantic for much of the time.

We would like to dedicate this book to all the politicians who have made the mistakes which made this book possible.

Contents

1
Pathology: The Medical Metaphor

Pathology is the branch of medicine which studies the nature of disease, especially its structural and functional effects on the body. It is essential for the treatment of patients, both by identifying disorders and by identifying the effects of those disorders which can be ameliorated or cured. Similarly, it is essential to understand the disorders which governments encounter in making and implementing public policies. But unlike medical pathology there is yet no agreed system of classification for the malfunctioning of policy-making. This book will develop, if not a complete taxonomy of those disorders, at least a listing of the most important, along with our understanding of the dynamics of the disease process involved. Related to these analyses will be some suggestions for cures, but, alas, no panaceas.

1.1 Medicine and policymaking: two inexact sciences

The analogy between the human body and the body politic has a long tradition in political philosophy. John of Salisbury, writing in the twelfth century, likened all the institutions of medieval society to various organs of the body (Dickinson, 1927). The present-day student of the policy sciences, or indeed medicine, is less likely to find this analogy appealing. The social scientist, after years of behavioralism, post-behavioralism, and increasing sophistication may be less willing to accept this metaphorical approach to understanding. The physician, with years of training, a specialized vocabulary, and some certainty in his craft, may regard social scientists as hopelessly unscientific. Our argument, however, will be that these two branches of enquiry—and action—have more in common than either would be anxious to admit (Axelrod, 1977).

The fundamental point of similarity between medicine and the social sciences is that they are both inexact sciences. The social scientist works with probability statements and statistics rather than with certainty, and works in a field cluttered with numerous

theories, paradigms, models, etc. Perhaps the fundamental characteristic of the social sciences—with the possible exception of
economics—is that there is no 'normal science' which provides a set
of intellectual puzzles, related to a comprehensive theory, for the
researcher to unravel (Kuhn, 1970). Some have argued that the idea
of a normal science in fact overstates the degree of complacency in
the physical sciences, but it is difficult to overestimate the degree of
confusion which exists in the social sciences (Feyerabend, 1978;
Blaug, 1980).

On the surface, medicine appears more certain and exact. The
training of physicians us now heavily concentrated in the fields of
biochemistry, microbiology, and a host of other 'hard sciences'.
The direction of training is so much in that direction that it has
prompted a number of people to argue that the art of healing is now
subordinated to science—to the detriment of patient care (Cousins,
1979; Illich, 1976). At a more fundamental level, medicine remains
very inexact and incapable of making the causal statements usually
associated with a science. We are all exposed daily to countless
microbes, but only a small number of us are infected. We are all
exposed daily to numerous carcinogens, but only a few of us develop
tumors. Medicine is still at the stage of making probability statements about the occurrence of disease, just as the social scientist
makes about the occurrence of crime, or the decision to vote for one
candidate or another. Likewise, the treatment of a malady, once
diagnosed, may be based upon trial and error as much as exact
knowledge. Medicine may not be, as Illich (1976) described it, a
'pseudoscience' but it lacks the certainty that many of its practitioners would ascribe to it.

Perhaps the fundamental point of tangency between these two
inexact sciences is that they both are concerned with the behavior of
humans, either as social or biological entities. Therefore, they
frequently are denied the experimental settings and the cooperation
achieved by the chemist, physicist, or even the biologist whose
subject will not talk back, does not complain about destructive
testing, and will not file lawsuits. The human element involved in the
work of social and medical scientists introduces a range of
variability that makes precise statements a virtual impossibility.

But the very factor which makes them inexact also makes these
two sciences important. Few people would deny the importance of
medical science, but a claim for the importance of the social sciences

appears to require some justification. The most fundamental justification for that claim is that if the social behavior of individuals—taken broadly to include their economic and political behavior—is understood then the possibilities of improving the conditions of society are enhanced. This raises a very important ethical point concerning the extent to which society should be manipulated by those who supposedly 'know' about how we as individuals and groups behave (Goodin, 1982, 49–54). We will leave that point for the time being, understanding that successful social engineering is almost certainly an impossibility with the current state of knowledge. What we will do is press on to explore the relationship between knowledge and action in the medical and social sciences. In both cases the practitioner would like to have firm evidence to support diagnosis and treatment, but in both the need for action may prevent that undergirding of 'hard evidence'.

1.2 As medicine is to biology, so is what to social science?

Medicine stands in close relationship to biology. Biology forms the underpinnings of knowledge for the more applied nature of medicine. Medicine could proceed without biology, by trial and error or by the belief that disease is caused by an imbalance of humors, or some other archaic model of causation. If medicine is to move beyond the stage of inexact science, it must do so by being firmly grounded in the pure sciences such as biology and chemistry.

The social scientist represents the 'pure' side of the study of human behavior (MacRae, 1976). Students are taught less about the applicability of findings than about the development of research designs to uncover the nature of underlying social processes. How are the social sciences to be applied, and in what form? We will be arguing in this book that the policy sciences, or simply policy analysis, represents the application of the social sciences to an important set of ongoing social processes. In particular, we are interested in the application of the social sciences to public problems.

Several points should be made about this application. The first is that policy analysis must by its nature cut across traditional disciplinary boundaries in the social sciences. The problems which confront the analyst rarely come in neat packages with disciplinary labels on them (Rose, 1976; MacRae and Wilde, 1976). Further, any 'solution' drawn exclusively from a single discipline is likely to be wrong, or at least incomplete. Almost any policy decision will involve economic, social, political, legal, and administrative questions which must be gotten right if the policy chosen is to be successful.

Further, the policy analyst must go beyond the social sciences and confront subject matter specialities (Hogwood, 1984). Policy is about something, and the policy analyst must confront and master at least a part of the specialized knowledge of the field(s) in question. A health policy analyst need not be able to perform an appendectomy but he must understand the basic structures of the health delivery system as well as some of the routines of treatment.

Also, the policy analyst cannot afford to be bound in a single cultural or political system. A patient is virtually the same in any country—a few genetic diseases such as sickle-cell anemia or Tay-Sachs aside—and a physician can function as well in New Delhi as in New York. A policy analyst must, however, have a complete and nuanced understanding of the culture within which he functions. But this is not enough: policy analysts must also be cognizant of policy developments in other countries and, to some extent, use the world as a laboratory for developing and testing new policy options.

Finally, just as the 'bedside manner' is important for the successful doctor, the ability to work with others in organizational settings is important for the policy analyst. The cleverest solution prescribed by the social sciences may be of little utility if it can not be 'sold' to the relevant consumers. Such salemanship depends less upon technical knowledge than upon empathy of the analyst for the problems of the client organization.

So, just as the physician frequently is called upon to be scientist, counselor, and secular priest, so too the policy analyst must be a consummate generalist. The argument can be made, in fact, that the speciality of the policy analyst is to be a generalist. If we continue the medical analogy, the relationship between the general practitioner and the policy analyst may be instructive. Medical specialists and policy specialists are certainly useful, but are useful only when there is a properly functioning referral system. The generalist in policy analysis needs to be able to identify the general nature of the policy problems and the techniques which may be appropriate for solving the problem, even if he can not implement the solutions himself. Similarly, the general practitioner in medicine would not undertake open-heart surgery although he can usually tell if the patient does have a heart problem. The generalist—medical or policy analytical—also acts as an interpreter of findings, both his own and those of specialists. As such he is the linkage between those who consume treatment and those capable of making specialized judgements and treatments. The one question which remains is whether this eclecticism is sufficient for the founding of a new discipline of its own.

1.3 Do we know what is health and what is disease?

Now that we have created this Superperson called the policy analyst we must give him or her something to do. From our perspective here, the first task would be to decide what is health and what is diseased. That is, he must decide when a policy or an organization delivering a policy has a condition which is sufficiently dysfunctional to hazard an intervention. The word 'hazard' is used advisedly, because there is no certainty that any intervention will be successful, and in fact, it may produce more harm than good. This would be what Sieber (1981) referred to as a 'regressive intervention'.

For the policy analyst, therefore, the earliest stage of analysis is 'problem search', the application of techniques to identify problems (Hogwood and Gunn, 1984). There is a danger that concentration on problems placed on the policymaking agenda by normal political processes will lead to the neglect of some issues altogether, or to others being neglected until it is too late for effective intervention (see chapter 4). Yet to suggest that professional policy analysts might supplement existing political processes and substitute their own judgement raises ethical and political questions about the role of policy analysis in a democratic political system.

No one would dispute, however, the role of the physician in diagnosing that a patient has a disease. Doctor's interventions are easier, however, because of more common agreement on what constitutes disease and because the majority of patients present themselves for treatment. Here we come to the end of the applicability of the medical metaphor. The body politic is not equipped for identification of symptoms in the same way as the human body. Further, the body politic itself is a metaphor, not a physical manifestation: policy is an aggregative concept and even when individuals do recognize their own problems they may not recognize them as policy problems. Even if individuals do identify what they consider to be policy problems, they may lack the mobilization or organization to perform the policy equivalent of 'going to see the doctor about a pain in my chest'. Bearing in mind these limitations of the self-identification of policy problems and the possibility of more active means of policy search, it is possible to point to indicators of policy problems. As these are discussed it will be increasingly clear that having established that there is a problem is merely the first stage; the next is to develop an acceptable definition of just what the problem is (Hogwood and Gunn, 1984, ch. 7).

One obvious indicator that something is wrong is where those involved in the policy area, either as clients or as members of an organization providing services, perceive that something is not functioning properly and seek changes in the existing pattern. The problem here is that there may be so many opinions about both what the symptoms of the disorder are, and what the underlying etiology is, that their reports may be less useful and more self-interested than might be hoped. Especially in social service agencies there will be conflicts over what is wrong with service delivery, and people at different levels and who perform different functions within the organization are almost certain to perceive dysfunctions differently (see chapter 3). While there is scope for analysis in problem definition, it is inevitably a value-laded and politicized activity (Hogwood and Gunn, 1984, ch. 7).

Another obvious indicator that something is not working properly is that an external body may intervene with its own perceptions that something is amiss. In the United States this is commonly the function of Congress, and more exactly the oversight organizations such as the General Accounting Office (Mosher, 1980). Likewise, other central agencies such as the Treasury or the National Audit Office in the United Kingdom may also have reason to question the activities of operating agencies and impose their conception that something was not functioning as it should. Unfortunately, just as there might be conflicts between the clients and the members of the organization itself over what the organization really should be doing, similar conflicts may arise between the operating departments and central agencies.

Organizations, just as individuals, also have their regular checkups, and diseases may be discovered then. The most common of these is the annual budgetary process, when the activities of the organization and its request for continued funding are reviewed. This offers a regularized opportunity to judge not only the financial probity of the organization, but its policy effectiveness as well. Also, an increasing amount of legislation now requires formal evaluations conducted regularly during the program's existence. This has been especially true of social legislation in the United States and has spawned an entire new evaluation research industry to service those demands (Weiss, 1972). But it is an industry with a monopsonistic purchaser, so that the doctor is less likely to deliver bad news to the client than to hand out sugar pills. Finally, there has been an increased interest in so-called 'sunset laws' which require organizations and programs to face periodic reviews with the presumption that they will be terminated if not positively renewed.

However, no procedural mechanism can answer the underlying questions about health and disease in public programs. Many of these questions arise from differences in perceptions and goals. County welfare offices may perceive that AFDC in the United States is working reasonably well, while both fiscal conservatives and clients of the program may perceive that it is disaster, although for very different reasons. Thus, to develop any definitive conception of disease in public programs may require at least minimal agreement on goals and minimal agreement on indicators of goal attainment. Neither agreement is very likely and we are therefore left with disputed goals and uncertain indicators.

Policy analysis, therefore, just as medicine remains as much an art as a science. The principal difference between medicine and policy analysis in identifying the existence of problems and correctly defining their nature lies not at the diagnostic stage but at the post-treatment or even post-mortem stage. To the previously ill-informed layman, the ability of doctors to diagnose correctly even routine disorders requiring surgery, e.g. appendicitis, may be frighteningly low. However, after treatment the doctor will normally be able to confirm or disconfirm the original diagnosis. By contrast, as students of policy evaluation are well aware, neither apparent success or apparent failure for a social program necessarily confirms or disconfirms the original problem definition.

1.4 Distinction between symptoms and disease

A physician examining a patient may discover conditions which are obviously indicative of disease, and then is forced to diagnose the disease in order to prescribe the appropriate treatment. On the other hand, the disease may be of a minor nature or so vague that the tried and true remedies, e.g. aspirin and bed rest, will produce a miraculous cure. The policy analyst is faced with a similar problem but may not even have agreement from those involved that something is wrong. Even if there is such agreement, it will be difficult to obtain agreement on what the most effective treatment might be. Organizational analysis and policy analysis tend to focus on the manifestations of underlying problems, e.g. conflict, lack of coordination, faulty communications, etc., rather than the causes of these disorders, and this may limit the effectiveness of the cures prescribed (see 1.8).

However, physicians uncertain about the cause of a disorder may succeed by treating only symptoms. The concept of 'supportive treatment' in which the patient is maintained without any attempt to treat the underlying cause of a disorder—probably because it is not known—is a useful one for the treatment of policy disorders. Intervention to address an underlying condition, if that condition is improperly diagnosed, may be disastrous and produce many more problems than it might have solved. This is especially true for organizations or programs which have been in existence for a long time and for which change might involve a major upheaval of existing understandings and upon which a significant cost would be imposed (Hogwood and Peters, 1983, ch. 6). On the other hand, if there is an underlying pathological condition producing the symptoms then delay can only postpone remedying the conditions and may allow the factors within the organization or program associated with the pathology to institutionalize themselves further.

A policy analyst will frequently encounter programs and organizations which manifest evidence of underlying pathologies. Some of the pathologies may be corrected simply by treating the symptoms. For example, if an organization which is divided internally into a number of bureaus is manifesting a lack of coordination, it may be enough simply to add a new procedure or a new routing of information which will improve that condition. Other conditions may be sufficiently advanced that the only way of producing the desired coordination is to reorganize completely the service delivery system. A careful decision must be made about just how extensive a treatment to prescribe since any intervention into an organization involves costs (Miles, 1977).

As well as the severity of the disorder, other factors must also be considered when contemplating how to intervene. One would be the degree of certainty on the outcome of the intervention. If there is good reason, based on past experience, professional advice, or whatever, to think that the intervention would be successful it may be worthwhile to intervene to attempt to attack the root causes of the pathology, otherwise not.

Finally, we may be concerned about who is harmed by a pathology. In most instances clients of the program would have the first claim that pathological conditions affecting them be remedied. However, if the program's 'clients' are recidivist offenders, victims would clearly have a stronger moral claim for altering the program. The taxpayer and the employee of the program should not be forgotten and changes which produce small benefits for the client at a large cost to taxpayers may not be acceptable remedies for policy problems.

1.5 Distinctions among diseases

The preceding section introduced a number of important questions about the nature of the disorders which might affect policies. Some disorders are relatively trivial, while others may threaten the very existence of the delivery organization. The classification of these disorders, much as human diseases, can be thought of as being on two dimensions. The first is a time dimension with short-term, acute disorders being on one end and long-term, chronic conditions being on the other (Rice, 1966). The other dimension is severity, with some disorders being terminal or possibly terminal, while others are self-limiting and ultimately not threatening. Each of these types of disorders has different implications for the policy analyst and a correct diagnosis is required in order to select an appropriate intervention, if any.

1.5.1 Acute disorders

One type of disease is the short-term acute attack. In policy and organizational terms this is a crisis. Something is going wrong, it is going wrong badly, and it is going wrong right now. These pathologies are most commonly found in the areas of defense, foreign affairs, and economic management where, because of the actions of an external force (the pathogen?) or because of the failure of the policies of the government, a crisis develops. An acute disorder tends to require swift action. Therefore, unlike most policy pathologies, there is a need for some pre-planning for coping with crises, much as hospitals have drills for the possibility of large-scale disasters. This, of course, requires that the crisis be anticipated and that its nature be correctly anticipated. With an inadequate or inaccurate definition of an impending crisis the response which would likely be worse than no response. Also, governments at times refuse explicitly to anticipate a foreseeable but undesired crisis, e.g. Harold Wilson's forbidding discussion of devaluation before 1967 in the UK.

Foreign and defense programs and organizations have the advantage in coping with crisis that they are predicated on dealing with acute situations. This is not to say that they do not fail because of inadequate information, reliance on outmoded responses, or whatever. However, most domestic programs can also confront crisis but are rarely equipped to respond swiftly and decisively. For example, in the swine-flu epidemic in the United States the dissemination of the vaccine was delayed significantly because no liability protection for the pharmaceutical companies had been planned before their asked to distribute a massive number of doses of a (relatively) untried product.

The crisis mentality may, in itself, be a pathology. If organizations are conditioned to respond only to crisis we would expect their decision-making to use inadequate information and to be based upon inadequate planning (see chapter 4). Consequently, crisis may rapidly follow crisis. On the other hand, crisis is a useful tool for organizations which want something from the policy process. It is easier to place your items on the agenda if there is a perceived crisis, and coalition-building in the legislature may be simplified.

1.5.2 Chronic disorders

Chronic diseases go on and on, and never appear to be cured. Similarly, some policy pathologies persist even after they have been identified and widely discussed. For example, a large portion of the population in the United Kingdom know about the 'poverty trap' and it has been recognized as pathological for some time, yet it persists. Likewise, the many failings of the welfare system in the

United States are widely known but there as well nothing has happened to improve the program (Tropman, 1981). How can policies which are widely recognized as poorly designed persist so long?

One obvious answer is that they do exist. That is, a program in operation requires political action to change it and inertia alone will generally keep it running. Second, as illustrated by the poverty trap, many policy problems arise from the interaction of two or more programs, each one of which may be doing a reasonably good job within its own domain. Also, as with American welfare, there may be no agreement on what the appropriate replacement for the existing policy would be, and there is a consequent fear that the replacement policy would be worse than the existing policy, especially given the upheaval required to implement the new program.

Chronic policy disorders may be more difficult to ameliorate than acute problems. After a time chronic disorders become a fact of life rather than a problem, and it is easy for policymakers to go on to something which is seen as an active, acute problem at the time. Also, policymakers may fear, when intervening in an area where many others are likely to have tried and failed, that they too may be burned by trying. Political leaders have limited resources of time and 'clout' and must decide how best to expend those resources for their own good and for the good of the nation (Lynn, 1981). Attacking an endemic problem may not be the best use of these resources.

1.5.3 Self-limiting problems

The majority of human diseases are self-limiting. That is, they will not kill the patient but will merely run their course and the body—if the body is basically healthy—will eventually throw off the disease with only supportive treatment. It is argued that this is a functional adaptation on the part of the pathogen, for if the host dies the germ or virus loses its home. This type of adaptation has been observed in some diseases, for example syphilis and tuberculosis, which when they first attacked humans produced rapid death. Over time, however, they adapted to long-term diseases requiring a number of years to produce a death if indeed they produced deaths at all (McNeill, 1976).

Almost certainly most policy disorders are also self-limiting. In most instances the policy, program or organization will continue to function even if it does not run at peak efficiency or effectiveness because of an inherent disorder in its operations. This is at once good news and bad news. It is good news because many of the newspaper headlines about crisis in this or that policy area are really journalistic excess. The Social Security system in the United States has been on the brink of disaster for the past decade but, with relatively minor adjustments, has been able to continue to send out checks regularly (Boskin, 1982). The bad news, however, is that this may lead to complacency and indeed Social Security may collapse some day. Likewise, the drain on the taxpayer's pockets from inefficient and otherwise suboptimal programs is frequently forgotten when the continuation of a poor policy is advocated on the basis that it '. . . isn't that bad'.

Self-limiting and chronic disorders have a great deal in common in that there may be a reluctance to attempt to remedy a situation because of fear that the results may be worse than the present policy and because it is known that the present system does work—after a fashion. The continuation of these policies can be explained in much the same way. Again, political leaders must question whether addressing such a problem where the results, if negative, are relatively benign, is really the best use of their limited resources.

1.5.4 Terminal diseases

Finally, some disorders afflicting policies are terminal, or potentially terminal. Such disorders so bring the utility or efficacy of a policy into question that attempts at termination may result. These disorders must be treated very differently from the self-limiting, chronic disorders mentioned above. Unless a political leader is actively interested in commiting homicide to the organization, then potentially terminal disorders will require intervention. However, it should be noted that a good number of the possible causes of terminal disorders involve environmental change which no political leader will be able to influence greatly. Thus, the threat of termination for environmental reasons may force organizations to rethink their goals and perhaps to develop alternative purposes for their existence. This has happened relatively frequently in the private sector, but less frequently in the public sector (Zald, 1970). Further, even though it may be directed at survival, some may regard goal-shifting as pathological. This would be especially true of long-term employees or clients of the organization who would feel threatened by the change.

1.6 Problems of diagnosis

The above discussion of different types of disorders in policymaking points to the difficulty of making accurate diagnoses about policy problems. In order to make a decision about whether to intervene or not, and if so how, the political leader or the policy analyst must make a correct estimation about the nature of the disorder and the likelihood that an effective remedy is available. This is difficult enough for the modern physician. even with the vastly increased range of medical hardware at his disposal. It is even more difficult for the policy analyst, who even more than the physician lacks a sure knowledge of the nature of disease and the nature of the underlying social processes involved in the generation of policy disorders.

1.6.1 Interaction effects

There is a human tendency, perhaps the result of laziness or congenital difficulties in dealing with complexity, to attempt to find a single cause for every observed phenomenon. This appears to be especially true for the problems of government where the media, citizens, or even trained analysts will attribute all the problems of modern government to the civil service, public sector unions, or whatever. Unfortunately, most problems in government lack a single, neat cause as more thoughtful comparisons of policy problems in different countries will quickly confirm.

One of the most common problems associated in making diagnoses is that two or more programs which themselves make a certain amount of sense within their own policy areas interact to produce severe problems. The poverty trap is the most famous of these. Another is the interaction of federally subsidized mortgages through the Federal Housing Administration and the Veterans Administration with new urban highways programs after World War II and the Korean War in the United States. Each of these programs was intended to assist citizens—the urban highways program being intended to help city-dwellers to go to the country at weekends, etc. However, as the programs interacted they made no small contribution to the decline of central cities in the United States. The problem for the policy analyst here is how to deal with two or more programs which are themselves not necessarily defective but which interact to produce harm. Frequently, as Wildavsky (1979) put it, 'policy is its own cause' and a new program may be required to attempt to correct for the problems created by interaction effects.

The above two examples are obvious cases in which two policies interact negatively. However, such interactions are not always so obvious, especially when they involve an interaction of some aspect of the central machinery of government with a program delivering a service. This is commonly manifested when some aspect of the civil service system interacts with a program and makes the actual delivery of the service difficult or suboptimal. For example, reliance upon personal accountability for errors made by civil servants, combined with a program allowing substantial discretion by civil servants may produce the unintended consequence of buck-passing and rigidity as opposed to the intended consequence of enhanced involvement of workers in policymaking.

1.6.2 Same symptoms, different diseases

Just as with human diseases, different underlying policy pathologies may manifest similar symptoms. A number of standard diagnoses of policy and organizational disorders, e.g. the lack of coordination, inadequate planning, or poor communication may result from very different root causes. For example, poor coordination may be the result of inadequate program design which decentralizes decisions too far, or it may be the result of inadequate attention to coordination by the management of the organization, or of conflicting objectives within the organization. Correcting this difficulty will require very different types of intervention depending upon which is the root cause of the problem, although there is a tendency simply to treat the symptoms by designing a new form of processing information within the organization. If top management is unconcerned with coordination, such a move might actually reduce coordination by giving them more information than they want and lulling others into assuming that the problem had been solved.

1.6.3 Changing symptoms and diseases

In some instances making a diagnosis and prescribing a treatment requires hitting a moving target. This is, in part, a function of the self-limiting nature of many disorders. Organizations may have mechanisms for adapting to difficulties which will at least ameliorate the difficulties if not solve them and, if the policy analyst acts after those immediately concerned with the problems have already acted, the diagnosis and remedy may be misdirected.

The problem of hitting a moving target is especially pronounced in policy areas which have a cyclical component, such as economic policy (Hood, 1976). Likewise, as both American and British educational systems have attempted to cope with changing school populations they have manifested the underlying problem of inadequate attention to well-known information first by under-supply of educational resources, and later through over-capacity.

1.7 Fashionable diseases

Diagnoses of policy disorders are cyclical, just as are some of the policy problems being diagnosed. It is simply fashionable to attribute policy disorders to certain causes at certain times. Likewise, certain treatments are fashionable at some times and not at others, just as X-rays and steroids have been in medicine. For example, during the early 1960s and early 1970s a common diagnosis for the problems of social and urban policies was inadequate participation by those most affected by the policies (Moynihan, 1967). This then led to the obvious prescription of more participation by residents of urban renewal or Model Cities neighborhoods, even though the 'cure' may ultimately have been more of a problem than the disease. Urban policies were also the victim of another fad in policymaking—area based approaches—which also have some dysfunctional characteristics (Booth, Pitt and Money, 1982). More recently, the policy fad of monetarism spread to a number of Western countries, being sold as a panacea for the economic ills of those countries and based upon the faddish diagnosis that what was wrong with the economies of these countries was an excessive growth of the money supply. These are but a few examples to illustrate the tendency of policymakers and analysts to follow the conventional wisdom of their time and to diagnose accordingly (Schon, 1972).

The examples provided above were largely failures. This was not entirely unintentional, for it illustrates that with hindsight we can see quite clearly that the conventional wisdom is frequently quite wrong. Further, even when it is right, it may be right for only a limited time or in a limited geographical or cultural setting. The number of examples of policies failing when extracted from their social and cultural setting is so large that we could not do it justice in several books (Mead, 1955). The policy analyst and the policymaker must therefore avoid being totally addicted to fashion when attempting to solve problems which confront them.

This may appear as a plea for greater conservatism in policy-making and a prescription to do nothing. It is not so intended, for indeed many fashionable ideas have a great deal of merit. But it may be instructive to look at a medical example, such as the debate over vaccination for whooping cough in the United Kingdom, to see the extent to which fashion can change and 'best practice' in medicine in one period becomes highly questionable in another. The dangers of being a slave to fashion in policymaking are even more pronounced than in medicine, assuming that medical fashion does not involve totally dysfunctional treatments such as leeches. This is because responding to fashion in policymaking frequently involves making a number of commitments to people—both workers and clients—and building organizations. Once those commitments have been made and the organizations are formed, reversing the process becomes more difficult (Hogwood and Peters, 1983). Further, even if it is possible to undo what has been done, and then to respond to another policy fashion, the clients of the program and perhaps its legislative sponsors will become disaffected and perhaps distrusting of the ability of those making policy to come up with the real answer—if indeed there is one.

On the other hand, in some policy areas fads and fashion may be the only guides. In some areas, where there is inadequate knowledge about underlying causes of the social problems being addressed, responding to fads may be seen as experiments in problem-solving. None is necessarily more likely than another to solve the problem, but government must respond. Perhaps by such a process of trial and error the real 'solution' to the problems can be found. Thus, rather than being a plea for the status quo, this section is a plea for some consideration of the reversability of the solutions arising from fads, the degree of knowledge about the policy area in question, and the intuitive appeal of a fashionable diagnosis and remedy before responding to the fad.

1.8 Sources of disease

To this point we have been discussing policymaking maladies without a real discussion of the causes of those maladies. In many cases the causes may not be known, just as the root causes of human diseases do not appear to be known (Cousins, 1979). However, we do have some idea of some of the basic problems which make policy-making such a difficult task and which appear to produce many of the disorders discussed in this book.

1.8.1 Collective problems

One of the problems of making public policy is that it is public. Many of the pathological conditions discussed in this book arise from the openness, accountability and democracy required to make and implement *public* policies as compared to making decisions in the private sector. Factors must be considered, for example distribution effects, which could be conveniently ignored were the decision to be made in the private sector. Likewise, controls over matters such as personnel systems, purchasing, freedom of information (at least in the United States), all make the conduct of public business more prone to pathological results than would be private decision-making.

A second aspect of the collectiveness problem arises from para-doxes of collective decision-making in which policies which are rational for individuals to follow, and which may maximize personal utility, become dysfunctional when they are pursued collectively. One of the most common of these is that the budgetary process becomes something akin to the 'tragedy of the commons' as too many groups seek their own ends through public activity (Hardin, 1968). It is perfectly rational for each interest group to seek benefits for its members from the public purse. They can receive a concentrated benefit and spread the cost of that benefit across the entire taxpaying population (Borcherding, 1977). However, if all organized interests engage in the same behavior costs mount and the taxpayer regards the entire system as irrational (Lewis, 1980). Some of the same occurs as 'pork-barrel' expenditures are extended across all or virtually all constituences. Total costs escalate and the impact which might be gained by a more selective program is lost.

The obverse of the collectiveness problem is the classic 'public goods' problem and the associated problem of the 'free rider'. Public goods here are referred to as those provided collectively and whose benefits cannot be withheld feasibly from any members of a group if they are provided to one of the group. The benefit secured by any individual is likely, though not necessarily, to be less than the cost to him of providing such a good for himself (and therefore to all members of the group). This may lead to the suboptimal position where, although the total benefit to members of the group is greater than total costs, the good is not provided. Except in small groups where social pressure plays a role each individual has an incentive not to agree voluntarily to contribute to the cost of providing the good since he cannot be excluded from consuming the good. Only if the state authorizes levying taxes on all those benefiting can costs be spread and the possibility of optimal provision result.

Despite the prominence accorded public goods in the economics and public choice literature, it is weak both as description and prescription for public policy. Classic public goods may not be provided by government (e.g. lighthouses in some countries at some times) or at all. Because of the poor practical guidance which the public goods concept provides for the appropriate level of provision there is a danger that the goods may actually be overprovided. Some public choice writers have argued that public goods are usually overprovided. In any case, public goods analysis does not necessarily provide a justification for taxing the whole community to provide benefits for only a part. This, then, is one aspect of the general pathology of collectiveness in that there is a mismatch between the costs and benefits accruing to individuals because of the activities of government.

'Public goods' are those where it is not practicable to deliver a policy to one member of a group without delivering it to all and where the benefit gained by any one recipient is not diminished by the fact that others are simultaneously benefiting from the same output. By contrast, with 'positional goods' the enjoyment of one person may be diminished as a consequence of other people also receiving or attempting to benefit from the good (Hirsch, 1977). The scarcity which brings this about may arise from physical limitations or social factors. A public policy example of a positional good with physical limitations is areas of outstanding beauty, such as national parks, where the satisfaction derived by any one person visiting them is decreased as more and more visitors seek to take advantage of the scenery. On the social side, attempts to increase the numbers holding educational qualifications may simply lead to higher entry qualifications at the next level being demanded, since one of the functions of such qualifications is to act as a selection filter (though education has other functions as well). The paradox of positional goods is that if government seeks to expand access to them it may destroy the value of them both to existing and new recipients. Affirmative action programs may fail to have the consequences intended because the existence of this paradox is not recognized.

1.8.2 Organizations

A second source of pathologies in the public sector is that most programs are delivered by large, complex, 'bureaucratic' organizations (see chapter 3). This is not, of course, confined to the public sector and many pathologies discussed are also found in large private organizations. The major difference is that public organizations normally lack a market to provide them information about their performance (Wolf, 1979). Lacking this, they must rely on internal control mechanisms which frequently exacerbate difficulties rather than eliminate them.

Organizations also interact with informational pathologies to make conditions for guidance and control more difficult (chapter 4). Difficulties in organizational communication have been widely noted but plague organizations nonetheless (Tullock, 1965). Even public sector organizations which might have reliable information about their performance find it difficult to use because of blockages which exist in the transmission of information up and down hierarchies. Thus, although etymologically 'government' refers to steering, it is frequently done by blind and deaf helmsmen.

1.8.3 Negative synergism

We have already alluded to this problem above (1.6.1) but we should include it in this catalog of woe. As the implementation literature reminds us, organizations do not exist alone but rather exist in large networks (Hjern and Hull, 1982). Thus, as with the poverty trap example, policies overlap and have possible negative effects when combined. Thus to understand effectively policymaking and policy pathologies we must understand the multi-organizational and multi-program environment in which policies are made and implemented, and understand the possible negative consequences they may have for one another.

1.8.4 Limits of control

Governments, perhaps even in totalitarian states, do not have total control over their citizens. This is especially true in democratic political systems where attempts are made to ensure the personal and, to some extent, economic freedoms of citizens. These freedoms, however, present difficulties for governments attempting to influence the behavior of citizens and as a result many negative consequences can arise from government interventions. For example, the State of Florida was attempting to save the wild alligator population of the state. One of the measures taken was to prohibit owners of wetlands from hunting alligators. Unfortunately, at least for the alligators, the owners of these wetlands were largely poor people who depended upon the income from alligator skins to make a living. When this was denied to them they sold off the wetlands to developers who drained them, leaving the alligators worse off than before. By failing to understand the number of options open to the landowners in a free-market society, the state government produced a negative effect rather than the intended effect (Sieber, 1981). This illustrates the general point of the inability of governments to control (although not necessarily to foresee) the behavior of a target population in reacting to policies and the perverse knock-on effects which can result.

1.8.5 Ignorance

Finally, governments can be pig ignorant about the problems they address through policies. This is not, however, entirely their fault as they frequently must make policies about events which will only occur, if at all, in the future. Governments must make forecasts about the future state of the economy, about the intentions of potential adversaries, and even about the weather, and then design policies to meet the predicted problem (Ascher, 1978). This is, to say the least, a difficult task.

In other instances, however, the ignorance of the public sector is less justifiable. At times governments choose ignorance either because they do not wish to make any reaction, or they believe the outlook is sufficiently gloomy that any reaction might only draw attention to the problem. The problems of communicating information upward in large organizations, especially information with high technical content, are well known. Consequently, while the entire structure may not be ignorant about the state of the world, those in central decision-making positions may be.

Our lack of *understanding* of social *processes* is even greater than our lack of *knowledge* of social conditions, and this lack of understanding may be greatest in the identification of aspects of the process which are malleable by policy. Even during or after program delivery our understanding may be little improved. To some extent this lack of understanding is an inevitable consequence of the complexity and dynamics of social processes. However, this is a poor excuse for designing large-scale programs based upon crucial assumptions which are unwarranted in light of current understanding. If analysis in the time available can not lead to full understanding of the likely impact of policy on social processes it may at least clarify the extent of our ignorance and the extent to which the policy initiative will be a 'leap in the dark' with possible pathological consequences.

1.9 Diagnosis as a precondition of treatment

The majority of this chapter has discussed the nature of diseases in the policymaking process and how they can be diagnosed. This is, of course, crucial since diagnosis is essential for effective treatment. The majority of the remainder of the book will be a more detailed exposition of the multiple types of pathological policies which exist even in well-managed political systems. These descriptions to some degree follow the medical metaphor which began this discussion, although we will attempt to keep the metaphor from interfering with the real policy analysis. We will conclude with a discussion of the possibility of treatment, although each section on pathologies will also contain some ideas about treatment. Our purpose is not simply to make a biological analogy for policymaking, but rather to use that as a beginning for a more complete understanding of what goes wrong with policy, and what the policy analyst can do to correct it.

2
Congenital Diseases

Unlike diseases which involve a virus infecting a body, some illnesses derive directly from the very instructions, the genetic code, which determine how a body is initially formed and subsequently develops, or are otherwise present at the moment of birth. An externally derived disease is much more susceptible to elimination by treatment or by the body's natural defence mechanisms. A congenital disease is by its very nature an integral feature of the organism. Advances in genetic engineering will make it easier to detect and forestall defects in births of future humans and other animals, but for existing beings with such diseases it may only be possible to treat symptoms or provide means of support to overcome the effects of the disease.

This is one area where the analogy between public policy and disease should not be pushed too far. It may well prove possible to alter the statutes and guidelines (the political genetic code) of an organization or program after it has already been set up. However, it may prove simpler to attempt a complete redesign. One medical analogy does seem appropriate, however. While the underlying causes are known for many congenital diseases it is often difficult or impossible to determine whether any given birth will be affected by them. However, just as genetic engineering techniques are greatly improving the chances of identifying potential offspring who might be affected, so the development of policy analysis may increase our ability to assess the likelihood of particular proposed programs suffering from particular problems.

The fact that a disease or policy problem is built into the very design of an organism at the moment of birth does not mean that its manifestations will immediately appear. A disease may not manifest itself until middle age or until triggered off by environmental factors. Further, while many congenital defects will reflect characteristics of predecessor programs, others will be specific features of the new program which did not obtain in predecessor programs. To reflect these differences, the discussion in this chapter is grouped under three headings: 'Crippled at birth', which considers features of the instructions built into the program from the start; 'Flawed inheritances', which concentrates on defects which were passed on from predecessor programs; and 'The genetic time-bomb', which considers defects which do not immediately manifest themselves, though this does not mean that they cannot be anticipated.

2.1 Crippled at birth

Programs may from the start fail to get off the ground or operate in only a limited form because of the nature of the instructions built into them. There may be too many, incompatible instructions; instructions which do not convey sufficient information; or instructions which are clearly specified but which are economically or technically infeasible.

2.1.1 Conflicting objectives

Even if we examine only official, stated goals, these are frequently multiple rather than single, and such multiple goals are often incompatible with each other. Prisons are given several goals, including the protection of society and the rehabilitation of offenders. However, the goal of protecting society may impose so many restrictions on prisoners that the goal of achieving rehabilitation is made unlikely.

It is worth distinguishing between programs which are merely 'overloaded' with multiple goals which it is not possible to achieve at once with available resources, and those which have inherently incompatible goals. Greater resources may ameliorate the first problem of multiple objectives, but not the second. Other problems of multiple objectives are merely tricky: try to design a program to alleviate family poverty which maintains a smooth and substantial increase in net income as gross income from employment increases.

Conflict among stated goals is, in principle, possible to remedy at the policy design stage. However, there may be differences between the stated and real goals of the organization, that is (to use Perrow's (1961) distinction between official and operative goals): 'what the organization is actually trying to do, regardless of what the official goals say are the aims'. Since any gap between official and real goals may not be understood even by members of the organization, it will be particularly difficult to bring the two into line. The development of alternative goals is particularly likely if the stated goals are vague (2.1.2).

So far, the discussion has been in terms of conflicts in the goals relating to individual programs or organizations. An even more widespread feature, discussed more extensively in 3.2.2, is the type of conflict which arises from the objectives set, perhaps at different times, for different programs, perhaps administered by different organizations. Such conflicts may arise between programs within the same policy area, such as the Office of Economic Opportunity (OEO) and Aid for Families with Dependent Children (AFDC) in the United States, or between programs which happen to bump into each other during implementation on the ground, for example, the Occupational Safety and Health Administration (OSHA) and the Environmental Protection Agency (EPA) in the United States.

Conflicting goals may be obvious where they are directly incompatible, but a more subtle form of conflict arises from 'multi-organizational suboptimization' (Hood, 1976), by which goals which separately sound highly desirable (minimizing length of patient stay in each section of a hospital) may have knock-on effects for the objectives of other sections or organizations, resulting in less than optimal performance overall. The conflicts and pathological effects may be different if the conflicting objectives are contained within a single organization or program as compared to conflicts across organizations. Given that governments tend not to be terribly tidy in objective and priority setting, conflicting objectives across organizations may not be terribly troublesome, while within one organization they may be disastrous.

Multiorganizational conflicts of objectives are particularly difficult to remedy either after the event or even when a new program is to be launched. There is no single moment of conception or moment of birth when the careful design of objectives can remove potential conflict. The second best approach would be to try to avoid adding to the accumulation of conflict when designing a new program (though this may be impossible if the point of the program is precisely to remedy perceived deficiences of existing policies).

Finally, we should avoid cures for conflicting objectives which might be worse than the disease. The elimination of all conflict between objectives may mean that some objectives would have to be given up altogether (would we want to abandon all attempts at rehabilitation of prisoners simply because they conflict with the protection of society objective?).

An alternative argument would be the 'survival of the fittest objective' one, recognizing that there are no mechanisms for resolving all conflicts of objectives and that there are considerable uncertainties about the achievability of objectives. By allowing the conflicts to be worked out as policies are delivered we can discover which objectives seem to have the ability to be fulfilled. By allowing all to be pursued, each group's pet objective has a chance to show its feasibility in an inevitably conflict-ridden policy world. While this may have some merit as description, the erratic nature of resource allocation and the timing of program launches casts doubt on the ability of some 'hidden hand' ensuring that intrinsically feasible objectives are achieved. In any case, while it is absurd to aim for impossible objectives (see 2.1.3), public policy is in part about aiming for difficult objectives which need special protection.

2.1.2 Vague objectives

Public policy objectives are sometimes specified vaguely (or not at all) for a number of reasons. A program may be a political response to a problem without any clear ideas about substantive outcomes (if any) expected. Alternatively, there may be conflict about objectives and values and therefore the deliberate use of a formulation which fudges these differences. Where objectives are vague but program design is specific this may cause few problems on the ground except when it comes to evaluating against one or more objectives.

However, vaguely specified objectives may be accompanied by only limited program design at legislative stage. Thus at implementation stage all the battles about conflicting objectives or values which were ignored or circumvented at the earlier stage will emerge at implementation stage instead, and program managers may have no authoritative statement to which they can appeal in seeking to resolve such conflicts.

Where there is little external concern about the operation of the program once it is under way, program staff will themselves by default have to set explicit or, more likely, implicit objectives for the program. Where, to use the British phrase, staff are good at 'reading the Minister's mind', the overall effect may be a smoother one than a formal procedure of explicitly specifying objectives. However, the

'Minister' may not have a mind to read in many instances, so that the vagueness is intended and may have been necessary to build a coalition to pass the legislation in the first place.

In other cases, program staff may input their own personal or professional values. Indeed, insofar as they were involved in decision-making about the program, they may prefer a vague formulation for that reason. Of course, the issue of objectives in the sense of overall goals and desired outcomes may never be raised. Emphasis may be laid purely on procedures. Issues such as whether to seek out clients or await applicants may be decided by default.

Whether vague objectives are regarded as pathological will depend on the perspective adopted. If smooth operation of the political system is the overriding criterion then vagueness of objectives in the absense of consensus may be desirable, though even here conflict may simply be postponed until a later stage of the process.

If substantive achievements from the use of scarce resources is the concern, the vagueness of specification of objectives may lead to resources being used to ends which would not be priorities if explicit decisions were taken. There may be different interpretations of vague objectives by different subunits, though this may be regarded as a desirable source of experimental variation rather than a problem. The idea of experimentation is one of the presumed virtues of federalism and the associated decentralized implementation of programs (see Wildavsky, 1979, ch. 6).

In circumstances where it is not clear what the purpose of a program is, it is difficult or impossible to judge whether it is 'working' or whether alternative programs would be more effective or efficient. The fact that vagueness of objectives arises from characteristics of decision processes in a number of Western countries means that attempts to remove the pathological consequences cannot be directed only at the specific programs concerned.

2.1.3 Impossible objectives

The world is full of clearly undesirable phenomena which public policy can be aimed at remedying. The temptation in launching programs to tackle such ills as poverty or pollution is to set as the target their complete elimination. Yet such absolute targets may be unattainable or attainable only at grossly disproportionate cost. The setting of such targets may engender cynicism because they are known to be unattainable. This cynicism may spill over from attitudes about a particular program to cynicism about public policy and the political process more generally.

Because the objectives are known to be impossible, there are no *useful* targets to aim for, and no realistic criteria by which performance can be judged. Relatedly, there can be no guidance about the appropriate level of resource inputs. The consequence is that the setting of an impossible target may actually lead to a *lower* level of achievement than is realistically and cost-effectively possible. In some situations, however, seemingly impossible objectives can serve as motivating devices. This would seem to be particularly likely for highly professionalized and capable workforces. An analogy with technology-forcing legislation can be made. When the Clean Air Act was passed in 1972 in the United States, the technology to produce the reductions of pollution mandated did not exist. Before the time mandated in the Act, however, it had been developed. This does involve something of a gamble, however, and if the firms had chosen to drag their feet, little or no reduction in pollution might have been achieved. The crucial condition for improvement-forcing objective-setting is that the objectives should not be intrinsically impossible, and should be attainable or approachable as a result of greater effort or innovations in approach.

The remedy may be to ask how much of something undesirable (or how little of something desirable) we are prepared to put up with given the costs (including opportunity costs) of achieving that level. To quote the title of an article in this vein: 'How polluted are we—and how polluted do we want to be?' (White, 1979).

Aaron Wildavsky (1979, ch. 2) suggests, in typically pugnacious style, that the problem of unattainable or difficult to attain objectives is best tackled by abandoning an objective-setting approach altogether and redefining the nature of a public policy 'problem': 'a difficulty is a problem only if something can be done about it . . . Analysis, in which solutions tell us whether we have problems, involves learning what we collectively are constrained to prefer by finding out what we cannot get' (Wildavsky, 1979, 42). This does not preclude a role for seeking answers to problems: 'Analysis also helps us discover what we might prefer by suggesting problems that might call for new solutions', but the focus is clearly on *what we can readily do is a solution, and anything else isn't a problem*. The idea of solutions chasing problems rather than *vice versa* is also a feature of the 'garbage can' model of decision-making (Cohen, March, and Olsen, 1972).

While we see an important role for seeking to identify potential opportunities as well as potential problems at issue search stage, we consider that a focus on objectives can be retained while still being practical. Objectives can be rescued from both over-optimistic planners and over-pessimistic sociologists (Hogwood and Gunn, 1984, ch. 9). A checklist of the kind of questions which would be asked in a realistic objective-setting exercise is suggested by Hogwood and Gunn (1984, ch. 9):

Where are you now?
Where do you want to be, and how will you get there?
What's stopping you?
What do you need from other agencies?
What is required of whom in your agency?
How will you handle multiple objectives?
What will you regard as success?
Should success be quantified?
On what conditions is success contingent?
What will you do if objectives are not achieved?

'To boldly go' is not the same as to blindly go. To be open-eyed rather than starry-eyed about objectives does not mean that programs to tackle important problems will lack impetus. Indeed, we have suggested that there may be a paradox: the higher you aim, the less you may achieve.

2.2 Flawed inheritances

We have noted elsewhere (Hogwood and Peters, 1983) that a large and increasing proportion of policy changes consists of replacement of existing policies, that is, policy succession, rather than completely new ones. To a greater or lesser extent, the 'new' program will be administered by the same staff as administered the old, take over organizational units and procedures and may have continuing commitments arising from the design of the old program rather than the purpose of the new. None of these features is intrinsically patho-logical. Indeed, the opposite is true in that the problems of launching a program at all would be much more severe if there were no personnel experienced in running similar programs. Nevertheless, there can be pathological features arising from these inheritances.

2.2.1 Inherited personnel

There are many ironical features about public policy pathologies and none more so than that success in generating commitment by staff to a program may make it more difficult to follow through a replacement program than if the predecessor organization had been less successful. Staff may feel that they or their clients have been betrayed.

Previous patterns of recruitment may have implications for an organization which is delivering policies which have subsequently undergone change. Organizations tend to recruit personnel based on their policy emphasis at that time. For example, the Environmental Protection Agency in the USA could have been expected to attract environmentally concerned individuals, as to some extent has the US Department of the Interior. As a consequence, any attempt to alter in any significant fashion the policies being administered by these organizations in a direction that would be less environmentally conscious could be expected to encounter opposition, and this is indeed what happened under the Reagan administration from 1981. Of course, from the perspective of supporters of the previous policy stance such resistance was the reverse of pathological, emphasizing that what counts as a public policy pathology is even more subjective than in the practice of medicine.

More subtly, certain types of professions tend to be attracted into particular organizations, bringing with them a particular conception of how policy problems should be approached. For example, an agency which has recruited physicians to treat mental health problems will find it difficult to escape the 'medical model' of mental disease in favour of a more social or community-based conception of the causes and treatment of mental disease (Foley, 1975).

With the increasing professionalization of society and the public service, the possibilities of conflicts among professionals have increased when a policy succession is undertaken. Each profession specifies how a particular problem should be defined and treated, and if different professions are forced to interact they will tend to conflict over control of clients. Since professional rigidities tend to be enshrined in law and in practice, policy successions may be expected to encounter these institutional problems as well as the behavioral problems arising from individuals (see 2.2.2).

For example, the Model Cities Program in the United States was intended to coordinate all the government services delivered to the residents of the model neighborhoods. In practice, however, the professionals within the program tended to define the problems of the clients according to their own specialities so that persons presenting themselves first to a health agency might be referred to other health agencies but rarely to other types of services. One of the main purposes of the program was effectively defeated (Bowman, Main, and Peters 1970).

The effects of the inheritance of personnel may persist well beyond the initial period of policy change. Organizations tend to recruit their personnel selectively and to train them to meet perceived organizational needs. However, those perceived needs may change, so that within a single organization there may be individuals who have been recruited under a number of different sets of values and policy perspectives. This 'age lump' phenomenon can be particularly troublesome when the leadership of the organization was recruited and trained in one era and the lower echelons recruited under a very different set of circumstances (see also 5.5).

2.2.2 Inherited procedures

All organizations develop routines and procedures in delivering public policy to meet a range of requirements from accountability to reducing the variety of individual cases to a more manageable set of categories, each of which will be dealt with in a certain way. An organization which unthinkingly inherits the procedures of predecessor organizations may find that these are being used intentionally or unintentionally to subvert the purpose of the new policy.

Some organizations, especially central agencies, may impose certain requirements on other policies which do not affect the carrier but do affect the receiver in the same way as a carrier of a congenital disorder, such as mothers of hemophiliacs. Similarly, some common statutes, such as the Official Secrets Act in Britain and the Administrative Procedures Act of 1946 in the United States, may have the same effect.

Organizational procedures used to slow down change can relate to internal staff or budgetary requirements or to relationships with clients. For example, an organization may slow down change by engaging in required consultation with organized interests affected by the succession. As these groups are apt to be as apprehensive as the members of the organization, the feedback from the consultation can be used to avoid the real intent of the policy succession.

Routines developed for different policy emphases may be inappropriate for the new. For example, procedures which relied on clients presenting themselves to the agency and the agency staff then selecting from among the potential clients those who would benefit most (who are not necessarily the most needy) would be inappropriate for a policy which sought to alleviate the most difficult cases (see also 9.4 on 'creaming'). A new policy which is implemented through procedures developed for other policies may well be unsuccessful, since the outmoded mechanisms may have the effect of keeping an old policy actually in operation.

2.2.3 Inherited commitments

Commitments entered into under previous programs may continue to entail financial outlays and the employment of administrators for years to come. This can arise either from legal or quasi-contractual considerations or from the more political consideration that if existing beneficiaries are allowed to continue under the terms of the old program then the new program will be easier to push through for the future, since potential beneficiaries will tend to be less identifiable and less mobilized.

An example of an inherited commitment of a quasi-contractual kind was the program of industrial investment grants which was replaced by the Conservative government in Britain in 1970. There continued to be a section of the Department of Industry responsible for administrating the grants up to the late 1970s (in the meantime there had been other policy changes). This continuation related to projects planned at the time of the change which were therefore eligible for assistance under the program.

In the United States, the 'grandfathering' of the clients of a program after it is scheduled for termination or replacement results in significant inherited commitments. (The term grandfathering comes from the *post bellum* South where, to prevent illiterate whites from being disenfranchised by literacy requirements, persons were given the right to vote if their grandfather had had that right. The term has now been extended to include any retention of rights or entitlements.) For example, dependents of Social Security recipients in the USA are no longer eligible for benefits for higher education—unless they began their education before 1 July 1982. Students who had begun were eligible for benefits for up to four years.

These leftover 'policy residues' (Hogwood and Peters, 1983, 81–3) may be less significant than the building in of inherited commitments in the replacement program. Because these inherited commitments have an already existing status and perhaps formal entitlement attached to them, they may be given priority over newer elements of a program. The accumulation of past commitments may severely reduce the scope for policy variation or innovation. However, any attempt to repudiate inherited commitments would raise both political difficulties and perceived problems of equity, especially if such commitments are an 'entitlement' arising from previous payment of contributions (for a fuller discussion of entitlements, see 7.2).

2.3 The genetic time-bomb

2.3.1 Delayed-action clauses

Policies may be designed with in-built problems which do not have an immediate apparent effect, but have delayed-action costs. This may be more or less deliberate in that political benefits are arranged to come early and costs later or represent a failure to think through long-term consequences or simply wishful thinking. Some degree of cost-shifting to the future is more or less inevitable; where it is relatively short-term and not disproportionately large relative to total government activity there may be few adverse effects—simply a constant shifting of costs into the future which more or less averages out over time. However, where there is a large time shift, with very large scale costs not directly offset by benefits and continuing into the long term, then the policy design can be said to be truly pathological.

One such example is the British 'second pension' system which started to come into operation from 1975. This provides for a second pension related to previous earnings on top of the existing flat-rate state pension. Employees have to join either a contracted-out private pension scheme (which is partly inflation-proofed by government) or the state second pension scheme. At first sight, this is a case where the costs to employees come first and the benefits only later—it will not be until 1998 that the first full pension will be payable. However, the government element of the second pension scheme is not funded; the actual payment of the second pensions will depend on the willingness of taxpayers at the beginning of the twenty-first century to pay from their wages for a higher level of benefit than those future beneficiaries are currently prepared to pay to current pensioners. The potential political problems depend heavily on the growth prospects of the British economy. The long time-scale involved—from 1998 onwards—might seem to indicate a lack of urgency in dealing with what is currently only a hypothetical problem, but the longer the current system is allowed to remain in place, the greater the sense of entitlement amongst those paying contributions nominally towards the second pension scheme—even though their contributions do not actually fund the state element of their future second pension.

Similarly, the pensions paid to state and local government employees in the USA have the same underfunding as the UK second pension. It has been common for both state and local governments, when faced with wage demands from their employees, to buy them off with generous pensions in the future. These were never funded since the governments were already suffering from fiscal stress, and there is a very big time-bomb ticking away. (For a general discussion of the pathology of entitlements, see 7.2.)

2.3.2 Threshold level effects

We have already commented that a number of public policy pathologies have particularly ironic features. A policy may be designed to try to avoid a threshold being reached yet actually increase the adverse effects if the threshold should nevertheless be exceeded. A classic case in counter inflation policy arose from Stage 3 of the incomes policy of the Conservative government of 1970-4 in the UK, which came into effect on 7 November 1973. Pay increases were to be allowed on the basis of up to £2.25 a week per head, which would help the lowest paid, or on the basis of up to 7 percent per head, subject to a maximum of £350 a year per individual. Retail prices in the year to October had been increasing by 10.3 per cent per annum. To make the proposed basic pay increases more acceptable, a threshold arrangement was built into the incomes policy by which increases of 40p a week were triggered if the Index of Retail Prices rose by 7 percent within twelve months, with a further 40p for every full 1 percent rise in excess of 7 percent. In the event, the 7 percent threshold was triggered by April 1974, and the year on year inflation rate by October 1974 was 17.1 percent. Leaving aside arguments about ultimate and proximate causes of inflation, this particular incomes policy, far from helping to reduce inflationary pressures, contributed to the very high British inflation rates of the mid 1970s. A policy which (allowing for various additional payments) provided for initial increases of at least the level of the triggering threshold and then provided for further payments to be triggered as soon as every additional percentage point was passed can be seen to be a poor policy design.

Threshold-triggering policies should be used with caution even in cases with a proportionately smaller initial increase if there is a high risk that the threshold will be triggered and the result of the triggering will feed directly back to the variable which the policy is trying to control. Against that, there is the problem of designing political incentives to make acceptable basic increases below the level of inflation during the previous time period. To include threshold triggers of this sort (especially multiple threshold triggers) may, however, be to build a self-destruct mechanism into a policy instrument.

A broader threshold problem (noted in particular by Hood, 1976) is the difficulty of introducing any cut-off point in respect of which benefits are made payable, taxation levied, or penalties imposed. This might be in the form of an absolute cut-off—for example, to exclude small-scale cases—or in terms of higher rates of benefit or taxation levied at different price levels or income levels. Where the behavior of those being taxed or provided with benefits does not alter, this can lead to apparently inequitable results, with two cases almost identical but on opposite sides of the threshold being treated differently. In cases where additional taxation is levied on the whole of an amount rather than the additional tranche, as in the case of British stamp duty payable on certain transactions, there can be perverse results, with taxation on the additional amount which has taken the taxpayer over the threshold amounting to several hundreds or even thousands percent.

Such inequities may be regarded as an inevitable consequence of having to design administratively workable systems. However, those adversely affected by such thresholds may alter their behavior so that they are no longer affected by the policy at all, or fall in a different threshold band. Thus lawyers in Britain handling the purchase of a house whose price was £500 over threshold level for paying stamp duty would ensure that £500 of the price was deemed to be for carpets and other 'non-fixed' fittings, so that the house part of the transaction will fall below the threshold for stamp duty beyond which tax is payable on the *whole* house price.

In the cases of taxation or benefit levels, the 'threshold effect' is a particular form of the disincentive effect associated with any non-flat-rate system. However, the problems associated with all-or-nothing or increased rate on the whole cut-off points can be particularly acute. There is no simple cost-free way of removing pathological threshold effects, but there is a trade-off between administrative simplicity and (a) the direct inequitable effects of thresholds; (b) the losses arising from adjustment behavior to avoid the adverse effects of a thresholds; (c) the increased costs of administration arising from attempts to counter avoiding or evading behavior.

Another form of threshold effect arises where a minimium level of resource input is required to obtain any meaningful level of policy outcome (see 7.6). The reverse pathology is to perceive the need for a large-scale minimum effort where such a threshold is arguably not necessary for progress to be made (if indeed, progress can be made at all). Schulman (1980, ch. 6) suggests that the large-scale commitment in the USA to the War on Cancer was inappropriate and may even have been counter-productive because the comprehensive planning generally associated with large-scale projects induces a rigidity of focus, which is functional for programs with a genuine large but minimum scale target, but inappropriate where there is theoretical uncertainty and a need for flexibility.

Thus we can see two main types of threshold where there can be pathological effects: (1) where the threshold is an artefact of the policy itself (pay thresholds, tax bands); (2) where the threshold relates to intrinsic features of the problem to be tackled.

2.3.3 Bumping into environmental changes

Policy problems may arise from characteristics of the design of a policy, but may come into effect only when some event or phenomenon external to government comes into play. The possibility of such external impacts and their implications for the program may be more or less foreseeable at the time of the policy design. Policies can be designed to be as shock-proof as possible, but, as we will see, this may be unacceptable if the design results in inequities across time or appears to contradict the basic purpose of the program.

One example of potentially vulnerable programs is the type of social benefit where the total budget is contingent on the number of people eligible. Vulnerability is further increased if benefit levels are inflation-linked, since inflation in times of economic depression may be higher than nominal growth of the economy or incomes of those paying contributions.

In the UK the contributory National Insurance system launched in 1948 was supposed to be designed to cover all major sources of loss of income, such as sickness, unemployment, and retirement. However, as economic problems grew in Britain the costs to the national insurance system grew at the same time as the basic concept of the system fell apart. The vulnerability of the national insurance system was limited by the built-in cut-off of benefit after one year (considerable savings were separately made by the abolition of earnings-related supplement to benefit). However, this meant that the unemployed then had to rely on the non-contributory but means-tested supplementary benefit, a classic case of cost-shuffling between programs. By 1983/4, of those unemployed receiving some kind of benefit only 39 percent were receiving unemployment benefit and 61 percent were relying on supplementary benefit only. Thus the vulnerability of the national insurance system has been contained, but at the expense of the fading away of one of its major purposes. The vulnerability of the social security system has been passed on to supplementary benefit, and attempts to reduce the vulnerability of supplementary benefit to economic problems would contradict its purposes as the ultimate safety net in the British system.

Despite initial smothering by the British government of a 'Think Tank' report, by the end of 1983 a debate had started about future economic and demographic changes which would have implications for public expenditure on welfare programs. Echoing the heading of this section, one newspaper headline was 'Thatcher floats her fears of benefits "time-bomb" ' (*The Times*, 25 Jan. 1984). She appeared to be particularly concerned about the cost of pensions and the

National Health Service in the medium term. In fact, official projections are for a slight increase in the number of pensioners until the middle of the 1980s, followed by a significant fall in their number until the second decade of the twenty-first century. Until the end of this century, the dependency ratio, that is the number of people of working age per pensioner, improves on current assumptions about birth rates (though whether those of working age will actually be working and paying taxes will, of course, depend on the state of the economy). However, a 'time bomb' effect subsequently becomes apparent, with the number of pensioners estimated to rise from 9.3m in 2001, to 9.8m in 2011, to 10.2m. in 2016, and 11.8m in 2033. Over the same period, the number of work force members per pensioners is estimated to drop from three to two.

Social benefits are particularly vulnerable, both on the benefits side and the resource base to fund them, to environmental effects, particularly demographic trends and the state of the economy. Policy design can in part contain such vulnerability (e.g. by funding for known demographic trends, by avoiding firm guarantees about rates of benefit), but to seek to eliminate vulnerability completely would defeat the purpose of the policies in the first place. At least part of such vulnerability will inevitably be passed on to the taxpayers of that time.

3
Organizational Pathologies

Governments are not monolithic structures marching to the tune of a single drummer. They are complex, composed of a large number of organizations with a variety of relationships to the central policy and coordination offices of government, e.g. the President or Prime Minister. Further, even those chief executives and their associated central agencies may themselves be highly differentiated and engaged in internal warfare (Porter, 1980, 221-3). The increasing size, complexity and technical competence of government may result in there being as many drummers as organizations, and in government by 'non-consensual directions' (Peters, 1982).

If we continue the biological analogy, the problem of coordinating organizations within government is analogous to the necessity of an organism having all its constituent subsystems coordinated, e.g. the respiratory and cardio-vascular systems must supply sufficient food and oxygen to muscle cells when they are working, but reduce that supply when the muscles are at rest. Unfortunately, coordination of government organizations is not as easy as coordination in biological systems. The components of the latter have no wills of their own and are designed to cooperate, having automatic triggers to produce coordination. Organizations, or their members, have the capacity for independent thought and may not want to cooperate or simply may not understand the signals sent attempting to produce coordination. The biologist may see an occasional case of an organism with internal coordination problems, but the policy analyst and public executive see it everyday.

3.1 Stereotypes of the pathological bureaucrat

The above statements should not be taken as an endorsement of the position, frequently expressed in both academic and popular media, that public bureaucracies are only concerned with their own interests and therefore tend to disregard 'the public interest'. One strand of this literature comes from public-choice economists who argue that bureaucrats (in most models the bureau head) are purely utility maximizers with the maximand being budget size (Niskanen, 1971). The bureau exists in bilateral monopoly with the legislature, with the bureau being the only supplier of services to the client and the legislature being the only source of supply of funds. The control of expertise and information by the bureau is argued to allow them to increase their budgets to a level up to twice as much as required to produce their services. Further, because of the imputed maximizing behavior, bureaus do not seek cooperation with other bureaus, but rather engage in a *bellum omnia contra omnes* for funds.

The elegant economic analysis developed by Niskanen and others is based upon very shaky foundations. The first and most basic is the assumption that bureaucrats have an incentive to maximize the size of their bureau. The individual bureaucrat has little to gain personally, given relatively inflexible pay scales and pay based to some extent upon longevity. While those at the bottom or middle ranks of an organization may be able to advance more rapidly due to new positions being opened, the bureau chief (the budget maximizer in Niskanen's model) could gain very little (Breton and Wintrobe, 1975, 204–5). In fact, in career terms, the bureaucrat's position may be improved by moving from a large and less prestigious organization to a smaller and more important one, e.g. the Treasury in the United Kingdom. Increasing bureau size may only generate managerial difficulties for the bureaucrat (Williamson, 1967), an outcome which could conflict with the other common stereotype of the bureaucrat as interested primarily in minimizing difficulty rather than maximizing budgets.

Even if the individual bureaucrat had incentives to maximize budget size, it might not benefit the organization. This is especially true as expansion might mean adding new functions to an existing structure. Empirically this happens rarely and new functions characteristically mean new organizations. Even if new functions are added to an existing organization (the power of organized interests will usually prevent it) it may weaken the bureau's position. The farther a new function is from the organization's 'heartland' the more the addition would weaken the organization's identity in the mind of its clients, and more importantly in the mind of its legislative sponsors. Bureaus may do better to do one thing and do it well rather than diversifying.

Finally, both empirically and theoretically competition does not appear the most appropriate course for bureaucratic action. Empirically, there is as much evidence of cooperation as conflict when organizations can make such decisions (Goodin, 1975; 1982). Theoretically, organizations may have more to gain by minimizing the resources used in competition and conflict and utilizing those resources for service delivery (Davis, 1973).

If the economic approach to bureaucracy disregarding the public interest does not appear sustainable, then a second approach may be. This approach argues that, instead of being budget maximizers, bureaucrats are change minimizers. Getting a bigger budget and more legislative authority is hard work, especially given the limited individual rewards which are likely to accrue. A simpler approach is to fight or ignore change and attempt to lead as easy a life as possible within the existing organizational framework (Peacock, 1983). This is similar to Allison's (1971) 'organizational process' approach to decision-making in which organizations code any new information or problems in terms of their existing procedures and problem definitions. This will obviously produce a stable life for those in the organization but will not be the best means of serving the public in a time of rapid change.

Another aspect of the slothful conception of the bureaucrat is discussed in a growing volume of literature, especially in the United Kingdom, arguing that the civil service dominates policymaking and that the 'departmental view' dominates over the policy ideas of elected politicians. The unwillingness of bureaucratic organizations and their personnel to respond to changes is argued to be a denial of the popular will (Kellner and Crowther-Hunt, 1980).

We do not impute such a willful denial of coordination or cooperation as the cause of all organizational problems within government, although we will discuss some aspects of these causes. Rather, we will assume that most organizations at most times are attempting to serve the public interest. In fact, many of the problems we will discuss arise from excessive zeal rather than the absence of zeal in pursuing the public interest. The central problem is the tendency of organizations to equate their own activities with the public interest. The majority of public organizations and their members believe in what they are doing and its contribution to the public welfare. But membership in an organization narrows the individual's vision and promotes a narrow perception of the public and public welfare. Thus, employees of the US Department of Agriculture may believe that the public is served by higher farm prices so that farmers can earn a better living, while all Americans are consumers rather than producers of food and would benefit from lower prices. As a detached observer we can see that 'healthy' policymaking involves balancing a number of interests. But working within the context of a single organization such global thinking may only cause doubt and confusion. Given our more benign perception of organizations and their behavior, the problems we will discuss arise primarily from the narrowness of organizational task definitions and from the inevitable rigidities within complex organizations, especially complex *public* organizations.

Several factors affect the extent to which organizations manifest these pathologies. One is the level of differentiation of organizations performing quite similar tasks. For example, a large number of organizations within the US federal bureaucracy provide social services: the Department of Health and Human Services (and its numerous agencies), the Department of Housing and Urban Development, the Veterans Administration, etc. An argument can be made that co-ordination would be improved, and services to clients also improved, by placing these agencies within a single large organization (Miles, 1977). While this would present numerous new problems of internal complexity and control, it might eliminate some of the contraditions and complexity of current social policy (Lynn, 1981, 26–33). But even within a single nominal organization there may be internal differentiation limiting the effectiveness of any reorganization. This would be especially true in the United States where cabinet departments are best viewed as 'holding companies' composed of relatively autonomous agencies (Seidman, 1980).

Organizations with readily defined missions, especially missions which result from policy initiations, present more difficulties in coordination and control than organizations with less clearly defined goals, or goals which have become a part of conventional government activity. As Downs (1972) discusses in a different context, there is an issue-attention cycle in which government and the public become highly agitated about an issue, but then gradually lose interest. While concern is at its height, those administering the program have a relatively broad mandate allowing them to evade control from above and from the interorganizational network. This freedom could be seen in the early days of the New Deal, and to some extent in the early years of the Environmental Protection Agency. Likewise, organizations with clearly defined clientele groups are more likely to present problems of coordination and to be hyperactive than organizations without clear environmental support.

This is true not only because such an organization is sure of support, but also because a powerful client group tends to constrain the conception of the public interest even more than is so in other organizations. For most such organizations, their legal mandate is to serve their clients to the greatest extent possible, but in so doing they risk societally dysfunctional outcomes because of higher taxes and incoherent services (Hardin, 1968).

Another factor affecting the behavior of organizations and potentially producing pathological behavior is the nature of the personnel employed. For example, organizations employing large numbers of professionals present different problems in coordination and control than do organizations with more 'bureaucratic' personnel. Professionals present difficulties because of their expertise, as well as their access to support and alternative normative structures outside the organization. A physician employed by government can always return to private practice and tends to rely upon professional norms for guidance when those norms and organizational norms conflict (Abrahamson, 1967). The stereotypical bureaucrat, on the other hand, presents difficulties because of permanence rather than the ability to depart. The bureaucrat often cannot leave, usually does not want to leave the organization, and may cling rather slavishly to formal rules which protect them from change and dismissal for inappropriate actions (Merton, 1940). Thus, in Hirschman's (1970) terminology, the problem with controlling the professional is a problem of exit, while controlling the bureaucrat is a problem of excessive loyalty.

The treatment of organizational diseases, just as the treatment of human diseases, may be iatrogenic. The treatment may produce as much or more harm as the disease itself. Organizational diseases, again like human diseases, are frequently self-limiting and intervention by an organizational superior to impose greater control over a subordinate may only produce less control and less desired organizational performance (Crozier, 1964). As in the classic Merton (1940) model of goal displacement, as superiors attempt to control subordinates those subordinates will focus attention on compliance with the rules rather than the ostensible purposes of the organizations. When the failure of the organization members to pursue stated goals becomes obvious, there may be increasing attempts by superiors to use authoritative control. This leads to declining performance and increasing rigidity and rule enforcement. Similarly, Crozier (1964, 110) found that if organizations attempt to impose control, subordinates attempt to locate areas of uncertainty and by controlling those areas exert power. Thus, somewhat paradoxically, managerial styles may influence the development of organizational pathologies, and attempts by managers to prevent or correct low-level pathologies may produce epidemics.

With this basic understanding of organizational pathologies in mind, and with some hypotheses about the causes of these pathologies, we will now discuss a number of specific pathologies. The majority of these pathologies do not arise from malignant desires of power hungry or chronically lazy public officials, but from the desire of organizations to accomplish their appointed tasks. It is not in the desire to perform the tasks, but in the excessive desire, that the pathologies arise.

3.2 Multiorganizational suboptimization

Organizations do not exist alone but rather exist in a very crowded environment populated by other organizations. This may be true even within a single large organization, and some classic pathologies of organizations, e.g. conflict between line and staff, occur within a single differentiated organization as well as between organizations. Thus, it is dangerous to try to understand organizational behavior as a 'single, lonely organization,' but rather that behavior must be understood as an attempt to reach organizational goals through an ongoing pattern of conflict and cooperation with other organizations (Porter and Hjern, 1978). The choice of conflict or cooperation depends upon particular contexts and circumstances (Davis, 1973).

The multiorganizational environment not only presents political problems of reaching accomodations with other organizations, it also generates several causes for pathologies. Pathologies arise as each organization pursues its own goals without reference to the overall goals of the political system (assuming those are known), or goals of other organizations with complementary functions (Hood,

1976). As in one of the fundamental paradoxes of social behavior, individuals or groups each rationally pursuing their own goals may produce results which are socially irrational (Hardin, 1968). One of the most important of these in present-day government is that by pursuing their own goals through increased budgets organizations produce an overall level of expenditure which many citizens regard as undesirable.

3.2.1 Lack of coordination

The simplest form of multiorganizational suboptimization is lack of coordination between two or more organizations whose activities might affect each other adversely without coordination. These adverse effects may negate the effectiveness of one or all programs because of their countervailing impacts. This is exemplified in the famous 'poverty trap'. In the United Kingdom—and to a much less extent the United States—the interaction of tax policies with means-tested benefits produces situations in which an individual who is economically deprived has little incentive, or actually a negative incentive, to earn additional income in the market (Piachaud, 1980). For example, if a family at an income level of £96 a week earned an additional pound of income the result was a net loss of almost two pounds a week because of loss of free school meals (*Social Trends*, 1982, 91).

Less seriously, the effects of the absence of coordination may be redundancy or inefficiency in certain services. For some government activities redundancy and an absence of coordination is desirable, e.g. the collection of intelligence (Landau, 1969). However, for many other services it only means wasting scarce resources. Such redundant provision of service has most commonly been cited in inner cities where a panoply of public service agencies may provide similar services to the same clients. Frequently organizations are imposed over existing organizations to attempt to generate greater coordination—commonly without great success (Booth, Pitt and Money, 1982).

Finally, an absence of coordination may produce wasted time and resources for citizens rather than for government itself. The most obvious example of such lack of coordination is the numerous reports which businesses had been required to file for government in the United States. Some reports merely duplicated information requested on forms from other agencies and at times asked for the same information presented slightly differently (Buchholtz, 1979). The net result of this data collection may be a great deal of wasted effort and exasperation for businessmen with little appreciable enhancement of the quality of information available to government.

How does the lack of coordination among organizations arise? The most extreme case is organizations not wanting to coordinate their activities. This reluctance may arise from factors such as jealousy, personality conflicts, or sincere differences of opinion over the best means of serving clients. For example, when organizations providing services to the mentally ill and substance abusers in a Southern state were encouraged to combine, the mental health centers and the substance abuse centers failed to coordinate their activities and move into common facilities, even though those common facilities and the cross-training of personnel would result in substantial financial savings. The ostensible reason was that substance abuse personnel believed their clients would be reluctant to come to a facility which might label them as being mentally ill. They were willing to accept the label of alcoholic or drug abuser but did not want anyone to think they were crazy. Consequently, substance abuse personnel did not believe they could adequately serve their clients if they coordinated their activities as desired by their superiors.

An absence of coordination may also arise from the simple failure to communicate. Organizations may not be sufficiently aware of their placement within in the interorganizational network, or they may define the amount and type of information necessary to transmit to their colleagues too narrowly. An organization such as a city water department may regard its repair schedule as of interest to no one but itself, but when the same street is dug up and patched by the water department one week and is dug up and patched by the sewer department the next week, it becomes clearer that there is some wider interest in this mundane detail. Within a single organization, it is sometimes considered that communication upward of information will be followed by the dissemination of that information among those with a need to know throughout the organization. That is rarely the case and individuals at lower levels must compensate for almost inherent faults in hierarchical communications (see chapter 4).

Associated with the above problem is the problem of secrecy.

Secrecy has obvious benefits in certain situations but may be counterproductive (see 5.2). It forces other organizations needing information kept secret to hedge their bets against the true nature of the world thereby perhaps unwisely using their resources. For example, secrecy surrounding the announcement of the Budget in the United Kingdom not only affects individuals who must decide how much alcohol and tobacco to buy before tax increases, it also affects other ministers and their ministries, especially social programs whose benefit structure might be improved by closer coordination with the tax system (Sandford, 1980).

Finally, the policymaking process may limit the ability of organizations to coordinate their behavior. This is best exemplified by the absence of coordination of taxation and social policy. In almost all countries tax policy and social policy are considered by different legislative and executive organizations. Individuals develop expertise in one or the other but rarely in both, so that the lack of coordination and resulting inefficiencies are not considered automatically by Congress or Parliament (Pliatzky, 1982). Mechanisms can be devised to consider problems of this type, e.g. Presidential or Royal commissions, but the quotidian process of government policymaking does not force, or even allow, consideration of such important coordination. It may be argued, in fact, that government is becoming less adept at coordinating policy areas. The familiar argument about 'iron triangles' in the United States, as well as the corporatist literature in Western Europe, all point to real and growing coordination problems (Jordan, 1981).

3.2.2 Conflict over goals

Organizations may not fail to coordinate, they may attempt to coordinate and find that they have fundamental goal conflicts. Or their goals may be so much in conflict that there is no possibility of coordination. Some classic examples of goal conflict among government organizations come from the United States, perhaps because the decentralized administrative structure allows organizations to pursue their own goals with less interference from executive departments or central agencies than would be true elsewhere. For example, at the same time that the Surgeon-General of the United States declares that cigarette-smoking is harmful to health and that all cigarette packages must carry a warning label, the US Department of Agriculture is spending millions of dollars each year to subsidize the production of tobacco. What is the policy of the federal government toward tobacco? It is obvious that there is no single policy but rather several in direct conflict. Likewise, during much of the 1950s and 1960s the Department of Agriculture was paying farmers to put a portion of their land into the 'soil bank' removing it from production to maintain prices. At the same time the Bureau of Reclamation of the Department of the Interior was spending large sums to reclaim arid land in the West for farming. As the reclaimed land was not always capable of producing the same crops as that put into the soil bank these policies were not always directly contradictory, but for some crops, e.g. cotton, they were. The goals of these organizations could be understood from their titles and institutional location. The Department of Agriculture had a major client group—farmers—whom it sought to serve through higher farm prices. The Bureau of Reclamation functioned almost entirely in the western United States and its major constituents were those states and their political leadership. Also, the Bureau of Reclamation had an ideological commitment to reclamation and a commitment to reclaim as much land as possible, regardless of the effect on agricultural prices.

How can goal conflicts be resolved without the waste and contradiction observed in these two examples? One means is an overt conflict in which one side becomes the winner and the other the loser. Resolution of the conflict may be administrative, as when an organizational superior decides between two subordinate organizations; it may be political as when the chief executive is forced to choose among organizations under his or her control; or it may be the result of market or quasi-market forces. The latter type of resolution is relatively rare, given that agencies are generally granted a monopoly in a policy area. One example, however, was the use of multiple organizations by Franklin Roosevelt during the New Deal. During the years leading up to World War II many of these agencies were determined to be less successful in producing benefits and were put out of business. Similarly, during time of war a very severe 'market test' may be applied to different organizations and tactics, e.g. the cavalry.

Another means of resolving goal conflict is for one organization to alter its goals. One dramatic example of this type of change occurred in the Army Corps of Engineers in the United States. The

Corps traditionally had been committed to using large engineering projects to solve navigation and flooding problems with little regard to the social and environmental consequences of their activities. This naturally brought them into conflict with other government organizations, e.g. the Environmental Protection Agency. During the 1970s, however, the Corps modified its goals toward more 'balanced' development projects, and their evaluation of prospective projects began to take social and environmental factors into account explicitly (Mazmanian and Nienaber, 1979). This change was brought about in part by generation changes within the Corps as well as some bruisings in direct conflicts with EPA. Interestingly, however, these changes have generated conflicts with other organizations, including the US Department of Agriculture over issues such as the channelization of streams. In this instance, the effect of goal change has been conflict-shifting. An organization which previously had been an ally, or at least neutral, became an enemy.

Finally, goal conflicts may be resolved by compromise and mutual accommodation. There is a tendency to regard government as a jungle inhabited by fierce beasts attempting to gobble up their companions. A more apt analogy, however, may be a gentlemen's club in which conflicts may exist but there are agreed-upon and pacific means of resolving conflicts for the good of the entire organization. Organizations may not wish to engage in a conflict which will utilize a great deal of their most scarce resource—time— as well as having some probability that they may lose. Therefore, they will seek accommodation and compromise—what Goodin (1975) refers to as 'bureaucratic back-scratching'. This type of resolution is favourable for the organizations involved but arguably not for political executives and citizens: it may simply institutionalize redundancy and contradiction.

One important instance of goal conflict, or at least goal ambiguity, arises when area-based programs are superimposed on existing functionally defined programs. This has been especially common for programs directed at the problems of inner cities. Booth, and Pitt and Money (1982) refer to the resulting redundancy as a 'Mango', or mutually non-effective group of organizations. They find, however, that although redundancy does occur, there is little overt conflict, in large part because of a consensual agreement on the lowest common policy denominator is reached. Also, these sets of organizations allow the central government to point to something being done for the inner cities, and allow local governments to extract resources from the center. Thus, although pathological, these organizational sets may persist for some time.

Government organizations will almost inevitably have different goals and many are in direct conflict. Organizations involved in such conflicts may well try to resolve the conflict by ignoring it, as the political process may allow them to do, or by reaching explicit compromises. But either of these approaches will only institutionalize the pathological features of goal conflict and produce government by 'non-consensual directions' (Peters, 1982). It is too much to hope that governments will decide what is important and what is not, but it is too little to allow them to persist with multiple contradictory goals and programs.

3.3 Goal displacement

Goal displacement is a very special form of goal conflict. It occurs not between organizations but within a single organization. The conflict is between the ostensible organizational goals and the personal goals of the members, or between the stated goals (ultimate goals) of the organization and more readily obtainable organizational goals (proximate goals). The pathological nature of goal displacement is obvious. If we assume that government does want the ostensible goals of the organization attained, then these will be pursued in name only and there is no room for alternative structures which would more actively seek to attain the goals. Even on the individual level, conflicts between reasons for involvement in the organization and organizational goals will reduce or eliminate job satisfaction.

Goal displacement arises from several sources. One is the process of personal and organizational maturation. Organizations and their members frequently pass through a distinct life cycle (Downs, 1967). They begin as activist 'zealots', committed to the organization's goals. This is especially true of organizations with clearly defined social missions, e.g. poverty or the environment. But this level of enthusiasm is difficult to maintain. Further, it may be counterproductive both for the individual and the organization. Organizations engaged in continual conflict with other organizations may not be as successful in attaining their goals as those which are able to reach mutual accommodations. A 'zealot' organization is almost by definition incapable of accommodation. Thus, it may be functional for the organizational to transform itself into an 'advocate', still interested in attaining goals but also willing to play the political game. An organization may be forced into accommodation by a fickle public not providing the continuing political support required by a zealot organization. But it is clearly only a short step from being an advocate organization to becoming a conserver organization, committed to the maintenance of the status quo. Once a stable pattern of accommodation is reached, the maintenance of that pattern and the place of the organization in the interorganizational network may dominate the purposive goals with which the organization began. Playing the game may dominate winning the game.

A similar process of goal change may occur within individuals. If initially strongly committed to organizational goals, the individual may soon learn that commitment is not enough for policymaking and that political skills and a willingness to participate in the 'game' are also necessary. An individual may therefore be faced with the choice of continuing purity or a compromise to attempt to achieve as much as possible. If the former is chosen it may mean leaving the organization. If the latter is chosen the individual, as did the organization, may become as committed to the process as to goals. In addition, individuals have individual goals and commitments— mortgages, children in college, pensions—which they would jeopardize by uncompromising commitment to goals. In short, individuals may decide that the maintenance of their position in the organization is more important than what they and the organization set out to do. Such a decision is rarely overt, but generally comes by rationalization or by interpreting organizational goals in a self-serving manner.

Goal displacement may be exaggerated when hierarchical authority is imposed. These tendencies are exaggerated by the permanence of civil service employment. Assuming that some initial goal displacement has occurred, and that some employees are pursuing more personal than organizational goals, an attempt of a superior to produce compliance with the stated goals of the organization may actually produce a retreat from those goals in favor of a strict adherence to rules and procedures which serve as protection for the employee. Especially in a civil service system, if the individual follows the rules to the letter, there is virtually no possible means of discipline—nor motivation. Rules beget rules and indifference begets indifference in an ever downward spiral of poor performance.

A special case of goal displacement has been referred to as the 'capture' of regulatory agencies by the very interests they were intended to regulate. The logic of this approach is that unless there is strong public support for the regulatory body and its goals, the principal group concerned with regulations are the regulated industries themselves. This is especially true when, as with many federal regulatory bodies, the regulatory bodies are independent and lack connections to bodies from which they could gain support—moral or political. In order to gain support for their budget and legislation the regulatory body has only one place to turn, the regulated industry. The classic example of capture is the Interstate Commerce Commission, established in 1887 to regulate the railroads. Over time the ICC was transformed into a virtual lobbying organization for the railroads (Huntington, 1957). As the ICC also came to regulate interstate trucking, it came to protect the trucking industry, so that the major opponents of deregulation of the trucking industry in the 1970s were the major trucking companies.

Capture by a regulated industry is a particular problem when field agents make the regulatory decision. Kaufman (1960) discusses the difficulty faced by members of the US Forest Service who make important decisions about lumbering and grazing on federal lands in Western states, but who were isolated in local communities which were affected by their decisions. Only through ardent socialization and frequent rotation in office was the Forest Service able to ensure that the criteria used in the rangers' decisions were the appropriate ones.

The licit or semi-licit exploitation of the agency (Sieber, 1981) described as regulatory capture may be contrasted with capture of an organization by professionals. Organizations which employ large numbers of professionals frequently have their goals subordinated to the professional goals and values of their members. Even if one does not adopt the extreme views of Ilich (1976), we can see that most health organizations in the public sector are oriented by professional values rather than cost-effectiveness. For example, Dr John Knowles (1978) of the Rockefeller Foundation has pointed out that the annual costs of developing an artificial heart are twice those of the most expensive preventive program for coronary disease. Yet health organizations go full-speed-ahead with high technology medicine and the orientation toward acute care which characterizes values in the medical profession.

Both regulatory capture and professional dominance represent licit exploitation of organizations by members. There can be illicit exploitation as well. This is most commonly reported in the police in which the power of the officer over citizens—especially known criminals—is used to extract money or merchandise (Reiss, 1971). These abuses are not confined to the police force, however, as recent scandals in the Federal Housing Administration and the General Services Administration in the United States and the Crown Agents in Britain have illustrated.

Government organizations are established to attain social goals, but those goals frequently become lost in the crush of business. Preservation, both for the organization and the individual—frequently becomes the dominant goal. Organizations which are zealously committed to their own narrow interests may not be politically effective and present numerous problems of coordination. But it is quite easy to go too far and to coordinate oneself out of all semblance of the original goal set. It is quite easy to say that organizations must strike a balance between their commitment to goals and their commitments to self-preservation and participation in the policy process. However, this balance must be struck if the organization is to avoid one or another of the pathologies identified here.

3.4 Procedures are the opiate of the bureaucrat

One standard complaint about the public bureaucracy is 'red tape', meaning that organizations are excessively committed to procedures to the detriment of actually getting anything done (Kaufman, 1974). In this procedural pathology, the development of procedures is another type of goal displacement. In the most extreme versions of this approach to organizational pathology, e.g. the humorous but instructive discussions of C. Northcote Parkinson, procedural complexity becomes a make-work scheme for bureaucrats. The more procedures and the more pieces of paper there are to be processed, the more people will be required to produce the same output for the society.

But we must remember that citizens are of two minds about the development of procedures in government. They may complain about the delay engendered by excessive procedural steps; they may also complain when not protected by adequate procedural safeguards (Peters, 1984). Citizens demand protection against arbitrary and capricious actions by officials, especially officials such as the police who may make extremely important decisions in difficult circumstances and who may employ force to implement their decisions. Also, citizens have been demanding increased opportunities to participate in the policymaking process and procedures which have been promulgated for this purpose have further slowed policymaking. Thus, if we are to accuse bureaucrats of being addicted to procedures, we may well accuse citizens of being the pushers.

Citizens do seek to have procedures developed for their own protection, but so do bureaucrats. One of the principal things which procedures will do is to protect the individual bureaucrat from the need to make decisions and from individual culpability. If procedures can specify adequately rules for making decisions in any case then the individual is not placed in a position of personally denying anyone anything. But it is in this that the pathology arises. Few if any rules or procedures can be well enough designed to take in all possibilities. There are then three options available when the unforeseen arises. One is to develop more procedures to take care of the case, leading inevitably to the escalation of the number of rules. A second is to refer the decision to a higher authority to avoid responsibility and to gain greater protection. The third, as in Allison's (1971) 'organizational process model' is to make all circumstances fit those which have been predetermined. Procedures may become the Procrustean bed which the real world is made to fit.

As with the imposition of hierarchical authority and goal displacement, a paradox arises in the enforcement of individual responsibility. One of the panaceas prescribed for the ills of bureaucracy is to make individuals responsible—even financially—for their actions. But if this is done, there will be an increasing proliferation of rules and procedures attempting to eliminate the need to make decisions, and a proliferation of hierarchical levels through which decisions must travel. If this analysis is correct, then *an attempt to make individuals more responsible for their actions may result in their being less so, and in even slower and more cumbersome administrative procedures* (Crozier, 1964).

But it is not only self-protection which produces a proliferation of rules and procedures. One of the most important is a tidiness of mind, or more elegantly, deductive logic. As administrators work with existing rules and regulations they find that certain things are not specified and that when a new case arises they have the opportunity to develop a new rule which can be applied in the future. Simply out of the desire to be comprehensive and professional rules, regulations, and procedures will tend to proliferate. Much of the proliferation of regulations under the Occupational Safety and Health Administration and the Environmental Protection Agency can be seen as a desire to be professional and complete rather than as a desire to impose unreasonable burdens on industry (Bardach and Kagan, 1981). This proliferation may even result from a desire to serve the client of the public at large by more completely specifying their rights and entitlements.

For whatever reason they may have been developed, attempts to limit discretion, which by their deductive and comprehensive nature may be labelled 'rational', may produce substantial irrationality. If we use the incrementalist argument that a policymaker is incapable of anticipating all possible situations in which the rule may be applied, then there will always be instances in which the rules devised do not fit. Thus, *general rationality may produce site-level irrationality when the rules are applied*. This logic would then call for greater flexibility and discretion for those applying the rules (Bardach and Kagan, 1981).

Here we return to problems of balancing the discretion of individual administrators with the rights of citizens to have equal treatment. There is concern not only about equality of treatment but also about the appropriateness of treatment for individual circumstances. In designing organizations and procedures to attempt to balance the competing pathologies of excessive proceduralism and excessive discretion, several factors might be considered. One is the extent to which basic rights of individuals are involved. Areas which involved those rights, e.g. activities by the police or domestic intelligence, should have more procedural protections than other decisions. Likewise, the more reversible a decision is the more it can be left to discretion with the possibility of correction. Also, the variability of the cases to be decided should be considered, with areas of greater variability having greater discretion for administrators to prevent excessive rigidity and misapplication of rules (Donnison, 1982). Finally, the quality of administrators making decisions should be considered, and those with more training and expertise should be allowed to use those skills in other than a mechanical fashion. These variables will not ensure that pathological responses will not be generated, but they should help minimize such responses.

3.5 Hyperactivity

One standard critique of bureaucracy is that it is excessively active, with the medical analogy being hyperactivity in children. This is manifested in the need of some agencies to promulgate rules and regulations (as mentioned directly above) but may go beyond that. As well as merely making more rules, organizations may attempt to do *something* even if something is not required, or even if the action may be counterproductive. Organizations concerned with a particular policy area may believe they have more than a watching brief over the area, and that they are required to respond to any problems which arise. This may be a manifestation of extreme organizational competition, in which the organization might respond to a problem if only to prevent a potential rival from gaining a toehold on their 'turf'. Also, problems are a useful commodity at budget time and if some response can be mounted then perhaps more money can be made to flow in subsequent budget years. More positively, the organization may feel a responsibility to react to a problem simply because this is their area of concern, or they may have pressures from politicians whose constituents want action.

A great deal of the hyperactivity observed in government organizations does not result from a need to extend their power and authority, or to prevent other organizations from extending theirs, but rather results from an ideological commitment to solving problems (Goodsell, 1982). The stereotype of the bureaucrat as slothful and uninterested, as might be manifested in the description of red tape and self-protection, may be contrasted with a picture of genuine interest and commitment to serving the public. The service which results may be narrowly defined and may actually benefit only a small percentage of the population, but it will be service all the same. For example, the Army Corps of Engineers, even after changing to a more environmentalist position, continues to believe in building large structures for flood control and navigation. The massive amount of money proposed for the Tennessee-Tombigbee waterway is indicative of their commitment to large-scale public works projects, even those with marginal social benefits. Of course, service provision need not be entirely altruistic, for the provision of services to a large number of people and geographical areas can build a powerful political constituency for the organization.

Hyperactivity also appears to result from reasoning by analogy. Government organizations lack a clear standard against which to judge their actions, such as profits or market shares provide private actors. They lack any clear criteria that would allow them to design programs for effectiveness or efficiency. Therefore, they must rely on analogies. One is that if it worked in X, it will work in Y, where X and Y may be geographical areas, policy areas, or organizations. More importantly for the study of hyperactivity, there is a tendency to think in linear terms; if a little of X helps, then a lot of X will help even more. Certainly no physician would prescribe in that manner, but government organizations frequently do. For example, lowering pupil-teacher ratios from very high levels, e.g. forty to one, to more moderate levels produces improvements in the quality of education, but there is little evidence to show that there are any improvements after more moderate ratios are attained. But improving the pupil-teacher ratio is frequently used by school boards to press for more funds.

Reasoning by analogy may be a particularly important means for coping with declining demands for services, especially for firmly entrenched organizations. With falling birthrates, schools have been faced with a falling demand for their services, but have sought to maintain employment through the intensification of services (CPRS, 1977). This has involved not only improvement of the pupil-teacher ratio but also adding new subjects, classes for the gifted, and federally mandated classes for the learning-impaired and non-native English speakers. Arguably schools have been willing to modify their mix of services away from strictly educational services in order to maintain their existing employment and structures.

3.6 Empire-building

Empire-building is closely related to hyperactivity. By empire-building we shall be referring not so much to the extension of services to areas where they may not be required and to where they may be counterproductive, but rather to the development of enhanced budgets and personnel rosters, either as a manifestation of machismo by officials who want to be able to say that they have a budget of an astronomical size, or as a hedge against future cuts. Despite arguments to the contrary, the personal emoluments of individual administrators are affected very little by the size of the organization. In fact, some schemes for rewarding government executives for performance, e.g. the Senior Executive Service, appear to reward those who reduce rather than expand their agencies.

Building insulation against future cuts may be a sound organizational strategy. This protection will almost certainly involve budget and personnel, but it may also involve program authorization. An organization may take on functions which are not clearly within its sphere of competence but which may be related, e.g. the Department of Agriculture being involved with Food Stamps, or with 'urban extension agents'. These ancillary programs provide protection and bargaining chips for the organization if they are confronted with cuts. They are thus able to protect their 'heartlands' from attack and to continue providing services to their basic clients.

The strategy of building organizational protection through empire-building has several risks, however. The most important is that by lessening the clarity of organizational mission the clientele which should be the basis of support will be either confused or alienated. The same may be true of workers in the organization who may lose any clear sense of mission. By attempting to protect against cuts the organization may actually make itself more vulnerable. This is especially true when active oversight bodies, which may themselves be connected to the clientele, become aroused by apparent changes in mission.

Also, building several missions within the same organization may make it a candidate for splitting (Hogwood and Peters, 1983). Once discussion of splitting is initiated, the existing management may not be able to control the outcome. This may result in more being lost to a new organization than would have been lost in the anticipated cuts. In short, the leadership may well outsmart themselves by building protection by empire-building.

Attempts at empire-building will also upset the balance of power within an interorganizational network. Mutual accommodation is the general strategy followed in such settings and anyone who is not playing by those rules is a threat to the system. Other organizations may gang up on the 'rogue' and prevent it from getting the money and authority it wants. Almost all government organizations have friends and supporters in the legislature who may be able to punish the rogue for its aggresion. There is a 'musk ox' phenomenon among organizations, meaning that they appear willing to band together to protect their fellows from outside attack and—given the connections of organizations with legislators—they make make a potential empire-builder worse off than before the attempt at expansion (Hogwood and Peters, 1983, 117). This is especially true given the importance of mutual trust in policymaking and that trust is undermined by empire-building (Heclo and Wildavsky, 1974).

The public as a whole may be disadvantage if the organizations created by empire-building are so large and diffuse that they are inefficient to manage and produce extremely high overhead costs. This was, in part, the argument against the continuation of the 'super departments' created in the United Kingdom in the 1970s, e.g. the Department of Trade and Industry (Pollitt, 1984). The question of just what is the most appropriate size for a government organization closely approximates arguments about angels on pinheads. There is clearly a trade-off between clarity of mission and (perhaps) lower overhead costs in smaller organizations versus the coordination and control sought through larger organizations. To avoid the wrong choice involves a careful understanding of the policy being delivered, the history and characteristics of organizations considered candidates for consolidation or splitting, and the political environment in which the organizational change is to occur.

If empire-building is tempting to bureaucrats and political executives, it carries a number of risks. Further, it is not clear that the risks are justified by what appear to be marginal benefits at best. We have no way of knowing what the right size government organization is, and if empire-building is potentially pathological, so too is the failure to develop a sufficient capacity to deliver required or desired services.

3.7 Atrophied muscles

The use of the term atrophy implies discussing once powerful organizations which have withered. This is true in part, but we will also discuss organizations which have not developed sufficiently to meet their demands in the first place. Unlike empire-building, atrophy (as used here) is rarely the fault of those within the organization, but rather tends to result from the actions of politicians or members of central agencies. The few cases of atrophy resulting from the actions of organizations themselves appear to result from extreme self-protection and conservatism on the part of the organization.

Atrophy may arise from several causes. The most common is the budgetary process, and the failure to provide enough money for the organization to do its job properly (see 7.5). This may be because of an inadequate knowledge of organizational needs, because of fiscal constraints requiring all organizations to work without all the resources they would like or, more pathologically, it may be a means of preventing the organization from stirring up too much trouble. For example, it has been argued that, despite the complaints about the Occupational Safety and Health Administration (OSHA) and the Environmental Protection Agency (EPA), neither organization had sufficient money to be effective even before the Reagan cuts. It has been argued further that this was a strategy calculated to appease unions and environmentalists without offending the business community excessively.

Atrophy may also be related to personnel problems. The number of personnel is in large part determined through the budgetary process, but the type of personnel may be determined by organizations such as civil service boards. For example, to return to our example of the mental health agency in a southern state, the director was attempting to improve the efficiency of his hospitals by providing orderlies and food service personnel minimal psychiatric training. With that they could provide some supervision while on the wards, thereby freeing professional staff for therapy, etc. The state civil service commission, however, continued to send him the traditional orderly, i.e. someone lacking the educational or intellectual background needed for such training.

In addition, organizations may lack the legal capacity to carry out their mandated tasks. Policemen frequently have argued that they lacked the legal capability to be as effective as they might be in preventing crime, just as organizations concerned with espionage have argued their domestic activities were too restricted. As with providing inadequate budgetary authority, providing inadequate legal authority may be intentional, either for protection of civil liberties as in these two examples, or to prevent the organization from offending powerful political constituencies.

Organizations may be forced into a form of atrophy which spreads too little 'muscle' over too much commitment. For example, the Elementary and Secondary Education Act of 1967 (ESEA) in the United States was intended as a program of compensatory aid to poorer inner city and rural school districts. However, in order to build a sufficient coalition for its passage it was transformed into a general subsidy for elementary and secondary education in even the most affluent school districts. The money provided might have been sufficient to make a major impact in poor districts if it had been confined to those districts, but it has not been when it is so widely dispersed.

Few organizations ask to be given a mandate to fulfil without the resources to do so. But it is a common outcome of the political process, as legislatures and executives attempt to balance the availability of resources with the competing uses of those resources. Further, they must balance the competing virtues of making no response, making a symbolic gesture (or a purposefully ineffective gesture) or making an effective and workable program (see 9.7).

3.8 Crises of succession

Organizations are means of routinizing activities and removing, insofar as possible, the human element in government decision-making. The standard Weberian model of the bureaucrat is of someone who works for government for the wage, obeys orders of a superior on a 'rational-legal' basis, and has very little commitment to the organization (Gerth and Mills, 1946). As well as being a dead bore for the individual bureaucrat, such limited involvement would be dysfunctional for the organization (Agyris, 1964). To be effective, an organization must generate commitment from its members, and they usually can do that. In this section, however, we argue that they may be too successful. The type of commitment which may be dysfunctional is not to the organization itself but to particular individuals within it. The conventional wisdom would find the idea of a charismatic bureaucratic oxymoronic, but there are indeed effective personal leaders in government (Lynn, 1981). Further, in the United States, political appointees head most government organizations and one of the characteristics by which they are selected is their leadership ability.

The problem with charismatic leaders in government organizations is that frequently leadership is not routinized. That is, organizational leadership can be too personalistic so that changing leaders involves not only his or her departure along with a second or third echelon of aides and appointees, but also a significant loss of organizational memory and continuity. One virtue of the bureaucratic organization which Weber identified was that the files serve as a memory and guide for future action. However, if the files which are important are the personal files of the agency head rather than the files of the organization itself then there will be a serious memory loss (see also 4.7). Issues in process may be lost and the effectiveness of the organization undermined by the crisis of succession.

The failure to routinize charisma may also result in political losses in the interorganizational network. If the contacts which the leadership has developed are personal, they will not be usable after a change in command. Further, if an organization becomes known as having chronic problems of succession, then it will not be able to deal successfully, for any deals made will not be enforceable. As trust and confidence constitute a major medium of exchange in the interorganizational network, leadership changes without proper continuity can only weaken the position of the organization.

The design of government organizations and the role assigned to leadership in the organization constitute a trade-off. Effective personal leaders will be able to exact higher levels of compliance and performance from subordinates in the short run. Also, everything else being equal, they will be more successful in the interorganizational politics so important to the organization. However, these short-term gains may have to be paid for in long-term losses, as structures and confidence developed by one leader may not be transferable to the next.

3.9 Summary

Organizations constitute the major means through which governments make things happen in society. But organizations also constitute a major source of policy pathologies. We have adopted the view that the majority of organizational pathologies arise from the characteristics of large organizations rather than the avarice or malevolence of the individuals who inhabit them. The majority of public employees are trying to perform their job adequately and are largely committed to public service. However, the nature of the structures within which they work—which would be almost as true in the private sector as the public—may prevent them from being as effective as they, and we, would like.

Unfortunately, there is no magic elixir to remedy the pathologies we have identified. In fact, several pathologies are linked, so that to avoid one is to encounter another. Leadership is often cited as a means of solving many of the problems of bureaucracies but this can itself pose difficulties when not properly institutionalized. Thus, if we have not provided the remedies, we may have performed a service by providing what appears a better diagnosis of the problems to be corrected, one which does not rely upon false assumptions of bureaucratic aggrandizement but rather more on structural problems.

4

Informational Pathologies

The obvious analogy to the information flow within government is the nervous system of a human being or other animal, a metaphor which was powerfully developed by Deutsch (1963) in his book *The Nerves of Government*. While recognizing the power of this metaphor and the way it fits in with the broader medical metaphor of this book, we realize the importance of not imposing it when it does not apply. Thus, we will not necessarily assume that there is a single organizational location corresponding to the brain in a human being: the absence of a single brain is, indeed, part of the problem.

4.1 Faulty receptors

To survive and operate, agencies need to collect and appraise a wide range of types of information coming into the organization, including from other government organizations. Government organizations are never so pathological as to attempt to insulate themselves from information from outside, since that is a method of committing organizational suicide. Indeed, an organization would have to take active steps to cut itself off from external sources of information, since all government organizations are continually assaulted with information of varying degrees of reliability from pressure groups, the media and elected politicians, as well as information routinely collected (though not necessarily utilized) in the course of the organization's activities.

In many government organizations a largely passive approach is adopted to the collection of information about the problems it is tackling, particularly once its programs have become established. This does not imply a lack of information, since much information may be thrown at the organization, and much routinely collected, and this volume of inputs may create the impression of adequacy. Indeed, in times of crises, the organization may suffer from information overload. Why then might it be suggested that these forms of information collection have pathological features?

Governments often become aware of problems or their ramifications (whether a new problem or a problem affecting an existing program) too late to act upon them in the optimal way (Hogwood and Gunn, 1984, ch. 4). Conversely, they may miss the chance to intervene to take advantage of an opportunity. The best time to start treating (or averting) a problem might well be before a crisis forced the issue on to the political agenda. Also, it often takes a considerable among of 'lead' time to set up or adapt the organizational structure to deal with a problem. If a decision has to be made very quickly once a crisis has arisen, it may be based on inadequate or misleading information. There may be insufficient time for adequate definition of just what the problem is and for exploration of the implications of alternative options. Many of the techniques available to policy analysts can only be brought to bear if there is adequate time for analysis; hence anticipation of occasions when decisions may be required is a precondition for effective policy analysis at other stages.

There are formidable technical and intellectual problems in devising methods of ensuring advance warning, or even adequate information about current developments. However, it is political factors which help to explain the relatively passive role of government organizations in problem search. There is a temptation for governments to concentrate on current problems requiring attention now rather than hypothetical problems where any adverse political effects of not taking action will not occur until the future, and perhaps affect a different political party. Yet failure to design information collection procedures in advance may lead to inadequate information being available when problems become current. For example, when the oil crisis broke in 1974 the US Federal government had no official source of information about oil supplies, leaving it to rely on the oil companies, who refused to supply the information. At present the rewards for foresight for both politicians and appointed officials are negligible, and are just as likely to be reaped by others as by those actually responsible for anticipatory information collection and appraisal.

To attempt to remedy these deficiences by introducing a comprehensive planning system to cover all information contingencies may itself have perverse pathological features. The type of information required for problem search by government organizations may differ from that required for strategic planning or forecasting, which tend to assume massive information input (see Ansoff, 1975, 22). If we are to be able to anticipate potential problems rather than merely identify problems which already exist, we need to be able to respond to 'weak signals', particularly when there is a discontinuity from the present pattern. There is a paradox that a comprehensive planning approach is easiest (and arguably only possible) when it is least necessary, that is, when there is plenty of available information and high continuity or certainty.

Another alleged deficiency is that access to the political agenda is currently unequal, and therefore there is variation in the extent to which problems affecting particular groups get on to the policy agenda and information about them is likely to be collected and given careful consideration. Insofar as social policy and policy analysis are particularly concerned with the problems of disadvantaged groups, then a passive approach to information collection is pathological, since information about these groups is less likely to be prepared and targeted at the relevant government agencies than is information about well-mobilized and affluent groups.

The extent to which information pathologies are likely to occur in information collection is likely to vary between policy areas and policy problems. For example, the type of information collection required for modifications to street-cleaning policies is relatively routine, relatively predictable and involves relatively short lead times (though even in normal garbage disposal pathologies can occur: see Bozeman and Bozeman, 1981). In the case of nuclear waste disposal the information requirements involve a much higher degree of scientific expertise, greater uncertainty about a higher risk issue, longer lead time to establish new disposal systems, and a high degree of scientific and political contention surrounding the issue. Indeed, such is the political sensitivity of the issue that the very collection of information may be a contentious issue. For example, the United Kingdom abandoned a program of geological test bores to assess potential underground storage sites for nuclear waste. In the meantime, nuclear waste continues to accumulate (itself a reflection of the fact that nuclear power policy was initiated before information about the problem of waste disposal and possible means of resolving it was collected). This provides tentative and worrying evidence that it may be precisely on those policy issues where information pathologies can be most damaging that they are most likely.

For any government organization data collected in the course of carrying out its activities, for example about clients, will be a major source of information. However, there is a danger that as a result of inertia (or lack of any thinking about policy relevance when the administrative data collection system was designed) inappropriate or inadequate sources of data may be generating misleading signals. If there are deficiencies in the present statistics, a number of alternatives might be considered. The type of information collected at the point of delivery or even the way the service is delivered might be altered to generate more meaningful information.

If this was inappropriate or would fail to get round the problem, consideration could be given to regular sample surveys to collect the necessary information. The number registered as unemployed or crimes recorded by the police are two notorious examples of the inadequacies of administratively derived statistics where sample surveys are arguably more accurate (see Rees, 1981; Stringer and Richardson, 1980, 26–7).

In the late 1960s there were some hopes that policy-relevant social data might be developed to the stage where they would not only identify problems needing to be tackled, but would provide measures of the success of government programs and might even be consolidated into a 'social report' or account corresponding to national economic accounts, which, it is argued, presented only a partial picture of the nation's well-being and led to excessive concentration on economic targets (see Olson, 1969). The original aspirations of this 'social indicators movement' have not been met, nor is it likely that they will be (see Carley, 1981). This reflects problems over *values* (disagreements about the normative implications of changes in indicators), problems over our limited *understanding of social processes* (which is necessary if we are to be able to assess the impact of government programs on indicators) and also more technical *problems of measurement* (selecting indicators which are both *valid*, i.e. meaningful measures of the problem with which we are concerned, and *reliable*, i.e. will consistently reflect changes in the problem). It should be noted that there is now much greater skepticism on all these matters about the economic indicators which the social indicators movement sought to emulate.

That said, there have been some advances in the collection and presentation of social data (for example, in the annual *Social Trends* published by the British government), and considerable scope for further improvements both in collection and consumption by policy-makers. This is perhaps particularly true of their role in alerting policymakers to problems which require further investigation, even if they cannot be used in undigested form for policy planning and evaluation. There would, however, be a danger even (or perhaps especially) with fully developed social indicators that they would fail to pick up precisely those new and unpredicted problems which it is a central aim of active problem search to identify. Social indicators must be supplemented by other methods, both formal and informal.

In considering what information is collected in practice and why, it is important to bear in mind the political setting of policy-making and the commitment of organization members to their work (see chapter 3). Naturally, a government organization will develop systems for monitoring data which advance the interests of the organization's members, for example, those that indicate rising 'demand' for its services. Conversely, data which would throw up problems whose consideration might work against the organization's interests might be neglected or even suppressed by the organization. Thus there are favourable problems (= opportunities) and unwanted problems from the perspective of particular organizations.

Might not attempts to remedy information deficiency problems lead to new pathologies of analytical and political overload? More active problem search would involve further problems receiving serious attention from government in addition to those it already considers (though in many cases it would simply be considering the same problems somewhat earlier). Even given a substantial increase in the analytical capacity of government, it would not be possible to bring costly analytical techniques to bear on all existing issues, let alone new ones thrown up by a deliberate search for more issues which might require analysis. However, this is really an argument for explicit priorities in deciding which issues should be subject to what kind of analysis and which should be decided by conventional routes (Hogwood and Gunn, 1984, ch. 6; Wiseman, 1978).

It could also be argued that policy analysts should not actively engage in seeking out new information and new problems for government, since this would entail increasing the demands on the political system without necessarily increasing the resources to meet those demands, 'supports' for the political system, or the capacity of the political system to resolve issues. Since many of the 'new' problems may be intractable (and this may be one of the reasons why information about them was not collected), the effect of creating new demands without necessarily providing the resources for corresponding solutions may be to create additional strain on the political system.

Not all potential issues are problems, however. Some provide opportunities and may provide cheaper or more effective forms of policy delivery. More broadly, it could be argued that better recognition of the problems that exist in a society would increase general support for the political system and therefore improve its capacity to cope with problems.

In efficiency terms it is normally better to avert problems than to fix them after they arise. If improved issue search was part of a wider improvement of decision-making, then fewer resources might be wasted on bad decisions (some of which arise from inadequate warning or definition of problems).

However, the idea of more active information collection and appraisal still has to be sold to the decision-makers who have to cope with more information and more issues. Their reaction may be that they have enough problems already, thank you. Advocates of more active information and problem search have to convince decision-makers that there are political and other benefits to them as well as to 'society as a whole'.

The task of ensuring that relevant information is collected is therefore a daunting one. Equally daunting is the task of filtering out erroneous information which would have catastrophic consequences if acted on: at a tense moment in the Berlin crisis in 1961, bombers of the United States Strategic Air Command were moved to the runways in response to an erroneous signal (Deutsch, 1963, 103) and this is by no means the only occasion when false alarms were generated by the early warning system. Less planet-threatening false inputs are a common, if under-reported, feature of other policy areas.

4.2 Failures in communicating information to decision-makers

Much of the information which is collected never reaches the parts of an organization which would find it most useful. Such failures of communication can be vertical (i.e. failure of front-line subordinates to report relevant information to superiors) or horizontal, as when a line unit fails to pass on information about opportunities to, say, a research or policy analysis section.

Front-line service delivery personnel, for example those paying out cash benefits to indigent families, may in the course of their work become aware of certain patterns of information (say, a rise in the proportion of blacks or Hispanics seeking benefit) but they may not pass this information on even to their immediate superiors (see Wilensky, 1967, 43). There may, indeed, be no formal means to enable or encourage this to be done. Front-line staff may, in any case, consider that this is 'not their job', and that it is up to management to spot such patterns. Such an attitude is particularly likely among poorly-paid workers who are in jobs which are interchangeable with other organizations and who lack a direct or financial interest in the broader purposes of the organization.

Staff at any level are likely to be aware that the passing of information may have direct consequences for them (Wilensky, 1967, 43). Where such information is likely to annoy a superior, it may very well be suppressed (see Simon, 1976, 163). Even when an organization member does have a personal commitment to the goals of the organization, information may fail to be passed on by default. One way in which this can arise is that 'the subordinate cannot visualize accurately what information his superior needs in order to make his decisions' (Simon, 1976, 163).

The bulk of the potentially useful information coming into an organization comes from informal methods (see Hellriegel and Slocum, 1974; Bardach, 1978; Simon, 1976, 160–2). Such personal, and often oral, information (including gossip) may not necessarily reach the relevant sections of the organization (especially if there is internal distrust) or may be discounted relative to supposedly harder, formal, printed information. Thus it is important to try to ensure that informal information and knowledge is injected into the overall policy information system along with formal techniques. What may be required here is not so much means of identifying new information as mechanisms (such as 'brainstorming') for making explicit the implications of information already held.

Formalized information-reporting procedures, designed to ensure that information is systematically passed from front-line units to the leadership of the organization, may have the perverse effect of systematically excluding available information. An office manager may be aware of a certain pattern in policy delivery in the area for which he is responsible, but this information may be 'summarized out' when he prepares the information in the form required by the report. Such standardized reports may also exclude the possibility of passing on information about unforeseen developments.

Even where information is passed on, it may do so in a garbled form (see Tullock, 1965, 137–9; Wilensky, 1967, 41). Details of the circumstances in which the information applies may be missing, so that false generalizations may be drawn from it. In other cases, the range and degree of uncertainty attached to a forecast, which may be at least as policy relevant as the size of the central forecast, may be omitted. (This is similar to what March and Simon, 1958, describe as 'uncertainty absorption'.) There is a danger that these caveats will be lost as forecasts pass up from the original forecasters to various policy-level officials, each of whom for the best of reasons may simplify and annotate the material (see Hogwood and Gunn, 1984, ch. 8). The danger of some form of garbling of information is particularly high when information has to pass through many levels (Tullock, 1965, 183).

Organizational leaders will not always want to have even important pieces of information passed on to them. They may prefer to maintain 'disavowability'. That is, the information would imply the need to take unpalatable action; if failure to take action later leads to criticism, the organizational leaders can claim lack of knowledge. This may itself lead to criticism, but this may be a risk organization leaders are prepared to take. Subordinates who are aware that their leaders would prefer not to know about a state of affairs (e.g. failure to implement an unwanted externally imposed mandate) may not pass such information on, and in turn may cover themselves by saying that they had not been given any instructions to do so (see e.g. Gonzales and Rothchild, 1979).

In other cases, superiors will attempt to guess what subordinates have filtered out, thereby introducing other types of bias into their decision-making (Tullock, 1965; March and Simon, 1958). Alternatively, where individuals or other organizations seek to control their own lives by withholding information, their hierarchical superiors (or anyone else requiring the information) may have to make concessions in order to extract the information from them.

Except in the very simplest organizations (and government considered as a whole is never that), the channels of communication are best considered as a network, with many alternative routes for messages from different sources to different ultimate destinations. There may therefore be 'the problem of choice between different possibilities of routing different incoming messages through different channels or 'associative trails' within the network' (Deutsch, 1963, 94). Where there are many alternative routes for incoming information, there may be indecision about which is the appropriate channel to use. On the other hand, if many messages have to compete for only a few channels, there may be a problem of the 'jamming' of those channels and this may have drastic consequences for the functioning of the network as a whole. To some extent these problems can be anticipated through careful organizational design and the establishment of operating rules about which types of information should be routed through which channels, but these are unlikely to cover all eventualities, particularly if there is a change in the pattern of incoming information.

Although at first sight wasteful, it is best in designing organizations to design in multiple channels, especially in more hierarchical, authoritarian structures where one view will tend to be adopted early and other information screened out (see Wilensky, 1967, 45). This involves the deliberate building in of 'functional redundancy' (see Landau, 1969). Such redundancy may also be a means of attempting to overcome the problems of restriction of information which may accompany the structuring of organizations into rival specialist units, as in the armed forces (Wilensky, 1967, 49–53).

Where decision-makers are concerned that important information about the organization's environment or internal operation is not reaching them or is reaching them in a form whose significance is difficult to interpret, there is a wide range of responses open to them (see Wilensky, 1967, 47–8). These include ensuring that there are staff lower down the hierarchy with personal loyalty to the top leadership or employees whose career pattern depends on the center but places them in close contact with developments in the localities. Franklin D. Roosevelt used this as one of a number of informal methods of short-circuiting hierarchies.

Where the concern is that only a single stream of advice and supporting information is reaching top decision-makers, those top decision-makers can insist that they have access to information lower down the hierarchy before these are homogenized out in the final briefing (Jenkins, 1971). Politicians, whether in the executive or the legislature can bring their own advisers and experts, either to provide direct information and expertise of their own or to double-check the information coming up through normal channels. This is particularly important where politicians come into office for relatively short periods as a 'Government of Strangers' (Heclo, 1977), who have not been plugged into the routine information flows of the organization which they nominally head and who lack the knowledge of past events which is essential for the interpretation of the significance of incoming information.

This use of a support team of personal advisers and experts is taken for granted in the United States, but in the United Kingdom many politicians have in the past been reluctant to introduce their own teams, and the civil service has, where it wished to do so, been successful in shutting out advisers from the normal information flow within departments (Klein and Lewis, 1977). The main problem in Britain has been a lack of clear specification of what types of information are needed to deal with each policy issue, whether such information is being adequately collected, appraised, and communicated to ministers, and, if not, what types of adviser or expert are required to overcome this.

Decision-makers who feel cut off from information flows can also seek their own external sources of information from interest groups, personal contacts, or journalists or academics (Wilensky, 1967, 179–80). However, these alternative sources of information would also contain a great deal of bias, perhaps of an unknown sort.

Patterns of hierarchy within an organization and associated formal reporting procedures may not correspond with the most sensible flow of information relating to a specific problem, particularly where specialist knowledge is held by a low staus employee or relevant specialists are separated out into a separate staff agency which does not fit into the hierarchy of line authority (Wilensky, 1967, 44). One way of attempting to resolve this is to set up project task forces, including the relevant expertise, so that information could be appraised and communicated to decision-makers in a way that short-circuited conventional formal communication channels.

In all these strategies for overcoming perceived deficiences in information collection or communication decision-makers have to strike a delicate balance between ensuring that adequate information reaches them and giving the impression of distrust of subordinates and the resentment and pathological behavior which may result.

4.3 Brain

The concept of a brain receiving information, taking decisions, and sending output to effectors is the least satisfactory part of an analogy between the policy process and the human nervous system. Normal and even damaged brains have the ability to act on information from a whole range of nerve endings and send instructions about actions to be taken to muscles which might be in completely different parts of the body.

In the policy process, by contrast, information-processing and decision-taking will normally be largely internalized within policy sectors, which will include the government organizations and interest groups with a particular concern in that policy area, be it agricultural policy or energy policy. Thus, normal decision-making in the policy process resembles behavior which would be regarded as highly pathological in a human being. For example, if the eyes saw someone about to aim a punch at the face the brain could only instruct the eyes to blink and not the legs to run away.

Some policy-relevant information may be received in more than one sector to which it is relevant, but be interpreted in different ways in the different sectors and induce different, sub-optimal and perhaps even incompatible responses within those different sectors. A policy example is the world economic recession which leads to attempts (often unsuccessful) by supporters of foreign aid to increase assistance to those countries most seriously affected by the recession at the same time as those concerned with protecting the country's own industries erect protectionist barriers which further damage the poor countries (and arguably help to prolong the world recession). The human analogy would be where in response to the eyes seeing some object the arms reached for it as the legs took the body away from it. Such uncoordinated behavior is relatively easier to observe in human beings; its pathological counterpart in government activities is often more difficult to diagnose and measure.

It is important not to exaggerate or overgeneralize about the lack of a unitary 'brain' in the policy process. Policy sectors are often not neatly defined but rather resemble loosely arranged, chaining, and overlapping networks (Jordan, 1981; Heclo, 1978), which it could be argued are analogues to pathways among brain cells tackling specific problems. The United States could be argued to conform to this 'network' image on some issues, whereas others are closer to the original 'iron triangle' image of a small exclusive set of participants in a decision. Other countries, notably the United Kingdom, with the integrative mechanism of cabinet governments based on majorities in the legislature, might appear to resemble a 'unitary' brain. However, this belief would be misleading, since there is a high degree of sectorization through government departments or inter-departmental committees, and those issues which do go to full cabinet are not obviously those in greater need of integrative decision-making but those of greatest political sensitivity (Mackie and Hogwood, 1984). In terms of policy outcomes, it is by no means obvious that the 'integrated' British system is better coordinated or less liable to produce perverse or bad decisions than the 'fragmented' US system.

In both Britain and the United States the increasing role of professionals in providing an input to decision-making as well as having considerable autonomy in implementation provides a further potential source of segmentation. This arises both in the way in which much information flow will be internalized within the profession and in the way in which jargon can inhibit communication with non-professionals.

It is important to distinguish between integrative *information-processing* and options-generating capacity at the center and integrative *decision-making* capacity—the ability to send out authoritative signals which result in action being taken (subject to the pathologies discussed in the remainder of this chapter). Through the Office of Management and Budget (OMB) in the United States there is at least as good an information flow in the federal US government as there is through HM Treasury in the United Kingdom, and the Executive Office of the President provides a more personalized integrating function for the chief executive than does the Cabinet Office for the British Prime Minister. However, in the British case a decision taken within the executive is likely to be the authoritative one, subject merely to legitimation by the legislature, whereas many but by no means all Presidential proposals are subject to modification and rejection by a Congress which, despite its own attempts to improve its integrative decision-making capacity, largely reflects a segmented approach to decision-making. In the United States, the courts constitute a further set of actors with effective decision-making power which may be used to overturn the decisions of executive or legislature on substantive or procedural grounds. Despite these comparative differences, most commentators characterize both process and outcome on most decisions in both countries as 'incremental'.

One possible consequence of organizational segmentation is the 'shunting' of low priority issues, with organizations exchanging information and views and giving a superficial impression of analysis and action, but with the issue failing to be resolved because of the lack of any authoritative mechanism to insist on its resolution. Only where there is conflict of a clear-cut kind do integrative decision-making mechanisms tend to come into play.

In order to get an issue off their agenda, organizations may be prepared to accommodate each other's views. This may have pathological results, with the resulting 'least unacceptable' policy failing to live up to the scale of the problem to be tackled (see 3.2.2).

Attempts to set up integrative units to funnel information, views and conflicts resolution up to a central decision-maker may perversely lead to a blurred consensus rather than the illumination of issues, since the representatives of competing organizations will prefer to arrive at a joint agreement rather than risk a settlement imposed from above (see Wilensky, 1967, 54). Wilensky argues that this is what happened in the National Security Council in the United States. It is interesting to note that the procedures for the Joint Chiefs of Staff in the UK were altered in 1982 to enable the overall chief of staff for all the armed forces to make his own recommendations, which do not necessarily reflect a consensual view of the heads of the armed services.

There are both absolute and behavioral limitations to increasing the degree of integration of information appraisal and decision-making. Absolute limitations refers to the limited time and intellectual capacity of top officials: communication is only completed if the recipient has time to read the message (see Rose, 1970, 136–7). The official also must have the ability to evaluate the information, which is especially difficult for technical information. Behavioral limitations refer to the ways in which officials respond when forced to integrate information or recommendations; this includes the accommodating behavior described above.

Where a decision does emerge, whether through fragmented or integrated appraisal, the question still arises of whether this decision is effectively communicated to those responsible for implementing it and actually results in those actions envisaged by those who took the decision—if, indeed, those who took the decision all envisaged the same action, since differences of opinion about the consequences of a decision may be blurred in order to secure agreement (see 2.1.2). One of the major pathologies of decision-making is the more or less deliberate ambiguity of the decision themselves.

4.4 Faulty nerve signals to muscles

Decisions are not self-implementing. They have to be communicated in operationalizable form to those who will be responsible for carrying out the necessary tasks. This will frequently require the production of guidelines and rule-books which spell out details of how actions should be performed. It is these guidelines and rules which individual public servants are normally asked to execute rather than the original decision itself. There is scope both in the writing of the guidelines and in the way they are interpreted for some 'drifting' from the original policy concept (see also Tullock, 1965, 138). This is true even when all concerned are conscientiously trying to carry out government policy.

Because each member of the intermediate level in a hierarchy (or in the case of intergovernmental policy delivery, the head of each of the agencies) may interpret the general policy directive in different ways, by the time the instructions reach the lowest level there may be considerable variation in the extent of selectivity or distortion.

It may be possible to reduce the extent of inadvertent policy drift by explaining the original purposes of the policy change at each level as guidelines and rules are passed on, but it may be difficult for individual public servants to relate their own work to broad policy statements. Further, individual public servants, particularly at lower levels, are likely to be held accountable on the basis of the detailed guidelines and rules rather than personal interpretation of broad policy, and, indeed, such personal interpretations of policy may be regarded as a threat by superiors.

It should not be assumed that information that a decision has been taken and the intent of that decision will necessarily reach all levels of the organization responsible for implementing it. Clear instructions may be given to executives, but not passed on in meaningful form to those responsible for day-to-day policy delivery.

Even when information is passed on, this may be understood as literally 'for your information', rather than as an instruction to carry out certain actions.

Wolman (1981, 452) quotes the example of the US Department of Housing and Urban Development (HUD) where a 1976 consultants' study showed that information from headquarters frequently did not reach the area officers or did not reach them in a timely fashion. The potential pathological consequences of this as listed in the consultants' reports were dramatic: 'changes in the delegation of authority could either be circumvented, miscommunicated, or not communicated at all'. In the large complex organizational structures common in public policy delivery, the communication of instructions or information necessary for public policy delivery cannot be taken for granted. The careful design of communications channels is as important as allocating financial resources to the program. The difficulties are all the greater when policy delivery is intergovernmental in character.

In addition to directions about the policies to be implemented, those at the delivery end of the policy process will also often require information to deliver the service. Simon (1976, 163) argues that the withholding of information from subordinates because the superior does not realize that this subordinate needs the information 'is of frequent occurrence in most organizations, largely because of lack of sufficient consideration to the needs of downward transmission of information other than orders'.

Attempts to avoid the problems of failure to communicate information or instructions by issuing very detailed guidelines may be counter-productive if public officials are overwhelmed by their volume. As Wolman (1981, 452) puts it, 'instructions issued by superiors may be so complex and prolific that they conflict with each other or are simply so unwieldy, that they are unusable in day-to-day decisions'. In other words, only by ignoring the guidelines and rules is practical implementation possible. Hence, we have the paradox that failure to abide by guidelines designed to ensure policy implementation, far from being pathological, may be functional to carrying out the original policy intentions.

As Hood (1976, 59) points out, 'Modern administration very largely proceeds by use of words.' The problem is that in order to make policies operationalizable, that is to convey information in a form which enables policies to be implemented, it may be necessary to categorize individuals or circumstances. Yet the range of variations in individual circumstances is likely to show greater diversity than is allowed for in the set of categories. As a result, there will be many 'hard cases' both in the sense of difficulty in assigning individuals to categories and substantially different treatment of individuals in very similar circumstances (Hood, 1976, 62).

The pattern of distribution of policy outputs which results may not be the same as that envisaged in the original policy (insofar as clear thought was given at that stage), quite apart from the perverse effects which may arise from 'categorization' or 'labelling' of individuals as policy targets (see Sieber, 1981, 140-9; Dexter, 1981). However, political or legal norms of due process or equal treatment may preclude a non-categorization approach which gives flexibility in individual cases (see also 9.4).

Vaguely defined policy objectives are subject to being interpreted in a number of different ways even by those responsible for actually implementing the policy. Where the program is administered through a number of different agencies, such as local authorities, a variety of different interpretations may be implemented. Despite the obviousness of the point that if it is not clear what is intended it is very difficult with the best will in the world to be sure that those intentions are carried out, the language of many policy decisions is unclear (Wolman, 1981, 452). Conversely, attempts at precise definition may lead to gobbledegook which, though legally correct, is nonsensical for those implementing the policy, and those who are policy targets.

The implementation structure may be ambiguously designed so that conflicting guidance is received from different superiors, either through inadvertence or disagreement amongst those superiors. An example of such conflicting guidelines would be where financial guidelines issued by the budget section were incompatible with procedural guidelines issued by a line section head.

A rather different type of pathology is where an instruction, guideline or information is received and understood by those responsible for implementing it but it is deliberately exploited to promote a pattern of policy outcomes divergent from that intended by the original decision-makers. Here we are referring solely to exploitation by service deliverers which is perfectly legal and within the remit of the institution (see Sieber, 1981, 89-90, 102-3). In the case of professions, particularly the health care professions, the government may deliberately refrain from detailed specification of the outputs to be delivered because it accepts the profession's case for discretion and autonomy. The sum of the actions taken by the profession's members are, however, unlikely to maximize the goals of improving the quality of health.

Finally, the intent of an instruction may be perfectly clear but because of the wording of the instruction, i.e. the 'information' actually conveyed, the intent of the instruction can be deliberately ignored or thwarted (see the example quoted in 8.5). In a context of such recalcitrance watertight wording is required.

4.5 Information failures in reaching policy targets

Front-line public employees may not have the information necessary to ensure that they can actually reach the policy targets. There may be a lack of information about what distinguishes target clients from those with otherwise similar characteristics (see 9.4).

For other programs, benefits may be delivered only to those who realize that they can get them and who identify themselves to the delivery agency as eligible. This is the classic problem of take-up rates, which occurs with a number of social and other benefits where some degree of initiative on the part of the target client is required. Both simple ignorance and confusion about complexity exist. Low income households with special problems which government has programs to ameliorate are particularly likely to be unaware of the benefits they are entitled to (see Field, Meacher, and Pond, 1977, 87). It is noticeable that take-up rates are low where benefits are targeted at, say, tenants in the private sector, whereas those so entitled in the public sector are more likely to be identified as eligible as part of their exchange of information with a public agency as landlord.

However, even businessmen, whom one might expect to be more sophisticated in their awareness of available funding, show a considerable degree of ignorance or do not fully incorporate the availability of incentives into their investment decision (Walker and Krist, 1980). For both social benefits and industrial investment incentives, simple ignorance about the availability of specific benefits is compounded by confusion about the complexity of the variety of sources of benefits and the way they interact.

Another type of problem is where someone else, either known or unknown, is acting in a direction which offsets the action of the delivery agency. The other hand or hands pushing in the opposite direction may be other public policy programs designed to fulfil conflicting policy objectives (see 2.1.1, 3.2). However, a focus on public policy alone carries the danger that it will exaggerate the extent of government influence. Government is only one of many sources of information and influence and may have to compete for the attention of its citizens (cf. Deutsch, 1963, 162).

We should not assume that making more information available about eligibility will necessarily improve policy delivery: in some cases it may make it worse. In section 4.4 we discussed problems of categorization from the implementing officials' point of view, but categorization is also very little help if in the real world individuals or objects or circumstances straddle these categories or can easily slip from one to the other (Hood, 1976, 60–6). Individuals may slip into categories which receive benefits and economic activities may be adjusted to slip out of the tax net. Here the pattern of 'information' implied in the policy is falsified through its very communication.

4.6 Learning disabilities

One of the major pathologies of modern public policy is the failure of government to realize that programs it is delivering are failing to achieve their objectives or are even acting in a way contrary to those objectives. If we lived in a world of complete certainty and perfect administration there would be no need for evaluation. Having selected the best option and put it into operation, we would know in advance what its effects would be. However, our understanding of many problems, especially social problems, is imperfect or even contested. Our understanding of how government intervention will work and what its effect will be is therefore also limited. Further complications arise because this government intervention may be only one of many influences on the target problem, because unforeseen changes may arise, and because it may be difficult to separate the effects of a 'new' program from the long-term effects of programs which have been replaced. All these problems make it both necessary to monitor the delivery of a program and evaluate its success and very difficult to do so.

The ability to secure feedback about the effects of policies through evaluation is therefore crucial to the whole operation of delivering effective policies over time. Deutsch (1963, 128) goes so far as to argue that as long as feedback channels remain unimpaired considerable damage to receptors or effectors may still permit steering. Despite the fact that the importance of evaluation is now strongly recognized, in the United States at least, evaluation is frequently something tacked on at the end of policy design rather than something integrated with it. Although evaluation is concerned with what happens once a policy has been put into effect, it is important that it should not be left until that stage before considering the issue of how to evaluate the policy (Rutman, 1980). If we wait until after program delivery has already started, we may find that evaluation is impracticable or produces inconclusive results. The time to consider evaluation is at the option selection and program design stages where the type of information required can be specified in advance. More dramatically, the extent to which an option is capable of being evaluated can be made one of the criteria for selection.

Of course, evaluation of some kind takes place for all programs. Many of the feedback channels involved in monitoring the behavior of subordinates may also provide sources of information on the impact of programs. Feedback, solicited and unsolicited, will also occur in largely anecdotal form through clients, constituency groups and the press. However, as Wolman (1981, 459) points out, 'these means of feedback have obvious limitations. Anecdotes, personal impressions, and group reactions may be biased in terms of unique interests or perspective of the recounter. Moreover, they are based on a small number of cases and are not easily generalisable.'

Systematic evaluation is often a difficult and uncertain enterprise (see Weiss, 1972), with much of the difficulty arising from informational pathologies. First of all, the objectives of the program may not have been clearly specified (see 4.4). In other words, insufficient information is provided in the decision itself. This in turn may reflect inadequate conceptualization about the problem at earlier stages of the policy process (see 4.1).

Second, although the term 'program' is frequently used, mainly in the United States, to designate a specific set of actions by public policy deliverers, the difficulty of clearly defining those actions which constitute part of the program is often much more difficult in the real world. This is particularly true where lower tier agencies use programs funded by higher-level governments to make up a cocktail to enable implementation of favored projects. In such circumstances it is clearly very difficult to specify what the effect of the program is.

Third, the types of problems of target identification listed in 4.5 also have problems for evaluation. If it is impracticable to identify all potential clients for service delivery, it is clearly also going to be difficult to identify them to be able to evaluate whether the policy has actually reached them, though survey techniques may assist the analyst to get round this problem.

Fourth, major difficulties can arise in *measuring* what has or has not happened.

Finally, the given program is likely to be impacting on its target clientele in conjunction with a wide range of other influences, including other public policy programs, whose overall effect may be extremely difficult to disentangle.

Learning is not just about the receipt of information but about drawing conclusions from it and acting on it. Not all feedback and learning will necessarily help the survival or development of the policy. We can distinguish three types of learning (cf. Deutsch, 1963, 169). First, there is the relatively routine feedback which neither adds to nor detracts from the subsequent capacity of the organization to learn or develop further.

Second, there is creative learning which increases the ranges of possible intake of information by the organization from the outside world and the ways in which that information is appraised.

Finally, there is pathological learning, when the lessons drawn from experience reduce the organization's subsequent capacity to learn and control its own activities. Pathological learning from complacency is the more subtle danger: a program or organization evaluated as a success at one period may as a result be reinforced to emphasize the apparently successful features, but these features may have reduced the capacity of the organization to identify further threats or adapt to them (see Deutsch, 1963, 227–8).

Pathological learning from 'getting one's finger burnt' is all too common. Adverse evaluations may be suppressed. The moral drawn may be to avoid involvement in activities with high political risk even where these are central to policy objectives. Overpessimistic conclusions may be drawn from setbacks (Sieber, 1981, 24). Learning involves more than merely reacting to experience.

Another pathological form of reaction to feedback is over-steering: moving back past the correct path to another set of mistakes in the opposite direction. This may also be associated with delay as a feature both of collecting evaluation information and reacting to it. The result of delays may be a program which produces perverse results in the opposite direction, whether because of over-reaction, or because the target problem has developed further during the reaction time (which includes both time to take a decision and the time necessary to implement it). This is notoriously a problem in 'steering the economy' (Brittan, 1971). Deutsch (1963, 226) provides a neat analogy: 'strong responses that come late are characteristic of oversteering, in the manner of the novice automobile driver who barely avoids the left-hand ditch by turning his car towards the right-hand one'.

4.7 Failures of memory

There are some rare occasions when a single person or group of individuals head an organization for so long that their personal memories contain much of the memory of past developments and the lessons that were drawn from them. Such memory makes for simple recall but leads to catastrophic loss of organizational memory when individuals leave, quite apart from the other patho-logical consequences of extended leadership by the same individual or group, as J. Edgar Hoover's leadership of the FBI exemplifies (see also 3.8). Even in such cases the bulk of records will be formal-ized and in written or other permanent form.

Such records are relatively easy to design and operate when we are talking about multiple files of a standard type, for example, client histories. However, the design of *policy* records, though far more important for the long-run development of policy, is far more diffi-cult and far less subject to structured analysis. Memory, of course, is not just about the storage of information but the retrieval of the *relevant* information at the appropriate time. Devising means of ensuring access to policy-relevant information about the past is particularly difficult.

Even in cases where an organization is considering a policy directly parallel to one it has operated in the past, memory may fail completely (Hogwood and Peters, 1983, 261–4). Rather dis-turbingly, such failures are most likely when effective memory is most desirable: when the organization has been engaging in a rapid sequence of policy changes, especially if these have been associated with frequent organizational successions. Even where great care is taken, some failures to draw appropriate lessons from past experience will occur. However, a major reason for memory failure is the lack of recognition that past experience may be relevant and therefore a failure to search for records of possibly relevant experience. Effective search is, of course, dependent on the previous design of systems to enable past experience to be identified. Despite the difficulties, the position is by no means hopeless; changes over considerable periods of time in complicated sets of programs can be summarized concisely in equation form (Hogwood and Peters, 1983, 53–9).

Careful design for organizational memory requires analysis of the various types of memory failure which occur. The first is simple lack of memory, where information about past experience is not recorded or has been discarded prematurely.

The second problem is the form in which the records about the past are maintained. Raw data in the form of, say, files about past clients are singularly unhelpful in drawing lessons about past performance, particularly when a policy decision has to be made quickly. It may even be that nowhere in the organization's records is there an adequate summary containing a clear specification of the components of past programs and how they changed over time. It is more likely that there may not have been any systematic evaluation of programs in the past (see 4.6). Poor feedback leads to poor memory.

Another type of memory failure is the failure to realize that there is a memory, that is to consult records about past experience. It apparently frequently does not occur to policy-makers or policy advisers that their predecessors had been there or somewhere similar before and that their consideration of the 'new' issue might benefit from learning about the outcome of the treatment of similar issues in the past. Of course, there is frequently 'folk wisdom' in an organization of the 'we-tried-that-before-and-it-didn't-work' variety, but this may be an impediment to examining what actually happened and trying to draw positive as well as negative lessons.

The most problematic type of memory failure is the inability to relate past experience, even when known, to policy issues currently confronting the organization. This is particularly likely to be a problem when the current issue and past problems are not directly parallel. This ability to recombine information from memory with information about new circumstances is ultimately a personal skill which the careful design of information systems can assist but not assure.

4.8 The paradox of improved information

In this chapter we have pointed to a number of potential 'second order' pathologies arising from attempts to improve existing information pathologies:

> Improvements in incoming information may clog internal channels of communication.
> Increasing the amount of information flow to decision-makers may simply overload them as may attempts to eliminate the fragmented features of decision-making.
> Greater clarity and detail in the wording of decisions may overwhelm implementing officials.
> Attempts to improve take-up rates may cause budgetary strain.

Above all, even, or perhaps especially, a program based on initially careful data collection and unambiguous decision-framing may continue to be delivered well after it is no longer appropriate if there is inadequate feedback about changing circumstances and program impact. More frequent response to recent feedback may strain the capacity of organizational memory to store and recall the relevant lessons of an increasing number of past program configurations. In all this it has to be borne in mind that improved data collection and appraisal may itself use up resources which otherwise would be available for substantive program delivery.

Further, improvements in the internal flow of communication within an organization should not be considered in isolation from their implications for external inputs. As Sieber (1981, 64) points out, 'excessive reliance on improvement of internal communication and collective decision-making can undermine the use of expert resources from outside the organization with the result that innovative effort is poorly conceived and carried out'.

Formalized information-processing procedures and the greater use of hardware such as computers have a considerable potential for increasing information appraisal and information flow within an organization, but used in inappropriate ways they also have capacity to inflict harm. As Wilensky (1967, 185) puts it:

Insofar as the managers ask the wrong questions and muster poor intelligence, wrong decisions will be more efficiently arrived at, and poor judgement, now buttressed by awesome statistics, will be made more effective. Wherever the new tools and perspectives are institutionalized, more weight will attach to data and systems analyses, whatever their quality. The chance is increased that information errors will ricochet at high speed throughout the system.

There is a danger that improved information technology may lead to 'hard' quantitative data driving out 'soft', but arguably more important, qualitative data. It is much more difficult to improve the preparation and use of qualitative assessments than to improve hard information collection and flow.

The flow of information and the uses to which it is put are as much a product of human behavior as of whether or not a particular piece of data has been collected by the organization. Given the importance of informal relative to formal methods of communication and of discretion in filtering information to be passed to and from superiors, attempts to remove information deficiencies through improving formal channels while neglecting the importance of mutual trust and advantage in deciding what information to pass on and what to withhold may lead to the perverse result of further information pathologies. To ignore the behavioral implications of proposals to improve public policy information is a recipe for failure.

5

Delusions and Other Mental Disorders

One affliction which often plagues government is delusions and misperceptions of the world within which it functions, and the nature of its own capabilities. Our chapter on information (Chapter 4) emphasized the problems associated with information flow to the 'brain' of government. This chapter will discuss the peculiar ideas which may be lodged in that brain that will make it react to information in apparently irrational manners—or which will make it impervious to information no matter how timely, correct, and compelling that information may be.

The majority of the delusions which we discuss concern the manner in which governments perceive their environments, with a general finding that governments tend to perceive their environments as hostile and threatening. This appears to be true both of their international and their domestic environments. These delusory perceptions of the environment then tend to produce patterns of behavior which are expensive and potentially dangerous.

Somewhat paradoxically, another group of delusions entertained by government is of great power and virtual omnipotence. The very size and the financial and legal resources of government may give those running it the feeling that their might is limitless and they may control whatever forces in the society and economy they wish. Thus, when governments seek to control the uncontrollable at times, their lack of success may in turn reinforce the other delusions that their environment is a very dangerous and wicked place.

The delusions which plague governments are often the product of their collective experience and are stored in a collective memory; a memory to some degree shared by all members of the society. Delusions appear to result from learning lessons too well, rather than not learning them at all (see also 4.6). Thus, the lessons of foreign policy before World War II led to the development of a 'Munich mentality' which regarded any attempt to negotiate with real or potential enemies as appeasement. Similarly, the successes gained by some governments in dealing with *some* social problems, especially the more tractable problems such as providing incomes to the elderly and unemployed, led governments to believe that they could solve *all* social problems. This led governments of many industralized societies to expect overnight success when they addressed problems which were in some cases centuries in the making.

5.1 Paranoia

We have nothing to fear but fear itself (Franklin D. Roosevelt).

Paranoia is the existence of unreasonable and ungrounded fears. It is quite normal for individuals to fear certain eventualities such as death, injury, or perhaps economic hardships. It is only when these fears have little or no grounding in fact—the millionaire fearing that he will die old and penniless—and become incapacitating that a pathology occurs. Much the same would be true for governments. Governments naturally fear invasions, civil unrest, and deposition but it is only when those fears dominate policymaking and prevent government from undertaking other necessary functions that we can see an analogous pathology occurring.

Pathological paranoia in government occurs primarily in international affairs. Governments may perceive even friendly nations as presenting a threat or they may perceive really hostile nations as presenting a much greater threat than they do. Such apparent paranoia may be the function—as mentioned above—of learning historical lessons too well and may therefore be seen as having some grounding in fact. For example, the Soviet Union's fears about any unrest in Eastern Europe and their very strong perception of external threats can be seen as the product of a long history of being invaded from the West and most specifically of the invasion during the World War II in which they lost millions of lives.

Paranoia, and paranoid behavior in international politics, may be seen as creating almost self-fulfilling hypotheses. Any nation which feels threatened by another will tend to arm itself to a greater extent than would otherwise be true and would tend to make unfriendly and/or threatening statements against its perceived threats. These actions may in fact *create* the very unfriendliness which was thought to exist in the first place.

In domestic politics, paranoia is most commonly manifested in fear of subversion and intrigue. This may, of course, be perceived international conspiracies, but may also be related to perceived internal conspiracies. One of the most paranoid periods in the history of any country occurred in the United States during the McCarthy period (Hofstader, 1968). There was the fear of the 'red under the bed' which seemed to captivate national politics and divert attention from more pressing problems. Paranoia in domestic politics is frequently directed against ethnic and religious groups who are perceived—usually incorrectly—as threats to the way of life of the country in question. Examples of this behavior include the Klu Klux Klan and the Know Nothing Party in the United States, and the speeches of Enoch Powell in the United Kingdom. Paranoia can be strictly personal as well and may lead political leaders, such as Richard Nixon, to extreme folly. Not only the Watergate break-in, but much of the conduct of his administration, demonstrated an extreme fear and mistrust of others in government (Aberbach and Rockman, 1976).

Information is commonly perceived as a cure for paranoia. If we learn more about our perceived enemies we may find that in most ways they are like us. Likewise, if we learn more about recent immigrants we may find that they are not a threat and desire much the same sort of future as we do. Unfortunately, as the next section will point out, governments may tend to compound their problems of paranoia with the use of secrecy.

5.2 Agoraphobia

> Once you embark on this business of striptease of government, where do you stop? (Burke Trend).

In medical terms agoraphobia is fear of open places. In policy-making, the obvious analogue is a fear of openness with the public and with the press, and the development of a mentality which regards secrecy as crucial to the development and implementation of 'good' policy. Secrecy is especially common in making foreign policy, but may be accepted even in making domestic policy. Further, although most countries readily accept secrecy as appropriate in foreign policy, there may be arguments that secrecy is as damaging there as in making domestic policy, or even more so.

The fundamental argument favoring secrecy is well-expressed in policymaking circles in the United Kingdom. It is felt by those who accept the prevailing doctrine of secrecy in all aspects of policymaking that if the public were aware of the manner in which decisions are made and the options which are being considered, or even that certain types of decisions were being considered, they would attempt to intervene and the resulting policies would be more the product of political pressures than of deliberation and considered judgement of those who have the responsibility of governing the country. Open government, then, would mean the abrogation of the constitutional duties of the Government to govern the country, and then be judged on their record at the next election. Further, it can be argued that the secrecy of certain types of decisions, e.g. the announcement of the Budget each Spring, makes those policies more effective and may prevent some misallocation of economic resources leading up to the announcement.

For individuals and groups, just as governments, secrecy can have a great deal of appeal; Shils (1956) referred to the 'fascination of secrecy.' Secrecy, with its associated control of information, means power over others. In addition, secret organizations may appear much larger than they are, thus potentially striking fear into their opponents. But secrecy is no undivided benefit. Organizations which by virtue of their secrecy do appear larger than they are invite overreaction from their enemies, e.g. a revolutionary group which appears large will be more likely to be repressed than a smaller one. Further, recruitment and communication among members is more difficult in secret organizations so that it is more difficult to coordinate the activities of the organization (Fidel, 1980).

The utilization of secrecy in government may produce a number of undesirable consequences. Of course, in democratic governments there is the fundamental problem that secrecy will mean that the public will not know what is being done in their name by government. Even if there are elections and a free press, the ability of governments to control the flow of information allows that government to manipulate the public to a greater extent than would be true with a more open government (Leigh, 1982). The majority of democratic societies now have quite open governments—one Swedish official likened working in Swedish government to working in a goldfish bowl. This may result in a good deal of embarrassing information coming before the public, but also may make democracy in its more plebescitary form more effective as well.

Secrecy may also impose some costs on government. One is a lack of coordination of organizational activities. While the Federal Bureau of Investigation (FBI) in the United States was involved in infiltrating domestic radical organizations—ranging from the Klu Klux Klan to the Communist Party—they often found after the fact that the people whom they had identified as the most important members of the organization were actually other FBI agents. It was natural for those attempting to infiltrate the organizations to be the purest and most outspoken members possible, and hence agents spent a great deal of their time and effort following and reporting on other agents (Wilensky, 1967). Similarly, with a number of organizations attempting to control the importation and distribution of narcotics into the United States there have been instances in which the undercover agents of one organization have attempted to entrap the agents of other agencies. Some amount of secrecy is deemed to be important to protect the safety of the undercover operatives, but excessive secrecy appears to produce inefficiencies.

Secrecy may also have the effect of removing a source of error correction for governments. When government decision-making is more open, there is an opportunity for outsiders to point out the errors which those in power may be making. This could be especially valuable when outsiders know of impending decisions long enough before the decision to be able to muster evidence in support of an alternative to the official position. In this regard Williams (1983) contrasts the experience of the United States with multiple advocacy groups and research organizations each attempting to have an influence over policy with the more hermetically sealed world of policymaking in the United Kingdom. Something analogous to a competitive market for information arises in the United States and although there may be confusion at times there may also be a great deal of useful information and opinion generated. In the United Kingdom the official view predominates with little challenge, except perhaps after the fact.

Secrecy may also mean that secret information sometimes becomes more valuable than openly collected information. In the intelligence community, or even in the criminal justice community, 'secret sources' and 'secret informants' have a particular appeal, and when the information derived from these sources is in conflict with information from open sources the secret information tends to be accepted. This is true even if the openly derived information can be verified whereas that from the secret sources almost by definition can not. For example, at the time of the Bay of Pigs fiasco, there was ample evidence from the media that the area to be invaded was defended and that the morale of the Cuban people and armed forces was high. 'Secret sources' used by the CIA, on the other hand, told them that the Cuban people were ready to rise in rebellion against Fidel Castro, and that the Bay of Pigs area was undefended. It is quite clear which information was correct in that instance (Wilensky, 1967).

As noted, secrecy has commonly been employed in international affairs and it has conventionally been assumed that a country should keep its enemies in the dark as to its military potential and the nature of available weapons. It can be argued, however, that secrecy tends to create even greater insecurity than would otherwise be the case, and hence tends to escalate tensions and increase the arms races which appear to lead up to actual violence (McGuire, 1965). Secrecy simply compounds the problems of paranoia and realistic fears which exist in international politics. In addition, inadequate information on the part of a potential enemy may lead that enemy to underestimate the potential of a country and lead them to believe that they could easily win an encounter. Thus, either by creating anxiety or by creating a false sense of relative power, secrecy may be counter-productive from the point of view of reducing the possibilities of war. The doctrine of 'open covenants openly arrived at' may have been a desirable policy after all.

Secrecy, or the fear of openness in government, is a widely accepted means of governments dealing with their international environments, but less commonly accepted as a means of coping with the domestic political and policy communities. In both cases, however, secrecy may produce undesirable results ranging from simple inefficiencies to the greater possibility of war. Both the persistence of secrecy in the government of the United Kingdom and the difficulty of developing effective inspection systems in international arms agreements indicate that despite these pathologies the fascination of many people with secrecy will tend to persist.

5.3 Delusions of grandeur

> It is the guarantee of due process, not the guarantee of infallibility, that democratic institutions require (Herbert Simon).

Theodore Roosevelt once referred to the presidency as a 'bully great pulpit' from which he could speak. To some degree government as a whole is such a pulpit and standing on high in that pulpit it is easy to believe in the power and majesty of government. But converting the power of government and all its other resources into action is not so simple as preaching a good sermon to the faithful. Governments and politicians frequently get themselves into the situation of promising more than they can ever deliver, and attempting to control more than they can ever control. These promises then get governments into situations which make them appear more impotent than they are, and certainly more naïve than many of the people who work in government are. To some degree the nature of democratic politics is such that in order to get something done a great deal must be promised; in order to get a small program established it must be made to seem as if it will solve virtually all of the problems of society.

The War on Poverty in the United States is perhaps the best example of a program suffering from delusions of grandeur. This was a series of programs—such as Model Cities, Head Start, and the Office of Economy Opportunity—which were supposed to 'solve' the problems created by generations of poverty and, for many of the poor, discrimination. Even a sympathetic analyst of the programs deemed the rhetoric 'flamboyant' (Aaron, 1978, 27). A somewhat less sympathetic analyst notes that:

This is the essential fact. The Government did not know what it was doing. It had a theory. Or rather a set of theories. Nothing more. The U.S. Government at this time was no more in possession of a confident knowledge of how to prevent delinquency, cure anomie, or overcome the midmorning sense of powerlessness than it was the possessor of a dependable formula for motivating Vietnamese villagers to fight communism (Moynihan, 1973, 240).

Rather naturally, conservative critics of the programs regarded them as large and wasteful exercises in futility.

We have already noted, however, that some programs must be carried on in a grand manner or they might as well not be carried on at all. The pathological element may arise, therefore, in one of two ways. One is by not matching the scale of the program to the problem being addressed (Schulman, 1980), or by addressing problems which governments do not have the methodology and means to solve, even if they could come up with the appropriate scale. As Moynihan has written, government in the 1960s in the United States simply did not know what to do about the problems it had undertaken to solve.

It should be noted, of course, that it is not always those in government who have the delusions of grandeur; at times those delusions are forced on to them by activists in the society, or simply by events which seem to beg for some policy response. Governments, then, have to some degree become the victims of their prior successes. From the time of the end of World War II until at least the first international oil crisis it appeared that governments in Western countries could do almost anything they wished and do it well. This was a period of unprecedented economic growth and government was quite willing to take the credit for the successes. Many citizens have now learned that government is not the panacea for all the ills which may beset their societies, but old habits are difficult to break. When a new or potentially expensive problem arises, the modal response remains to give the problem to the public sector and let them struggle with it.

A variant on delusions of grandeur is manifested primarily in policy analysts, although it times is seen in politicians as an occupational disease. This is to assume that there is a solution to every problem, and not only a solution but a relatively simple and painless solution. Thus, policy analysts, because of their rationalist training, and politicians, because they have to 'sell' programs to citizens and to other politicians who do not want complexity and indeterminacy, will either assume that if they can think hard and long enough they can come up with the right answer or that simple answers are always to be preferred to complex answers (see also 5.4).

Another variation of delusions of grandeur is to build monuments to grandeur, either national or personal. There is a common delusion that building a great building, ship or airplane will establish the place of a country in the world hierarchy. One obvious example was the building of the Concorde by France and the United Kingdom. There appears to have been an assumption that developing this plane would refurbish some of the lost glory of these two countries after having lost their former colonial empires and their place as world superpowers. Other obvious examples are the numerous cities who clamor to host the Olympics and World Fairs every few years even though these events are almost invariably economic nightmares. It is deemed that to host an event such as this is to get City X 'on the map'. These monuments are almost invariably costly and may not even create the symbolic benefits intended. One lesson to be learned, however, is that, if you want to build a monument, a statue requires only periodic cleaning to remove the homage paid by pigeons; an airplane, or a hospital, or a university imply large running costs in addition to the initial investment (see 5.7).

5.4 Idées fixes

Analysts as well as governments can have delusions about their importance. Expert advisers to government trained in a specific discipline may, without realizing it, suffer from the delusion that a single methodology can solve the problems of society. This has been seen most clearly in economists (Self, 1975), but at times those who construct social indicators and those who are keen on statistics and operational research will assume that their particular methodology holds all the answers for public problems. This is almost certainly delusory, since the majority of public problems come in complex packages which cannot always be split up into conventional disciplinary problems, much less soluble through a single discipline's approach.

In their analysis of public policy, academics of various disciplines implicitly or explicitly assume models of policy based on sets of premises and relationships (Hogwood, 1978). These models may be *analytical*—designed to help us to understand issues in the abstract; *descriptive*—that is statements, generalized to a greater or lesser extent, about how a government policy operates or what its impact is; or *prescriptive*—about how a government ought to act. The use of analytical models is an accepted part of developing theories in the social sciences; by isolating a particular set of relationships from the interplay of a much wider range of relationships in the real world, we can make much stronger statements about those particular relationships. However, considerable caution is necessary in drawing prescriptive conclusions from analytical models. Where analysts interpret the world only in terms of their discipline's models they are subject to a delusion which can be pathological if others confer on them expert status.

Different disciplinary perspectives focus on different types of objectives, but this reflects much wider differences in terms of which facts and which outcomes are considered important as well as desirable. If models are selective in their focus they may neglect important values and assumptions employed by other analysts or policy actors. If all relevant analysts or political actors are agreed that analysis should take place in terms of a particular model then there will be few intellectual or practical problems arising from incomprehension at the sets of assumptions or definitions of policy offered or implied. However, this is likely to be true only in fairly limited circumstances.

These disciplinary boundaries were, of course, supposed to be straddled by the 'policy analysis' approach, but unfortunately much of the straddling has been rhetorical rather than substantial. Both the teaching and the practice of policy analysis have, with honorable exceptions, failed to achieve integration (Hogwood, 1984). At best, what is often achieved is a multi-disciplinary rather than a genuinely interdisciplinary training. Even within associations with policy analysis labels, much of the communication is between persons of the same discipline. The temporarily fashionable nature of policy analysis led to a number of disciplinary monoglots jumping on the bandwagon.

An important reason for this continuing fragmentation and the danger that it may be handed on to the next generation is that few current teachers and practitioners of policy analysis ever did a policy analysis course as part of their own training. Perhaps the greater number of trained policy analysts coming out with policy analysis degrees will gradually overcome this, but this will only occur if the courses themselves are both integrated and related to an understanding of public policy in practice.

5.5 Senility

The aging process in humans tends to create a number of mental problems generally lumped under the label of senility. Senility is not so much a disease as a set of symptoms resulting from the aging process. The most common of these symptoms is the loss of memory, especially memory for recent events. It is not uncommon for the senile to be able to remember events which occurred in their childhood while forgetting the events of the day before, or even the same morning. It would appear that those earlier events were more strongly imprinted on the brains of the individuals than the more fleeting images of their life at present.

Governments and governmental organizations appear to exhibit similar behaviors. It is not uncommon for governments to rely very strongly on the principles which they manifested, or thought they manifested at the time of their foundings, even if some of those ideas may have become increasingly meaningless as the world about them changed. In the United States, some arguments over the constitutionality of particular activities by the federal government have centred on the intent of the framers of the Constitution rather than on the meaningfulness of those procedural and substantive restrictions in a world some 200 years later.

At the organizational level, the existence of standard operating procedures is in part a similar manifestation of senility. Once a procedure is established it tends to persist and to persist without serious reexamination. Having the procedure is evidence that the problem has been solved and the organization can go on to something else. These standard operating procedures then enshrine what the organization learned once, perhaps very long ago, and thus may make the organization less sensitive to their current environment and its opportunities and constraints.

Organizations tend to enshrine ideas as well as procedures. They tend to adopt ideas about the nature of the world about which they make policy relatively early in their existence and then continue to make policies based upon those ideas. Downs (1967) discussed the existence of 'age lumps' within organizations. The majority of organizations take in a large number of people when they are first formed, or when they undergo rapid expansion. These groups of employees carry with them the ideological and policy ideas of the time at which they are recruited and despite their learning, their perspective on policy issues is to some degree a function of their socialization (see also 2.2.1). Thus, the original members of the Environmental Protection Agency in the United States would be expected to be ardently committed to the environmental movement and to be less willing to trade environmental values for economic development than would people recruited to the agency during the more economically troubled 1980s. Thus, as noted previously, pathologies in policy may arise not only from governments not learning their lessons but from their learning a lesson all too well and failing to forget the older lessons in favor of new lessons arising from new circumstances.

5.6 Megalomania

Megalomania is the obsessive seeking of power. Among individuals it is said to describe people who seek to dominate others about them or to dominate their physical environment. It tends to be especially prevalent in political leaders, and even more especially among those with aggressive and ambitious personalities. While usually considered to be pathological (Hitler or Stalin), this tendency may also produce great political leaders with somewhat more conventional policies.

For government as a whole, megalomania may be manifested in the desire and virtual compulsion of government to attempt to dominate its society and to control virtually all aspects of behavior within the country. As noted above concerning delusions of grandeur, this may mean that governments get into the business of attempting to control the uncontrollable. In addition to that fundamental problem, attempts on the part of government to control large areas of their economies and societies may produce other pathological results. The first is that exercising broad scale control is simply terribly expensive. It is often said that totalitarian societies have a tremendous advantage as compared to more open societies because of the degree of control which the government has over citizens. However, it is terribly expensive to keep a policeman or a tank on every street corner and to attempt to monitor all aspects of the behavior of citizens. The ability—or willingness—of more open societies to allow many behaviors to be unregulated, or to be coordinated by market and social forces, allows them to manage their societies with considerably less direct cost.

In addition to the costs which exercising control imposes on a government, megalomania produces a certain paradox of power: the more things which a government controls the more things it has to control. This can be seen especially clearly in the area of economic policy. Leaving aside for the moment how well it works, the economy can be seen as a self-regulating system (Dornbusch and Finster, 1980). However, when government (or private forces such as cartels) choose to intervene they will upset the internal mechanisms of control and then require even greater control. Intervention with a wage policy requires in turn a price policy. Those two together may require a greater level of intervention into the labor market to make sure that firms which need more labour are able to acquire it. These things in turn may require even greater government intervention in the form of indicative or command planning. In short, when governments choose to intervene they may create the need for even greater intervention to attempt to solve the problems created by the first intervention. The search for power over a policy area may merely indicate how little power governments have when attempting to control complex social and economic forces.

5.7 The delusion of sunk costs

One delusion which governments frequently encounter, especially with large capital projects, is the 'sunk cost' problem. Once a project is initiated, there is a tendency to want to bring it to completion even if the assumptions underlying the project have changed drastically. There may be instances, for example, when it is better to leave a dam or a ship half-completed, take the losses which have already been sustained, and not throw good money after bad. To do so, however, invites the scorn of citizens and the attention of auditing or other oversight organizations. Building any large project involves forecasts of the future and despite the best efforts of those in charge of the project forecasts can be wrong (Hall, 1980). Projects initiated prior to 1973 with assumptions of cheap energy prices, or projects initiated before Three-Mile Island with assumptions about the safety of nuclear power plants were likely simply to be wrongly conceived for the period in which they would be completed, and indeed it may be better not to have completed them.

A variation of the sunk cost argument concerns running costs. The Anglo-French Concorde project (see 5.3 above) demonstrates this point rather well. The Concorde is an engineering marvel but an economic nightmare. Whether or not it should ever have been built is questionable, but it seems relatively certain that after it was built there is little justification to keep flying it. Given its capacity, energy prices, and the nature of the airlines industry in the mid-1980s it is likely to make a loss almost every time it takes off. However, in part because the costs of building it have already been sustained—as well as for symbolic purposes—it continues to fly.

The Concorde is a project where it is relatively easy to avoid adding operating costs to sunk capital costs. All that is required is to mothball the aircraft and put the personnel onto other assignments within British Airways and Air France. For some projects, however, the operating costs may have significant social and economic importance. Take, for example, the controversy over closing coal-mines in the United Kingdom during 1984. In this case, the sunk costs are truly sunk—into the ground—in the form of existing coal pits. The proposals of the National Coal Board to close uneconomic pits would first deprive a number of currently employed miners of their traditional employment and probably convert a number of villages—especially in Wales—into virtual ghost towns. In addition, once the mines are closed it will be difficult or impossible to reopen them. In such instances, sunk cost arguments, or variations thereon, may have more weight. There is certainly no guarantee of employment for miners nor is there economic justification for mining coal which loses money on each ton mined. What are important are the political difficulties encountered when trying to deal with such sunk costs. Thus, governments should remember that to some of their citizens' entitlement programs (see 7.2) have the form of jobs as much as social benefits.

6

The Problem of Obesity

6.1 Is government obese?

The complaint most commonly voiced against present-day governments is that they have become 'too big'. The analogy with human physiology would be that governments have become obese. However, unlike humans for whom there are accepted tables of desired body weights by height, there is no agreed standard against which to compare the size of governments. In fact, there is really no agreed system for measuring the size of government (Peters and Heisler, 1984; Aronson and Ordeshook, 1980). Thus, those who discuss the 'bloating' of government and complain about its size are begging the questions of both measurement and evaluation.

We can think about government, or a program within government, becoming obese (leaving aside the exact meaning of that term) in one of two ways. The first, which we will call gluttony, would be through government absorbing an increased shared—a 'too large' share—of the goods and services in the economy. This pattern of obesity would be manifested by government taking more, spending more, and employing more people, even though the functions of government have not increased. Some programs, if not whole governments, appear to have grown in this manner. For example, Social Security in the United States, while enhanced since the 1930s (Hogwood and Peters, 1983, 101–4) is essentially the same program with drastically increased costs. Gluttony has been blamed on aggressive bureaucratic entrepeneurs (Niskanen, 1971) as well as on demographic and production cost changes (Larkey, Stolp and Winer, 1981; Baumol, 1967). In any case, government programs simply cost more.

The second type of obesity is termed 'ramification,' the taking on of new programs and policy areas. Naturally, if this type of growth is seen as producing obesity, then it must be said that the program areas into which government is moving are inappropriate and represent government involvement in issues where it has no rightful place, or where its intervention may produce more harm than good. Given the 'tools' (Hood, 1983) available to government, growth by ramification may occur without any significant increase in public expenditure. In fact, it is frequently those areas which involve relatively little direct public expenditure, e.g. regulation, which generate the most complains about government growth.

Gluttony and ramification need not covary, although governments which are involved in more policy areas tend to spend more money. The United States, despite complaints from some citizens and some notable politicians, spends rather little money through the public sector for an advanced industrial society. However, the government of the United States—especially if state and local governments are included—actually is involved in almost as many policy areas as other industrialized democracies. Frequently, however, the mode of intervention is different and US government becomes involved through regulation, loan guarantees, tax incentives, or other indirect mechanisms. If the impact of these activities could be effectively costed, as the impacts of regulation appear to have been (Weidenbaum and DeFina, 1978), then the actual 'size' of US government might be more nearly like that of other industrialized nations which, on the basis of expenditure and public employment, appear much larger (Peters and Heisler, 1984). At the other end of the spectrum a 'warfare state' with a large military budget but few other programs might be a gluttonous but unramified government. Some governments in Third World countries might fit into this category.

6.2 Assessing obesity

If we are to declare a government or government program 'obese', or simply too big, then we must have standards which permit such a judgement. This is difficult, especially if one is trying to be objective rather than simply relying upon political rhetoric. The difficulty is compounded by the availability of at least four alternative methods of evaluating whether public expenditure or other public interventions are too large.

6.2.1 Politics

One means of evaluating the size of government is strictly political, with the political criterion coming directly from the mass public;

government expenditures or interventions are too large if they exceed those desired by the public. In a large and complex government dealing with equally large and complex problems such a criterion may appear naïve or even undesirable, but it is certainly a test of the functioning of a political democracy.

The problems of reflecting the wishes and desires of the mass public through the political process are numerous. To the procedural difficulties must be added the problem of interpreting what appear somewhat ambiguous ideas about the size of government. Free and Cantril (1968, 32) described the attitudes of Americans toward government as 'operational liberals' and 'ideological conservatives.' That is, at the program level, e.g. Food Stamps or Social Security, most Americans favor preservation of the programs. However, when asked general questions, Americans will express opinions condeming 'big government' and wanting lower taxes and less government intervention. This separation in the minds of individuals was nowhere more evident than in the results of surveys of Californians who had voted for Proposition 13, severely limiting state government revenues from property taxes. When these voters were asked which programs they wanted cut as a result of the tax cut there was a majority in favor of cutting only one program—welfare, or Aid to Families with Dependent Children—and that was not an overwhelming majority. In fact, more voters who had voted for Proposition 13 wanted programs *increased* than wanted them cut (Sears and Citrin, 1982).

Ambiguous conceptions of the proper role of government are not confined to the United States. For example, Taylor-Gooby (1982) found that his British respondents gave the welfare state 'two cheers'. In this case, however, the survey respondents appeared to be ideological liberals and operational conservatives. They liked welfare state programs but at the same time expressed an interest in having the benefits of private services—fee paying schools, private medical insurance, etc.—for themselves. Other surveys of British attitudes have, however, found patterns more similar to the United States, with a desire for lower taxes and a smaller state but continuing support for most, if not all, welfare state programs and with a desire to spend more money on almost every program except defense (Gallup, 1983; Peters, 1984).

Support for government programs and for the 'size' of government is also a function of how questions are asked, and the specific programs mentioned. Questions asked in surveys which have no consequences attached, e.g. 'Would you like to have your taxes reduced?' tend to produce the most extreme response patterns. Who doesn't want their taxes lowered? On the other hand, respondents asked if they want their taxes reduced even if it means a reduction in certain services tend to be more moderate and responsible. The same pattern emerges when asked about expenditures; citizens want to preserve and expand programs but may not always be willing to pay for them.

There are also marked differences in the support given different programs. For example, in research identifying program support in eight industrialized countries Coughlin (1979) found that in every country there was strong support for old age pensions while only in France was there significant support for public assistance. Only in the United States was there less than strong support for publicly provided health programs. Thus, a government which spent heavily on public assistance might be regarded as too big, while one that did not spend much of pensions might be regarded as too small.

We must remember that the political process tends to favor those with expenditure programs against those who would like to maintain or reduce expenditures (Kristensen, 1980). The consideration of legislation is generally subdivided functionally and advocates of a program can generate support and lobby in a constrained arena. In addition, it is generally easier to organize citizens benefiting them directly as opposed to the more diffuse benefits of reduced taxation. Further, at least in the United States, legislators whose constituents are most directly affected by a program tend to sit on committees making decisions about the programs. Even when there is not a natural majority favouring a program in committee, legislators who can benefit politically from the passage of the legislation have the opportunity to form coalitions by 'log-rolling' and vote-trading with legislators indifferent about that program but with pet projects of their own.

In summary, political criteria for determining the appropriate size of government are ambiguous. The mass public tend to oppose expenditure and taxation on principle, but favor certain programs, or frequently *all* programs. Elite opinion is assessed directly less frequently, but when it is it tends to be somewhat more pro-expenditure (Aberbach, Putnam and Rockman, 1981). In addition, the demands of the job for many political élites generate pressures for them to spend even if the majority of their constituents are in principle opposed to higher expenditures—except of course the ones which benefit them.

6.2.2 Economics

A second set of criteria for how much government should spend comes from economics. There are at least two sets of criteria here which can be used to determine if government is becoming obese. The criterion most often discussed when thinking about obesity in government comes from macroeconomics: does the size of government affect rates of economic growth, inflation and unemployment? The other criterion is from microeconomics and concerns the economic merit of each individual project proposed by government. The microeconomic criterion has become increasingly familiar in the form of cost-benefit analysis, which seeks to determine if a proposed project can make a 'profit' for society, i.e. will it produce a net benefit for society, and will it produce a greater net benefit than alternative uses of the same funds?

Evidence on the macroeconomic criterion is somewhat mixed, and has been shrouded in intense ideological and professional rhetoric. The Reagan and Thatcher governments represent the manifestations of some of that rhetoric, with the simple assumption that the cause for all the economic woes in both countries has been government expenditure. There is some evidence that larger government expenditure, especially for consumption purposes, does retard the rate of economic growth and especially capital formation (Smith, 1975). Although he quite rightly notes that the *impact* of the relationship may be meagre, Cameron (1982) does report a strong negative correlation between public expenditure and economic growth, and an even stronger relationship with reduced capital formation. On this basis, however, he argues that a larger public sector may in fact promote economic growth in advanced capitalist societies in that it can be used to bargain with labor over the social wage in order to gain wage concessions. Similarly, Cameron argues that the public sector will become the means of overcoming the principal economic problem of these societies—a dearth of capital formation.

While Cameron's arguments are unconvincing in several places, the basic point that there appears to be no strong relationship between the size of government and economic conditions does appear to stand. One can find countries with large public sectors which have been slow-growing (the United Kingdom) and those which have grown relatively rapidly (Austria). Likewise one can find countries with small public sectors which have been fast growers (Japan) and those which have been slow growers (the United States). Perhaps the only agreement in this literature on obesity is that a government which is large enough to inhibit capital formation is too large. There is as much support for that contention from neo-Marxists as from the ideological right (O'Connor, 1973; Gough, 1979).

One means by which large government, and especially social welfare expenditure, is supposed to inhibit economic growth is through making work unnecessary for large numbers of people. Those on the political right have argued that a large Welfare State will make it as attractive not to work as to work. However, the present size of social benefits in Western countries do not appear sufficient to deter anyone from entering the labour market. For example, Kahn and Kamerman (1984) found that on average in eight industrial countries a single woman with two children (the stereotypical 'welfare mother' in the United States) was 46 percent better off working at half the industrial wage than receiving social benefits. In addition, there is some evidence of large numbers of people working even at income levels below the benefit level they would receive if out of work (Field, Meacher, and Pond, 1977, 150). The work ethic appears sufficiently ingrained in most citizens to keep the economies functioning.

The microeconomic criterion for government intervention appears more precise. If a proposed project produces a net social benefit then it is worth doing; from among a set of projects producing new social benefits, choose the one which creates the greatest net benefit. This deceptively simple set of criteria actually contains several important pitfalls, to the degree that cost-benefit analysis has been referred to as 'nonsense on stilts'. This is not the place to engage in an extended discussion of the method itself (Mishan, 1973; Self, 1975; Kelman, 1981). Rather, we only point out that there is a great deal of subjectivity involved in applying these criteria. For example, for the criteria to be applied in some public programs requires a valuation of human life. Even leaving aside ethical difficulties in doing this, there are marked variations in the valuation assigned which in turn have significant effects on the analytical results (Graham and Vaupel, 1983). Further, these criteria only assist in making decisions on individual cases; they provide little guidance for making cumulative decisions about the aggregate of public projects.

6.2.3 Ethics

Another possible source of guidance for how large government should be comes from ethics. The role of government and the obligations of the State have been constant subjects of enquiry for political philosophers. As with the economic answers mentioned above, answers of philosophers as to how big government would be in order to be obese have been varied. Even leaving aside the Marxist analysis, ideas about the appropriate size of government range between those who see anything more than a simple 'Nightwatchman State' pathological to those who would regard a government which did not use its powers to create greater interpersonal equality as pathological.

The 'conservative' position has been championed by (among others) Nozick (1974), who has argued that individuals who gain any property by lawful means have a special claim to that property; any attempts to remove that property therefore must have overwhelming merit. Such a position obviously assigns government a very limited role, especially in the redistribution of income.

On the other hand, Rawls (1971), through the 'difference principle' and the 'veil of ignorance' has argued for a more equitable distribution of income, and for a stronger government to produce that distribution. He has argued that in principle any actions which seek to benefit the worst off in society are preferred to other activities. In addition, individuals would choose a more equitable society were they to make decisions about income distribution without knowing their own position in that distribution (behind the veil of ignorance). Few would be willing to select highly unequal systems if they knew there was some chance they would be in the poorest elements.

Some of the confusion surrounding the role of government from the ethical perspective results from two principal ethical criteria for the actions of government—the preservation of life and the preservation of individual autonomy—frequently being in conflict

(Glover, 1977). Does taking tax money to preserve and extend the life of a poor person deprive the more affluent person of the right to make autonomous choices about their wealth? Should the State act *in loco parentis* in order to prevent individuals from abusing their own lives and bodies? We have no definitive answers to these philosophical and legal questions. Rather, we can only recognize that the conflict exists and persists, and that as a consequence ethical criteria are not the philosopher's stone which would allow us to determine when government has become obese.

6.2.4 Policy analysis

Policy analysis involves the application of the three sets of ambiguous criteria already mentioned. However, it also provides its own deceptively simple answer to the basic question of the appropriate size of government: government is too large when it becomes incapable of attaining its goals because of its size. To a great extent the rest of this chapter will be an explication of that criterion. We should, however, point out that for many programs anorexia may be as much a problem as obesity. That is, government may be *too small* to reach its goals. The problem of malnutrition is discussed at length when discussing budgeting (see 7.5). There are, however, several points to bring out here. One is that there is a tendency in political life to look at costs and benefits of public programs from a very short-term perspective. Further, there is a tendency to concentrate attention on a single policy area rather than looking at the more diffuse impacts of public programs. These difficulties are especially evident in social and health policies.

If we adopt a long-term perspective on social expenditure as investment in human capital—an approach common in education but less common for other social expenditures—then what may appear as 'too much' in the short-term may be 'not enough' in the long-term. We begin with the knowledge that most social welfare programs, especially in the United States, have been failures in their stated goals of providing short-term relief, with the recipients soon returning to the 'mainstream of American life'. Rather, the programs have been constant facts of life for generation after generation. Poverty and dependence have been inherited like eye color. This is true in part because of the social and cultural aspects of receiving welfare, but may also be physical. Children born of poorly-nourished mothers and who are themselves poorly nourished have more learning disabilities, are less healthy, and are more likely to fall into (or not escape) poverty, than children from more affluent homes. Thus, spending money for social programs in the short term, and breaking the cycle of poverty for some, may reduce the long-term costs of the same programs so that from a strictly analytic perspective—the humanitarian perspective aside—government may not be obese but rather too lean.

The second policy-analytic point is that one policy does not exist in isolation from all other policies, and apparent savings in one program may induce costs in another. For example, a number of other programs may be impacted by a failure to spend adequately for social programs. Poor nutrition and housing produce more demand for health care, and perhaps money wasted in education. The most obvious impact of failures of the social welfare system may be manifested in the overflowing criminal justice system in the United States. Some of the blame for massive increases in crime must be borne by the continuation of poverty for a large segment of the population. Of course, even the most lavish welfare-state programs will not eliminate poverty and crime, but they do appear to eliminate some of the need for theft and some of the frustration which engenders crimes of violence. Again, leaving aside the humane elements of the argument, in simple policy terms this may mean that money spent for social programs may reduce total government costs. For example, the estimated cost of incarcerating one criminal in New York is $48,000 per year. This is greater than the average family income in the United States (approximately $23,000). It is very much greater than the average social benefit ($3,500 nationwide; $4,500 in New York). The fundamental point is that a failure to examine the amount spent for social programs in light of other programs and their costs, and the interactions of programs, may result in the faulty conclusion that social expenditures are excessive and government has become obese.

6.2.5 Summary

None of our four sets of criteria for obesity is definitive and all are subject to objection. Most fundamentally, the size of government, unlike the size of humans, is very much a matter of perception. A government which is too large for one citizen and taxpayer will be too small for another. Further, just as humans can wear dark colors and vertical stripes to make themselves appear slimmer, so too can governments adopt strategies designed to make themselves appear leaner to the public (see also 7.7). The ability to move programs to 'off-line' agencies and to address public problems through mechanisms involving little direct utilization of money and personnel allows governments to deceive, at least in part, their citizens. The problem with trying to reduce the size of government, if indeed that is the aim, is to try to get the patient to take the cure; there are any numbers of ways of avoiding the foul-tasting medicine.

6.3 Difficulties in moving quickly

One of the difficulties commonly associated with obesity is difficulty in moving quickly. For individuals this is a problem of physically moving quickly. For government, the analogous problem is difficulty in responding to new problems, or changes in old ones, and in making timely and effective responses. Size, and more specifically excessive size, affects this ability in several ways.

We should point out, however, that obesity resulting from gluttony may not present such difficulties in responding rapidly to environmental change. Paradoxically, it may create an *improved* capacity to respond. By definition, a gluttonous government has a very large amount of money and personnel at its disposal, and by definition more than it needs to fulfill its mission. In the case of obese organizations, there is budgetary 'fat' which clever managers have been able to wrest from the legislative sponsors of the organization (Niskanen, 1971). This fat, then, is an organizational resource available for responding to real or perceived problems (or opportunities) in the environment. The presence of fat is important for response because it is relatively free money which the organization may be able to expend without extensive additional involvement with the legislative sponsor. Without the need for approval from another organization, especially one as cumbersome as a legislature, the organization can respond more rapidly and perhaps more effectively. Thus, as many students of organizational behavior have argued, it is rational for leaders of organizations to accumulate as much fat as possible, in order to have the latitude to deal with eventualities, as well as to be able to cope with any budgetary cuts which maybe imposed.

Obesity resulting from gluttony might influence the ease of movement of government, or a particular organization within government, by creating a large organizational structure which is itself more difficult to cause to respond. As an organization increases in size it tends to respond more slowly to stimuli in its environment. There are more hierarchical levels through which information about the environment must filter, and back through which a decision must pass. Further, even if the organization does reach a decision, the organization is not an organism in which all parts march to a single drummer; there are still possibilities and even probabilities that some members will overtly or covertly oppose the decision (Hood, 1976; Pressman and Wildavsky, 1973). Opposition is easier to carry off in a large organization where there may be less direct control by top management, and within which it may be accepted that size produces some loss of coordination. Indeed, management may accept the lack of close coordination, knowing that the costs of imposing greater control may be prohibitive.

Obesity resulting from ramification may increase response time to emerging problems. First, as government expands its activities, there are fewer totally new things with which it can become involved (Hogwood and Peters, 1983) and, as a result, any new problems which arise will probably impinge on the 'turf' of an existing organization, and there may be 'turf fights' to decide who has jurisdiction over new problems. Even if the problem *is* totally new, the response may be delayed by the belief that with such a large government it must be someone's turf. In an obese government, not only are there numerous organizations, but a whole fourth or fifth branch government consisting of interorganizational committees coordinating the activities of other organizations. The necessity of these committees, and the bargaining associated with their decision-making, will almost certainly delay government response to problems.

As a result of the few really new problems for government, it is more difficult for governments to respond effectively to such problems. The typical response of government organizations, or other large organizations, is to categorize a new problem as an old problem and to deal with it through standard operating procedures (Allison, 1971). This in a way will speed the production of *a* response; unfortunately, it is not likely to be the *correct* response. That is, a problem which is treated incorrectly may be worse than having received no treatment at all. Policy analysis as well as medicine may be iatrogenic (Illich, 1976).

In summary, the major effects of obesity on response speed is an organizational one. The size of the budget of the organization may make little difference to its speed in responding, or may actually improve the response speed. On the other hand, obesity which results from government organizational and program ramification will, in all likelihood, produce greater degradation of response time and a government which finds it difficult to make decisions. In many present-day political systems these internal difficulties are being compounded by the close connection between government and private organizations which are virtual veto groups of government activities. While this has, at times, simplified the decision-making of individual organizations, the result at a systemic level has frequently been conflicting decisions and massive incoherence in government (Peters, 1982).

6.4 Vulnerability to heart attacks

A principal physiological problem associated with obesity in humans is vulnerability to heart attacks. These result from the clogging of arteries carrying blood to the heart and the death of a portion of the heart muscle. We have already mentioned (chapter 4) a number of problems with the flow of information in organizations—perhaps the best analogue of the flow of blood in humans—but here we are interested in the independent effects of size on these problems.

One effect of gluttony is to increase the number of hierarchical levels in an organization, thereby increasing the number of steps through which information and decision must flow, and reducing the response time of the organization. This will produce negative outcomes in and of itself, but at times responses by organizational managers may exacerbate problems. When those in charge of an organization perceive they are not receiving adequate amounts of information, there is a tendency to centralize and force all information to flow to the top. This is likely to produce more communications problems, as those lower in the organization lose the ability to sort information and select the relevant bits for transmission. If channels had been selective and incomplete, they may become very complete and very clogged. This places great strains on the information-processing and decision-making capabilities of top management with resulting analogous (or real) heart attacks.

Much the same phenomenon can be seen operating in government as a whole, or in large subsets of government, in response to growth by ramification. One of the characteristics of growth by ramification is a lessening of central control, and government by 'non-consensual directions' (Peters 1982). If those at the top of government —either elected officials or members of central agencies (Campbell and Szablowski, 1979)—wish to regain control, they must behave at a large level like a manager in any organization who is losing control. That is, they will attempt to gain control over the flow of information and ensure that they know what is happening and can try to influence events; this may be only way they can ever impose their priorities. Of course, this can produce massive congestion and perhaps even less control than in more decentralized systems.

One option for dealing with the problems of information heart attacks—as well as with real heart attacks—is the development of a bypass system. This can be done either through the development of mechanisms for identifying important materials which must be transmitted, as well as relatively automatic means for those materials to reach the top, or the use of informal techniques such as Franklin Roosevelt's alternative communicators located well down within their organizations. As with real arteries, two may be better than one and although redundancy has been criticized by advocates of efficiency, it may be valuable as a means of ensuring that vital information is transmitted and reaches its intended target (Landau, 1969).

6.5 One sip at a time

Obesity in government does not occur overnight. Rather governments and their component organizations grow slowly and (dare we say it) incrementally. For example, the data in Table 6.1 demonstrate the slow but steady growth of public expenditures in the United States and the United Kingdom during the post-war period. Obesity in goverment comes in small sips rather than in big gulps, with the principal exception being massive increases in expenditure in wartime, and the associated tendency of governments not to return to their pre-war size after a war (Peacock and Wiseman,

1967). The pattern of slow growth is found whether we think of obesity resulting from gluttony or ramification. In the case of gluttony, numerous studies of budgeting have demonstrated that the most common pattern of budgetary behavior is gradual increases in appropriations for programs and organizations (Davis, Dempster, and Wildavsky, 1966; 1974; but see Wanat, 1975; Natchez and Bupp, 1973). In the case of ramification the discontinuities and growth spurts will be more obvious, but even then 'new' programs are often simply clones of old programs.

Table 6.1
Growth of public expenditure, 1950–81
(percentage of GDP)

Year	United States	United Kingdom
1950	20.6	30.1
1955	22.8	29.0
1960	25.2	29.6
1965	25.4	30.9
1966	28.5	31.4
1967	28.9	33.3
1968	28.9	33.7
1969	28.7	33.0
1970	30.3	33.2
1971	30.2	32.9
1972	30.4	34.5
1973	29.7	34.5
1974	31.2	39.1
1975	33.6	41.0
1976	33.0	40.9
1977	32.1	39.7
1978	31.2	39.7
1979	31.4	40.0
1980	33.5	42.2
1981	34.2	44.6

Source: OECD, *National Accounts of OECD Member Nations* (Paris: annual).

The rapid expansion of government is rarely a planned outcome of the policy process. Rather, it tends to result from a large number of decisions made independently of each other. The organizations within government which make the majority of decisions about expenditures do not take into account—at least not as a first priority—the size of the public sector. Rather, they are concerned about delivering the mail, delivering bombs, or delivering babies. If all their decisions taken together add up to a larger public sector, then each organization will want to make sure that any cuts which have to be made will come from other organizations. Larkey, Stolp, and Winer (1981) liken the expansion of the public sector to the development of cirrhosis of the liver in alcoholics; it is an unplanned outcome of a set of decisions (to have a drink or two). The victims of the disease certainly do not choose the disease in the conventional sense of making a conscious choice in which the outcome was relatively certain and plain. Rather, the individual made a set of choices with a net, undesirable result.

For government, the decisions which result in a larger public sector are made across a long period of time and across a large number of organizations. Thus, political leaders at the present are paying for choices made by political leaders before them. Mayors and governors in the 1980s are beginning to face the consequences of their predecessors' failure to spend money for maintenance of public works in the form of massive bills for replacing decayed infrastructure. They are also facing the consequences of their predecessors willingness to buy off municipal unions with pensions, pensions which were not funded on an actuarially sound basis. As Larkey, Stolp, and Winer (1981) point out, the time required for the chickens to come home to roost is a limiting factor in government's responding effectively to their own decisions. Further, even if political leaders did want to avoid the types of errors mentioned above, they have powerful political incentives to commit the same errors. They can create benefits without having to impose the costs upon their voters.

Government also grows because of sips being taken at a number of different levels of government. Especially in federal governments, levels of government make relatively autonomous decisions about how much to tax and spend. Even in unitary governments, if a local authority wishes to tax and spend, and the citizens are willing to support the authority, central government may find it difficult to restrain the locality. Not only may there be no hierarchical control over taxation and expenditure in such situations, but a certain amount of psychological and political control is undermined. If many different governments are all taxing and spending, it becomes difficult for the average citizen to know what his or her total tax bill is. The little sips may not appear as much as one big gulp, and a 'fiscal illusion' is created (Wagner, 1976). This fiscal illusion may make the task of those in government seeking to have their own programs funded that much easier.

Another means by which government expenditure may grow a sip at a time is evident in military procurement, and is commonly referred to as 'goldplating'. Many weapons systems begin life as simple, functional designs, and end up as extremely complex, multi-purpose systems. As a result, many systems emerge from the procurement process more expensive than when they began, and frequently less effective than when they began. This was evident in the attempt of the US Army to purchase the MBT-70, a new main battle tank with a very simple design stressing reliability; it emerged from the procurement process as a hodge-podge which was potentially so expensive and unreliable that it was never built. This is hardly a planned process, but as designs are passed through the military bureaucracy and discussed with civilian contractors, all are able to add their own pet ideas to the project. This is a special problem when a weapons system is potentially useful to more than one of the armed services, but winds up really useful to none.

6.6 The problem of slimming cures: the problem is to take the cure

Just as television and magazine advertising offer any number of nostrums to help individuals lose weight, so too there are a number of slimming cures offered to presumably obese governments. Further, as with obese individuals, the trick to make any cure work is to take it seriously.

As with individuals, the simplest cure for obesity in government is willpower. Governments or their constituent units may be advised simply not to ask for any more more, or any more legislative authority. If this is applied to government as a whole it appears simple to implement, but may actually produce a large-scale redistribution of resources. If some organizations have to 'hold the line' on spending this may result in a cut in services, as they have rapidly growing client populations who believe themselves entitled to services (see 7.2). And if the expenditures for those programs are allowed to increase to meet the increase in clients, there will be a shift of resources away from other programs. For individual agencies, budgeting is perceived as a *bellum omnia contra omnes* and any self-denial simply means that another agency will get funds which the virtuous organization might have received. As with the famous example of grazing on the commons, individual rationality may produce collective irrationality (Hardin, 1968).

Any number of 'simple' cures have been proposed to assist gluttonous organizations in quelling gluttony. Analytic programs such as PPBS and PESC (Schick, 1966; Wright 1980; Ashford, 1981) have been devised to provide 'scientific' advice on how to reduce public expenditure and to make the use of public money as efficient as possible. Other devices, such as taxation and expenditure limitations in the American states and the balanced budget amendment at the federal level (Wildavsky, 1980) are attempts at placing somewhat arbitrary ceilings on gluttony. The 'cures' are often most unpleasant for those in government, as they attempt to impose technical decisions into a complex and highly politicized decision-making environment.

In the United States federal government the Grace Commission is a larger version of a phenomenon which has occurred in more than 30 states. Commissions of citizens—usually businessmen—are loaned to government for a short period to investigate how to reduce the costs of government. These recommendations can be quite substantial; the Grace Commission recommended cuts of $424 billion in a federal budget of $800 billion. In one southern state, there were recommendations for cutting over $380 million from a state budget of over two billion dollars. These commissions are usually well-intentioned and (from the personal experience of one author) quite hard-working. They can, however, have the opposite problem of the technical solutions discussed above and may appear excessively simplistic to those well-versed in the operations of government. Those suggestions simply may not fit into the tough political world in which policy and expenditure decisions are made. Governments often have difficulty in swallowing all the medicine which is offered to them from the private sector.

6.7 Conclusion

In thinking about obesity in government, we must remember that few governments and few people in government wish to spend money for the sake of spending money: spending money is hard work. Rather, they spend money either because they believe that they can improve the lot of some portion of the society, or because there are political pressures for them to spend. This is not to say that some individuals and organizations do not attempt to create demand for their programs, but rather that most have a sincere belief that they can help individuals and the whole nation with the programs. Thus, government expenditure should not be regarded as a public bad, but as simply government's attempt to meet the demands of citizens. There are gluttonous programs which could be as effective with less money, and at times government appears to wander into policy areas about which it knows little and over which it has little control. In addition, an increase in the size of government tends to produce increased difficulty in public management. However, big government does appear to be a feature of life in the last decades of the Twentieth Century, and should not be considered a pathology by definition.

7

Pathologies of Budgeting

It should not be surprising that budgeting exhibits a large number of policy pathologies. Given the central position of budgeting in the policy process, and the intense competition for public funds, it is understandable that there would be a number of pathological outcomes. The majority of these outcomes stem from difficulties in rationally allocating public funds. This is true at a macro-level in deciding how large the public sector should be relative to the entire economy, and is also true at the micro-level of deciding how much to spend for particular programs. Unlike the private sector, there are no agreed guidelines for success or failure and political considerations tend to dominate economic or analytic logic. To some degree this is to be valued in a democratic society in which elected officials are supposed to make decisions. But this also points out that the old aphorism that the price of democracy is high refers to more than losses in war. Thus, pathological outcomes such as hiding, earmarking, choking, and bleeding (see below) all result from using political considerations to guide budgetary choices.

A second source of pathologies is the budgetary process itself, and especially the separation of revenue and expenditure decisions in most governments. This tends to produce higher levels of public expenditure than might be expected otherwise, and allows subsidies to be attached to the tax system which might fail if they were considered as expenditures. The complexity of the modern public sector, and the overload of its decision-making structures, may make the separation of the two aspects of governmental financial policy desirable from a decision-making perspective, but it may well produce undesirable results from a policy perspective.

7.1 Earmarking

Some taxes are referred to as being 'earmarked' for certain purposes. That is, all the revenues from that tax will be devoted to a particular expenditure program. For example, all the revenue from alcohol taxes in several Scandinavian countries is used for the prevention and treatment of alcoholism. Earmarking may produce a misallocation of resources with programs receiving the earmarked revenues having more revenues than needed, and other programs being starved for resources. Or, if a program is entirely dependent upon a single revenue source, it may become starved.

Earmarking may occur in two ways, which we will refer to as 'strong' and 'weak' versions. The strong version of earmarking has the proceeds of a tax, and *only* those proceeds used for a particular expenditure program. An example of this would be the Social Security program in the United States where, unlike the majority of industrialized countries, only the proceeds of the payroll tax are used to provide social security benefits. The weak version has revenue from a particular tax devoted entirely to the program, but other funds may be used as well. Again, in the United States, the proceeds of the gasoline tax are placed in the Highway Trust Fund for the purpose of building and maintaining highways, but other funds are also used for that purpose.

Earmarking taxes has been adopted for several reasons. One is to impose restraints on expenditures. For example, it has been argued that the principal reason for maintaining Social Security financing in its current form is to prevent either a President or Congress from raising benefits in order to gain votes. With the restraints imposed by the 'strong' version of earmarking there is little enough money to pay existing levels of benefit, much less add new benefits at election time.

A second reason for maintaining earmarking is to make expenditure programs appear like insurance programs. Much of the potential ideological opposition to Social Security in the United States was defused by making the program appear as much as possible like a private insurance program. Individuals pay a 'premium' or 'contribution'; during their working life and expect to receive benefits when they retire just as they might from a private annuity. If money from Society Security contributions were intermingled with other government funds the insurance principle would be weakened or lost, and with it some support for the program.

Earmarking is also useful for generating and maintaining support for programs, especially tax programs, even if not analogues of insurance. Taxpayers and voters can see an earmarked tax producing demonstrated benefits, whereas general taxation goes into a large hopper and the connection between the tax price and benefits of a program is lost.

Despite the apparent, and real, reasons for earmarking, some pathologies may result. One, which has been all too obvious with Social Security in the United States, is that dependence upon a single form of taxation may starve the program of resources (see 7.5), especially when the economic and demographic assumptions upon which the program was founded alter significantly. For most of its 50 years Social Security actually ran a surplus of receipts over expenditures. However, as the population has continued to age and more and more people are living longer, the program faces a continuing and growing deficit, with a number of attempts, e.g. 1983 legislation, to patch up the system. It would appear that no amount of patching will solve the underlying problems of inadequate funding resulting from reliance upon a single, rather inflexible, revenue source.

Earmarking also may misallocate resources among different programs which may be substitutes for each other. For example, the gasoline tax provides a stable source of revenue for highways, but there is no comparable source of revenue for mass transit. The favoritism given the automobile may reflect accurately the preferences of most Americans, but it may also be a self-fulfilling prophecy. People may not, in fact, like to ride mass transit because it is not readily available and not very comfortable. That may be because it is underfunded. Attempts have been made to divert some resources of the highway trust fund to urban mass transit, but these encountered opposition from powerful lobbies, e.g. the trucking industry. In this instance it would appear that the utilization of an earmarked tax has produced a misallocation of funds which has adversely affected urban areas. Further, this earmarking has produced difficulties because of increases in energy prices and the failure to shift to more energy efficient means of transportation.

The utilization of earmarked revenues may also make policy successions more difficult (Hogwood and Peters, 1983). Those who have paid into an earmarked trust fund may feel that they have 'bought' the right to have a certain type of service and will protest changes. In addition to perceived rights, there may be justiciable rights as well, as in the Social Security system. Therefore, rather than receiving revenue as a fungible asset, governments, by earmarking revenues, limit their policy options.

Finally, earmarked taxes may produce delusions of various sorts (see also chapter 5). One delusion is that problems have been solved simply because a source of revenue has been dedicated to them. Again, Social Security is the obvious example of the failure of such a 'solution'. Also, as Social Security has been modified by indexing benefits, it is delusory for individuals to think that his or her contributions actually pay for their benefits. In fact, contributions of those still in work are used to pay for current benefits. Likewise, there may be delusions in the case of 'weak' earmarking that the program is entirely self-financing and does not constitute a drain on the public purse. In the first place, this may be wrong because other revenue is used to finance the program. Second, just because a program is self-financing does not mean that resources are being used in the best way. Money collected from the gasoline tax could still be collected but rather than being used for highways could be use for mass transit or other good purposes. Thus, earmarking may reduce the degree of thought and analysis in policymaking by being so automatic, and in so doing may reduce the quality of decisions taken.

It is not, however, so easy simply to say that earmarking of taxes should be eliminated. There are several good reasons why this approach to revenue collection has been adopted and been continued. What appears to be required is more careful attention to the reasons for adopting earmaking, and the negative effects which may accompany the positive effects.

7.2 Entitlements and other uncontrollable expenditures

One major factor affecting the ability of governments to budget their resources effectively is the large number of entitlement programs and other uncontrollable expenditures. The terms 'entitlement' and 'uncontrollable' are both somewhat overstated and the rhetoric associated with the names has become a part of the problem itself. The idea behind the phrase 'entitlement program' is that once programs are established citizens believe that government has a continuing obligation to provide benefits; once a program such as Social Security is established, it is believed that government has made a virtual contract with citizens to continue the program. Consequently, if a government were to attempt to eliminate the program, or even eliminate some feature such as indexing, it would be portrayed as having broken a solemn bond between the governors and the governed. Further, it is frequently believed that the initiation of a program binds future governments to continue it, rather than accepting a program of any government of the day as being as temporary as their position in office. One such elective official (and academic) lamented his fate in living in a 'pre-planned society' where even though his government wanted to alter programs and policies, their latitude was constrained by existing commitments (Tarschys, 1977). There, are, however, varying degrees of entitlement and both the Thatcher and Reagan governments have chipped away at various components of their social security systems, while leaving intact the basic pension program with its indexation features.

The concept of uncontrollable expenditures is closely related to entitlements. This concept, as developed for the US federal budget, is that expenditures for certain programs cannot be eliminated in any one year without a change in law so that any political leader has little control over how much will be spent for programs. In addition to entitlement programs, other uncontrollable expenditures are debt interest, a number of subsidy progams such as those in agriculture, revenue sharing for states and localities, and long-standing categorical grant programs. In effect, the only significant controllable elements of the federal budget are defense expenditures and raises for government employees. LeLoup (1975), however, found that many components of the budget which were called controllable in fact were quite difficult to control and, of course, all programs deemed uncontrollable—with the possible exception of debt interest—are in fact controllable. What the terminology means is that politicians do not want to have to make tough decisions which would result in reduced expenditures. The acceptance of the terminology for the programs, however, can easily result in a sense of helplessness in the face of rising expenditures, as well as a lack of responsibility for increases in expenditures.

In addition to abandoning the terminology, several other things could be done in the design of programs to make them more controllable. This is not, it should be clear, a simple ideological plea to reduce levels of public expenditures, especially for entitlement (read social) programs. Rather, it is a plea for maximizing real choices about what will be spent through the public budget rather than merely accepting decisions of previous governments.

One thing which can be done to make expenditures more readily controllable is to abandon linkage between taxation and benefits (see 7.1). So long as citizens believe that the payment of a certain tax or fee guarantees their receiving a benefit—and rightly so—many entitlements are indeed created and many programs will be uncontrollable.

In addition, programs are more likely to be considered entitlements if they completely supplant a private program, or they alter the behavior of citizens in ways that can not be reversed. Again, Social Security is an apt example because, once the program was initiated, individuals changed their means of planning for their retirement or possible disability. Any major program change therefore would have individuals without adequate funds for retirement, or at least without the levels of income they had planned. This would be true even for the more affluent who may have private pensions but who regarded Social Security as a significant component of the package which would support them in retirement. Similarly, a program such as federally funded flood insurance for people choosing to build houses or business in flood-prone areas could be withdrawn only with the possibility of great financial loss as most or all private insurers would not write policies for these areas.

Both Social Security and flood insurance are 'stock' programs. That is, they affect the stock of resources which individuals or organizations build and where they build them. On the other hand programs such as Food Stamps are 'flow' governments providing a continuing stream of benefits without any capital stock on the part of recipients. In general, 'flow' programs can be altered more easily than stock programs simply because there are no long-term assumptions in the planning of citizens and individuals are able to alter their behavior. A reduction in a flow program such as Food Stamps would, of course, produce hardships but the possibilities of adjustment are greater than with a stock program.

Controlling expenditures is also more difficult for programs provided by outsiders rather than by government itself. The contrast between the expansion of health expenditures in the United States and the United Kingdom is instructive in this regard. Health care in the United Kingdom is supplied by government through the National Health Service and most health practitioners are government employees (albeit at arm's length). They have little or no in centive to provide more services than required as would doctors being paid on a fee-for-service basis. They do place pressure on government for increases in budget and personnel which governments resist with varying degrees of success.

In the United States, on the other hand, health care is provided through an open-ended commitment to Medicare and Medicaid programs on a fee-for-service basis. There is therefore a very strong incentive for providers to supply as many services as possible and thereby to escalate total costs (Friedson, 1970). There is, however, little or no evidence to indicate that health in the United States is any better because of the additional funds being spent. The fundamental point, therefore, is that open-ended commitments to outside suppliers of goods and especially services are to be avoided if the controllability of expenditures is to be increased. These programs become entitlements to suppliers as well as to clients.

Other forms of uncontrollability occur within government itself, and between governments in federal systems. First, at least in the United States, large amounts of unspent obligational authority exist 'in the pipeline'. This is money appropriated in a previous budget year but not spent (Figure 7.1). The money has been obligated, i.e. a contact has been let or some expenditure purpose had been assigned to the money, but it continues to languish in the

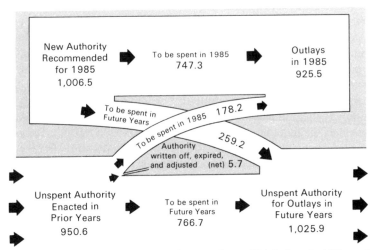

Figure 7.1 Relation of Budget Authority to outlays—1985 Budget (in billions of dollars)
Source: Office of Management and Budget, *Budget of the United States, FY 1985.* Washington, DC: Government Printing Office.

Treasury vaults. This present no particular problem unless the government is attempting to use the budget as a mechanism for controlling the economy. In that case, those attempting to plan the surplus or deficit (to the extent possible otherwise) are faced with huge amounts of money which program managers can spend and thereby destroy economic management assumptions.

Likewise, in a federal government, central government budget-makers have little control over fiscal decisions of subnational governments (Hansen, 1983). Although the central government decides on a tight budget to attempt to restrain inflation, subnational governments may decide to tax and spend large amounts on their own. The ability of subnational governments is to some degree restricted by the need to raise new taxes and constitutional provisions in most states prohibiting state and local governments from running deficits. The federal government has some means of controlling such taxing and spending, e.g. the stimulative effects of grants, but these are indirect. Other federal governments, e.g. the Federal Republic of Germany, have developed means of dealing with this problem by imposing central fiscal control in times of economic crisis. The controversy over rate-capping in the United Kingdom illustrates that even in unitary governments local authorities have some taxation and expenditure powers which central governments seek to control.

Altering program design may make expenditures more or less controllable but only programs with contractual obligations, e.g. debt interest, are truly uncontrollable. Other program costs can be controlled and presumed entitlements can be revoked. No government or politician wants to do that, but so long as government has authority they can. The use of the phrase 'uncontrollable' therefore, acts like labelling theory in medical sociology. That is, if a person is labelled 'sick' they will adopt the sick role and act as if they were sick; if a program is labelled uncontrollable it will act that way.

7.3 Creating dependency

A budgeting problem closely associated with the problem of entitlements is that of public programs which create dependency and eliminate traditional means of coping with problems. Dependency is created for individuals who rely upon any of a number of social programs. Certainly most citizens receiving these benefit need them and have no alternatives. However, the dependency created and the absence of private alternatives may create problems both for the individuals and government itself. One example of this counter-productive dependency is council housing in the United Kingdom. Programs of council housing were developed to address the needs of many British citizens for good, affordable housing; a need that apparently was not being met by the private sector. However, over time, the program has created a large portion of the population which will be born, live and die in council housing without the opportunity to own their own homes. Furthermore, despite pressures from Conservative governments to sell houses and raise rents, local councils are still laden with large expenditures for the maintenance of housing which is not necessarily being met from rents. Finally, the dependence of many citizens upon council housing has limited the mobility of labor so that at times there have been jobs going begging in some parts of the country while unemployed in other parts were unwilling to give up council houses in order to accept a job. This type of program differs from an entitlement program in that all citizens are not eligible for the benefit by citizenship. However, once a person begins to receive the benefit they find it difficult to return to private alternatives; in the French term in becomes a *droit acquise*.

In addition to direct dependence on government created by programs such as council housing, these programs interact with other legislation to create even more pathological results. For example, in the housing market the availability of council housing, combined with rent controls and other regulations of the private rental market, and with tax subsidies for owner occupation, has produced an immense reduction in the amount and quality of private rental accommodation. This may ultimately produce a situation in which council tenants are in relatively high cost accommodation (because of energy costs and transportation costs as well as increased rents) with few private alternatives available to them. They would then be locked into the council house system and into effective poverty even with medium income levels.

As well as affecting ordinary citizens, dependency can be created for organizations and subnational governments. In the United States, the existence of a number of grants from the federal government, especially categorical grants, has made local governments dependent upon central government for the continuation of certain programs (Wright, 1983). Several processes have created this dependency. Categorical grants, e.g. grants given for a specific purpose, created a certain amount of 'priority inversion' in local government (Wolman, 1983). Local governments use their own money to match money which they can get from the federal government—as they are required to under most grant programs—rather than doing what they might prefer to do; the money available from the federal government become almost an end in itself rather than the means to the end of providing desired local services. Further, once a local government begins to provide a certain service using grant money, they find it difficult to withdraw the service at a later date, even if federal funds are no longer available. Thus, dependency in the short run may generate fiscal stress in the long run.

Even more fungible grants, e.g. block grants or the availability of cheap labor through programs such as the Comprehensive Employment and Training Act (CETA) may create long-run dependency. Local governments have a tendency to divert their own resources into functions which can not be supported by grants. For example, with CETA, much of the money available for public employment was used to support normal city services, e.g. refuse collection, where many of the workers had some of the characteristics of the population CETA was intended to serve. This released more local government own-source revenues for programs that could not be supported by CETA funds. Therefore, as CETA money dries up, a strain is imposed upon local governments. They must try to maintain the programs they initiated during a period of relative grant affluence while maintaining basic urban services.

Thus, for local governments as much as individuals, once a program is initiated it becomes difficult to terminate. The problems facing an individual are great in adjusting personal revenue and expenditure plans to meet a drop in income from public programs. The problems of local governments may be even more intense as they must continue to provide services to thousands of citizens with lost revenue and increasing expectations. This is not an argument for abolishing programs which create dependency for either individuals or organizations. Rather it is a plea to the recipients of these programs to understand their potentially ephemeral nature and to plan accordingly. Many indigent individuals have no planning options, but most local governments certainly do, as do private organizations dependent upon government subsidies or favorable regulations for their profit or positions in the market.

We must be careful not to place all the blame for the creation and perpetuation of dependency relationships on clients and legislatures which write legislation. Organizations administering programs of this type typically serve as advocates of their own programs, as do professionals delivering the services. It is, of course, difficult to separate genuine concern for clients from more self-serving advocacy; the commitment of professionals to their programs has been argued as one of the reasons for the perpetuation of institutionalized treatment for somatic, and particularly for mental, diseases.

Dependency may be inevitable for some public programs. However, care should be exercised in program design to minimize dependency, especially if the dependency created is likely to be permanent and private alternatives are likely to be foreclosed by the public program. These considerations should be taken for the sake of the government which may have to continue to pay benefits for those dependent upon it. More importantly, however, care should be exercised for the sake of citizens who by becoming dependent and eliminating any alternatives may become as much victim as beneficiary of a program.

7.4 Separation of expenditure and taxation

One of the most commonly cited difficulties with budgeting in almost any country is the separation of the expenditure process from the process of revenue-raising. Some political systems, e.g. the United States, attempt to bring the two totals together in budgeting, whereas in others, e.g. the United Kingdom, they are widely separated in both time and space. Even in the United States, the only times at which revenue and expenditure figures are considered together are in the President's budget statement and the two concurrent resolutions which Congress must pass on each year's budget. Further, even in those three places the revenue figure used is a notional one. Apart from those three instances different committees in Congress (Ways and Means or Finance for revenue and Appropriations for expenditure) and different actors within the executive branch are concerned with the two figures, and tend to work in isolation from one another. Every household, or at least every one seeking to avoid bankruptcy, must balance revenues and expenditures. However, the structures and processes of government do not make that balancing very likely.

The most obvious pathological result of the separation of revenue and expenditure is the tendency to spend more money than is received and as a consequence to have deficits even in prosperous years. For example, in the United States, in the thirty-four years from 1950 to 1983 the federal government ran a deficit in thirty years, even though many of those years were years of rapid economic growth. This is not an appeal for a balanced budget in all circumstances; it is an appeal for improved budget planning so that if a deficit is to occur it is within the limits of fiscal forecasting—a planned deficit. Regardless of one's position on fiscal probity and Keynesian economics, the ease with which deficits can occur is a cause of concern, and is indicative of the ease of public spending in the absence of a revenue constraint (Buchanan and Wagner, 1977). Spending is always easier politically than raising revenue and the separating of the two processes eliminates a major constraint on the joy of spending (Downs, 1960).

Associated with the ease of running deficits is the loss of signalling on how much to spend through the public budget, and for what purposes. Taxes constitute the analogue of prices in the market. As with the price mechanism, therefore, taxes may serve as a means of helping those in the public sector to decide how much to spend. The process of authorizing public expenditure could introduce a price-type signal if revenues were related—either as taxes or fees—to expenditures. This need not imply earmarked taxes, but only that the revenue implications of the expenditure be associated with the expenditure. Without such a linkage, it is difficult for decision-makers to know what utility public expenditures have for citizens. Of course, there are a number of difficulties associated with using a tax price for signalling collective preferences—public goods, disguised preferences, etc.—but a closer connection between the two fiscal decisions could only help to improve the signalling.

A somewhat less obvious point, perhaps, is that both taxes and expenditures have effects on the distribution of goods and services in the society, and on the incentives of individuals to engage in certain types of activity. As has been noted in the study of social policy, taxes and expenditures may cancel out each other's presumed distributional effects—the result being the 'poverty trap' or other pathological outcomes. It is not clear whether simply changing the manner in which tax and expenditure decisions are made would be sufficient to eliminate such anomolies entirely, but apparent contradictions between the two sets of policies might be more obvious. The more general point is that now governments intervene in their economies and societies in a number of ways and without proper coordination, and their net effects may be negative or nil. In fiscal terms, this means that a great deal of money is spent, and a great deal of revenue is collected, with a net effect that is either diminished or absent. It further points to the need to consider together not only the aggregate revenue and expenditure but also the types of revenue and the objects of expenditure.

At times, even revenue policies themselves are not coordinated; Tarschys (1982) discussed the idea of 'fiscal cannibalism' in which attempts to raise one tax may reduce the yield on other taxes, and perhaps the total tax yield. A sales tax increase may reduce consumption which in turn will reduce production and the payrolls and incomes which are the subject of other taxes. As the decision-making about these different types of taxes may be done in different organizations even in unitary governments (Customs and Excises handles VAT in the United Kingdom while the Inland Revenue handles the income tax) it is quite possible for different revenue units to be working at cross purposes. This is, of course, especially likely when taxes are levied by different levels of government. One special example is that in the United States some state income taxes are levied as a percentage of the federal income tax. Thus, President Reagan's income tax reductions at the federal level produced fiscal problems for those governments. Working the other way round, since state and local taxes are deductible against federal income tax, an increase in state and local taxation may reduce federal taxes takes.

Several mechanisms have been advanced for 'solving' these problems, but there is always the danger that the solution may be a new pathology (Hogwood and Peters, 1983). For example, one possible solution to these problems might be an earmarked tax, which would require expenditure decisions to take into account the revenue constraints of a single revenue source. We have already shown, however, that this form of taxation may present difficulties for government and for citizens (see 7.1) . As with Simon's (1957) 'proverbs of administration', many of the problems and solutions of problems in budgeting are mutually contradictory.

Another solution proposed for the separation of revenue and expenditure decisions is the 'balanced budget amendment'

(Wildavsky, 1980). This would require the federal government to pass a balanced budget each year, no matter what the state of the economy, unless a special majority of Congress declares an 'economic emergency.' This measure, supported by influential conservative politicians, would obviously require that revenue and expenditure decisions be brought together. It would, however, also have some undesirable consequences. The first would be to remove one important, if sometimes blunt, economic management weapon from the arsenal of government. Whether conservative leaders approve or not, governments have been handed the task of regulating their economies, to the extent possible to do so. It cannot be denied that governments frequently practice 'one-eyed Keynesianism' (Rose and Peters, 1978) but that may be preferable to total blindness.

A second undesirable consequence of a balanced budget amendment might be that the balancing would become a shambolic rather than real exercise in fiscal control. Governments encounter great difficulties in predicting their revenues and expenditures from year to year (Penner, 1982). Both sides of the budgetary equation depend upon too many factors to be predicted accurately. In addition, forecasts must be made many months in advance of the time the budget goes into effect (Ott and Ott, 1977) and any number of conditions can change during the year in which the budget is executed. As shown in Table 7.1, over the past 10 years the federal government has missed its revenue estimate by an average of 2.9 percent and its expenditure estimate by 3.4 percent. The direction of error of the expenditure estimate in the politically desirable direction indicates that the error may not be entirely random, but even those with no political stake have encountered difficulties in forecasting revenues and expenditures (Penner, 1982). Similarly, in the United Kingdom, the Public Sector Borrowing Requirement from 1967/8 to 1982/3 has been missed by an average of 1.4 percent of GDP or approximately 3 percent of public expenditure. If we assume that the difficulties in forecasting would persist after the passage of a balanced budget amendment, they may put the President and Congress in the position of appearing to have violated the Constitution if the actual out-turn of the budget is unbalanced. If the out-turn is not meant to be balanced, but only figures on a piece of paper called the budget, then the exercise can only enhance the already growing cynicism of citizens.

Table 7.1
Errors in US Federal budgetary predictions
(in percentage)

Fiscal Year	Outlays	Receipts	Deficit
1969	0.9	– 5.4	141.3
1970	– 0.7	2.5	– 185.3
1971	– 5.3	6.8	– 186.9
1972	– 1.2	4.1	– 101.7
1973	0.1	– 5.2	43.8
1974	0.2	– 3.5	66.9
1975	– 6.7	4.7	– 322.4
1976	– 4.3	– 0.8	– 23.6
1977	– 2.1	– 1.9	– 4.4
1978	– 2.3	– 2.3	– 2.3
1979	1.5	– 6.0	54.9
1980	– 9.0	– 3.5	– 105.9
1981	– 7.3	– 0.4	– 268.8
Mean absolute error	3.5	2.9	116.0

Another possible pathological result of a balanced budget amendment might be that expenditures would *increase* rather than decrease. Most balanced budget provisions have an override provision. By a special majority Congress would be able to pass an unbalanced budget (presumably to meet the needs of an economic crisis). However, a coalition for an override must be constructed in the same manner as other coalitions in Congress, that is by log-rolling and pork-barrel legislation allowing members of the coalition to spend for their pet programs. To create a coalition of one-half plus one of a legislature requires spending a substantial amount of money; to create a coalition of two-thirds may require that much more expenditure. Unfortunately, the passage of a balanced budget amendment will no create saints out of practicing politicians in Congress so that many of the traditional means of forming coalitions will be unaltered and the price of government may actually increase.

Another possible remedy for the mismatch between revenues and expenditures would be to require each expenditure proposal to have its revenue implications directly associated with it, along with some idea of where that revenue would come from. Further, attention should be given to the long-range revenue requirements of an expenditure proposal, not just requirements for the first year. This might prevent the 'camel's nose phenomenon' or 'wedge' which has been encountered in many expenditure programs (Wildavsky, 1984). Zero-base budgeting contained provisions of this sort, but since there were no means of preventing appropriations committees and sub-committees from ignoring revenue implications those provisions had little apparent effect in reducing expenditures. A somewhat similar provision was included in the COPE (Committee on Programme Evaluation) program in New Zealand which required those proposing new expenditures to say what existing programs might be scrapped in order to fund the new program. This 'scrap and build' approach to budgeting was not popular with many civil servants for it created high levels of uncertainty, but it did relate revenue and expenditure quite directly.

In summary, the separation of revenue and expenditure decisions in government may produce pathological results, e.g. continuing deficit spending with little or nor regard for the economic justification for the deficits. However, the majority of 'simple' remedies for this problem may themselves have pathological results. As in many other cases, the simplest solution may be the best: do what must be done without a formal program. Political leaders and administrators may choose to hide behind institutional and procedural excuses, but if they wish to consider revenue and taxation together they can.

7.5 Malnutrition

From the perspective of those in government, malnutrition is probably the most common budgetary disease. Some programs are simply not given enough money to function properly, and then the programs are deemed failures. Malnutrition in public programs appears to come about in two manners: not being given enough (wasting in medical parlance) and not being fed long enough (stunting).

Some programs simply are never allocated a sufficient amount of money for them to accomplish their stated goals. This simple malnutrition may result from several factors. There may be no intention on the part of the legislature passing the program to put it into effect—the intention may have been entirely symbolic. For example, the United States Congress passed a tough coal-mine inspection act in 1977, but refused to appropriate enough money to hire more than a few inspectors for the thousands of mines covered

(Edwards, 1980). The effect was to improve mine safety very little, although Congress could point to the existence of a program.

In other instances, those funding a program may assume that the problems being addressed are solved easily and consequently that not much money is required. This has been quite common in social programs which attempt to solve long-standing social ills on a shoestring budget. One extreme example is the assumption of early planners of the National Health Service in the United Kingdom that after the first few years the volume of work for the service would decline—a backlog of disease having been eliminated—and there was no need to plan and build more hospitals.

Finally, private-sector analogues may be used to plan programs and it is possible that public programs—because of personnel policies, procurement policies and other restrictions—may be more expensive. Also, public programs find it difficult or impossible to exclude anyone from participation and consequently the level of funding be insufficient for those who decide to use the program, e.g. in recreation. Further, publicly-sponsored health programs may be the last resort for those whom private health programs will not serve and as a result public programs may attract the illest segments of the population with associated higher costs.

Long-term malnutrition is a problem affecting programs whose benefits accrue to beneficiaries in the future, or which require a long time span to be effective. This problem was encountered by programs in the War on Poverty in the United States, intended to alter or break the cycle of poverty rather than providing transfer payments to eliminate the hardships associated with poverty. As such, these programs required longer time spans and more follow-up than most social and educational programs. Unfortunately, because they did not produce the immediate results desired, perhaps naively, by some, the programs were considered ineffective and were either gradually eliminated or merged with other, less innovative, programs.

It may be easy to say that a program was malnourished after it has been terminated. It is more difficult to make those determinations while the program is being planned or while it is operating. The budgetary process itself has somewhat ambiguous impacts on the tendency of government to malnourish programs. In particular the annual, repetitive budgetary process encourages decision-makers to underfund programs initially, with the possibility of adjusting funding later. It may be rational for programs to receive very modest funding until they begin operations and obtain some idea of true costs and benefits. This, of course, runs the risk that the program will never appear effective and consequently will never receive the funds to make it effective. On the other hand, the annual budget allows, in the best incremental fashion, for decision-makers to learn from experience and adjust expenditures according to apparent needs and apparent benefits.

7.6 Choking and bleeding

Choking and bleeding represent two ends of a dimension concerned with the timing of budgets and public expenditure. Choking implies the authorization of more spending than the agency in question can effectively spend within the time allowed. Bleeding, on the other hand, implies continuing to spend relatively small amounts of money for a continuing problem when a large-scale infusion of funds might eliminate the problem. Bleeding differs from malnutrition (see 7.5) in that expenditures for a bleeding problem are sufficient to meet social needs in the short run but are not sufficient to eliminate the problem and save money in the long run, while malnutrition means that there are insufficient funds to meet the needs even in the short run. There are, of course, instances where this distinction may be difficult to identify or sustain.

In choking, governmental decision-makers attempt to provide too much money to fast and create inefficiences in the manner in which money is spent. Some programs are sufficiently popular to attract as much money as they can use, and more. Further, programs which are capital intensive tend to have difficulties in absorbing large new budget authorizations; at least they have difficulties in creating outputs which appear commensurate with the amount of money spent. Further, there is a tendency to choke certain types of programs which are relatively 'high profile' while simultaneously starving other programs, even in the same policy area, which may ultimately produce greater social benefits, e.g. the availability of large amounts of money for acute medical care while preventive health programs are starved.

Defense policy provides illustrations of choking on money. In testimony before the Senate Armed Services Committee Admiral Hiram Rickover argued against the proposed increases for the military in President Reagan's 1983 budget. He was not doing this from a sudden conversion to unilateral disarmament; he was convinced that there were not sufficient good weapons systems available in the short run to justify the proposed increases. The result of the proposed increase would therefore have been either a simple waste of funds or the procurement of substandard weapons systems which would ultimately require even greater expenditures for repair or replacement. Further, the procurement of substandard weapons systems creates a 'stock' problem and, for policy as well as financial reasons, reduces the future procurement of better systems.

The general point made by Rickover is to some degree reinforced by figures on defense appropriations and outlays under the Carter and Reagan budgets. Despite the rapid increases in budgetary authority (the right to spend money) under the Reagan budgets (21 percent from FY1982 to FY1983) there was a more modest increase (15 percent) in actual outlays during that budget year. Similar disparities between authority and outlays were projected for the FY1984 and FY 1985 budgets (Office of Management and Budget, 1983). The military procurement process simply could not respond rapidly with enough high-quality programs. When public funds must be spent or at least obligated during a particular budget year, rapid increases in expenditure authority can produce massive waste and sub-optimal use of scarce resources.

The War on Cancer, initiated by the Nixon administration in 1971, illustrates the problem of choking in domestic programs (Rettig, 1977). Many health researchers believed that the money spent on the War on Cancer could have been better spent on basic biomedical research than on a task-oriented 'war effort' (Cohen, 1971). Their argument was that since the causes and possible cures for cancer were by no means agreed upon, the possibilities that a large-scale program would create waste and follow blind alleys were very great (Schulman, 1980). Basic research, on the other hand, provided a broader approach to the problem which was more likely to discovery the underlying causes of the disease. Likewise, a 'War on Aids' would encounter many of the same problems of uncertainty and the possibility of massive mistakes consuming both time and money.

The problems of bleeding are best illustrated by expenditures on social programs. In principle, social programs are intended to provide temporary aid for citizens in times of distress so that they can get themselves back on their feet and participate in the economy. In practice, however, many social programs have become permanent subsidies for the poor. Despite their permanence, however, the programs are not addressing the underlying causes of poverty but merely keep the recipients alive at a minimal level. At that level many of the problems of ignorance, disease, and alienation are transmitted from generation to generation. Thus, many social programs do not solve social problems but perpetuate them. However, a dominant (in the United States) ideological coalition tends to restrict both the funding and creativity of the programs.

Choking and bleeding point to a very fundamental problem of finding the appropriate scale of public programs (Schulman, 1980). There is, at times, a tendency to attack peanuts with steamrollers, providing the peanuts are sufficiently popular. Conversely, there are programs which attack four-alarm fires with seltzer bottles. Leaving the analogies aside, the fundamental problem is one of identifying a scale for a program which provides sufficient resources to meet needs without providing more resources more quickly than can be absorbed by the organization charged with spending the money, or assimilated by the program's clients. In addition, it is important to understand the nature of the program in question. Schulman (1980) points to the necessity of addressing indivisible problems with large-scale programs. It would do little good to get a man half-way to the moon and then wait for more appropriations. Similarly, Etzioni (1976, 99) points out that rehabilitating one block in a slum area would be likely to fail in at least some of its goals. Other programs, e.g. biomedical research, lack a sure technology or even agreement on goals so that a centralized, large-scale program such as the space program could not be successful. The War on Poverty, on the other hand, was both uncertain about its methodology and caught in a web of multiple goals and interests. Everything else being equal, the large-scale approach may have been suitable for problems of poverty but political realities and the tendency of politicians to 'think small' led to the cannibalizing and eventual death of the program (Aaron, 1978; James, 1975).

7.7 Hiding

One the many things which the public budget should do is to provide both decision-makers and citizens information about the financial operations of government. As the 'size' of government has become an increasing concern in Western nations (Peters and Heisler, 1984), it is important to measure accurately the amount of money which flows in and out of the public purse. Unfortunately, public budgets often are not very good at supplying that information and, even leaving aside other operations of government which may have some economic impacts (Weidenbaum and DeFina, 1978), much of what government does is not completely reflected in the budget. Further, in some instances, the information in the budget does not correspond to conventional understanding of what a budget should contain and the real impact of public spending and revenue is hidden from the public.

The simplest means of hiding public expenditures is to place the activities in off-budget, debudgetized organizations. This is most commonly done for public enterprises which operate largely with self-generated funds, but means can be developed for hiding other public activities. For example, social security funds in a number of European countries are nominally private or quasi-private and as a consequence their transactions do not appear as a part of the public budget. In fairness, international organizations such as OECD which provide the major data sources for cross-national comparison of public revenue and expenditure do include social security funds no matter how they are counted by the individual countries.

Significant amounts of public expenditure occur outside the bounds of the traditional definition of the public budget. For example, the operating expenses of off-budget activities at the federal level in the United States (which in fairness are reported in several appendices to the *Budget of the United States*) were over $32 billion in 1983. Their loans and other obligational authority amounted to an additional $14 billion. One study of off-budget enterprises in state and local governments in the United States found almost 26,000 such enterprises (Bennett and DiLorenzo, 1983). In New York state alone these organizations spent more than $6 billion in 1980 (Bennett and DiLorenzo, 1983, 73–5). In some countries, e.g. Israel, off-budget activities of government are almost as large as the budgeted activities (Sharkansky, 1979).

Another type of hidden expenditure is actually revenue which is forgone; the common name for these foregone revenues is 'tax expenditures' (Surrey, 1969). The idea of a tax expenditure is that if government allows its citizens not to pay taxes on money spent for certain purposes this amounts to a subsidy for those purposes. For example, the willingness of the US federal government to allow citizens to deduct interest they pay on home mortgages amounts to a subsidy for housing—primarily middle-class housing. Again, we are talking about significant amounts of money. Table 7.2 shows levels of expenditure and tax expenditure for the seventeen functions into which the federal budget is usually divided. In two of the categories tax expenditures are greater than direct expenditures. This is especially pronounced for commerce and housing credit where tax expenditures are 95 percent of the money 'spent'. In a number of other areas tax expenditures account for at least 10 percent of the total federal involvement in the policy area. This is true even in areas such as health and income security where public expenditure is a major political issue.

Table 7.2
Expenditures and tax expenditures by function
(US federal government, 1983)

Function	Expenditure (bil $)	Tax expenditure (bil $)	Tax expenditure as percent of total
National Defense	209.9	2.4	1.1
International Affairs	9.0	2.7	23.0
General Science, Space, Technology	7.7	0.6	7.7
Energy	4.0	5.1	56.2
Natural Resources and Environment	12.7	2.1	13.8
Agriculture	21.2	1.8	5.1
Commerce and Housing Credit	4.4	92.1	95.4
Transportation	21.4	0.0	0.0
Community and Regional Development	6.9	0.3	4.8
Education	26.6	12.8	32.5
Health	28.7	23.8	45.3
Income Security	122.2	87.0	41.6
Veterans Benefits	24.8	2.3	8.5
Justice	5.1	0.0	0.0
General Government	4.8	0.2	4.0
General Purpose Financial Assistance	6.5	29.3	81.1
Net Interest	89.8	0.4	0.5

Source: Office of Management and Budget, *Budget of the United States Government, FY 1985*, Washington, DC: Government Printing Office, 1984.

The United States is not alone in having a great deal of revenue foregone by government in order to subsidize certain activities. In the United Kingdom in 1983/4 there were £25 billion forgone in tax expenditures (Cmnd. 9143, 1984). Many of these tax 'loopholes' were similar to those in the United States. For example, in the area of housing, despite large direct expenditures for council housing (£2.76 billion in 1982), some £2.75 billion was forgone as tax relief on mortgages.

Merely examining levels of public expenditure hides a great deal of government activity from proper consideration by decision-makers and citizens. This is especially true given that tax policy making tends to be more specialized and less subject to detailed scrutiny than making expenditure decisions (Good, 1978; Hansen, 1983). Thus, hiding a subsidy in a tax bill is easier than hiding it in an expenditure bill.

Loans are another means by which governments may become involved in the economies of their countries without commensurate increases in public expenditure. This is to some degree dependent upon the manner in which loans are treated in public accounts. It is not uncommon for loans not to be counted as expenditures; the assumption is that they will be repaid. Therefore, to the extent that a government changes a program from one operating through direct expenditures to a loan program, the public budget will reduced although the role of government in the economy will be unchanged (Hogwood and Peters, 1983, 193 ff.). In some instances in the United Kingdom loan repayments are counted as *negative* expenditures so that the apparent size of the public budget may fluctuate quite widely depending upon the composition of loans and direct expenditures.

If government loans are a means of actually dispersing money without that money actually appearing in the budget, then loan guarantees are an even more indirect means of moving money. With guarantees government itself does not actually expend any money. Instead it insures private lenders who lend the money to the individuals or firms. The largest example of this type of program was the guaranteed loan to the Chrysler Corporation, intended to prevent firm from declaring bankruptcy. Other more mundane programs, e.g. student loans and housing programs, operate in a similar manner. As of 1982, the federal government guaranteed loans for $353.1 billion, a figure almost half the public budget of that year. If everything goes well government will not have to pay a cent to guarantees on these loans (Chrysler actually repaid its loans early). However, government still incurs a great liability and this liability does not necessarily pass through the same appropriations process as expenditures. In some instances, e.g. the United Kingdom, the magnitude of the total commitment is not even publicly known. Much the same can be said of government insurance programs, e.g. flood insurance and crop insurance in the United States. In good times such programs generate premium revenues for government but there is always the threat of having to pay very substantial claims.

In summary, it is at times very desirable politically to hide the true size of the budget. This can be done in a number of ways, all of which are perfectly legal. However, all these methods to some degree deceive decision-makers and citizens into believing that the public sector is not as large as it really is. In addition, some programs which are virtually cost-free in the short run have potential expenditure liabilities of massive proportions. Such attempts at deception, and self-deception, are pathological for they allow governmental decision-makers to escape the true importance of their actions and to continue to pursue policies which have potential dangers for their societies.

7.8 Corruption

The most flagrant pathology in public budgeting is corruption or the misappropriation of public funds. However, unlike the majority of other pathologies we have been discussing, the impact of corruption does not come in determining how much money to spend either in total or for a particular program. Rather, it arises in the execution of the budget and in decisions about who will receive the appropriated money. The receipt of the misappropriated money may be by a public official who is using the public funds for his own purposes, or it may be a contract awarded to an individual for political or other non-commercial considerations. It may even be by a client who receives public benefits with the implicit or explicit promise of political support (Merton, 1940). In each instance, public money is either spent wrongly, or spent with the types of strings attached which are unacceptable in most political cultures (Heidenheimer, 1973).

We must be careful, however, to differentiate real corruption from activities which are regarded as corrupt by many citizens, and which may well produce sub-optimal expenditure patterns, but which are not patently corrupt. In particular, 'log-rolling' and 'pork-barrel' legislation are frequently decried as corrupt. These means of conflict resolution in legislatures result in more spending for some programs than might otherwise be the case, but are not corrupt *per se*. In fact, the argument can be made that they are means of increasing the total utility of public expenditures. If Congressman A and his constituency are indifferent about program b while Congressman B and his constituency are passionately committed to b, and at the same time Congressman B and his constituency are indifferent about program a which Congressman A is attached to, then they can increase total utility by trading votes. This does result, of course, in many more governments being passed than would otherwise be, and constituents of A and B, not to mention $C, D, E, \ldots$, may feel worse off because of increased taxes.

Relatively few citizens of industrialized countries favor corruption in government. However, corruption may serve as an alternative means of allocating resources or escaping administrative barriers to performance. Blau (1956) reports that some FBI agents found it convenient to violate the stated rules of the bureau about accepting bribes in order to gain control over those suspected of other crimes. Similarly, centralized mechanisms designed to reduce possibilities of corruption may result in very inefficient government procedures and in large amounts of wasted time. For example, one Southern US state with a history of significant corruption established centralized purchasing and procurement agencies in an attempt to eliminate those problems. Because of the inadequate knowledge of the centralized purchasing agents this resulted in, among other things, non-sterile dressings being purchased for hospitals, police cars without lights and sirens, and all police uniforms being purchased with the same length trousers. The elimination of corruption and the misappropriation of funds is an important value in public administration; the problem is that legal misappropriation, if that is not a misnomer, may result from some efforts to eliminate corruption. It is not clear that a cost-benefit analysis of many procedures used to eliminate corruption would show a positive balance. The time spent filling out forms, account in triplicate for travel funds, etc. may take much more time (and its associated expense) than is saved by catching the few dishonest people in most public organizations.

The one area in which what is nominally corrupt has received some accolades is big-city political machines in the United States, and to some degree political machines in Third World countries. The argument made by Merton (1940) and others is that these machines served as a alternative means of providing social welfare and as an initiation into American life for large numbers of immigrants who otherwise were outside both the economic and political life of the country. In exchange for their votes, the machines provided their adherents with employment (Irish policemen and Italian sanitation workers, etc.) and political access. Of course, the leaders of Tammany Hall and other machines received even greater benefits as a result of this process but not everything which the machines did was evil. Under perhaps the last of the machine politicians, Chicago was proud to be called the 'City that Works' (Royko, 1971). What is perhaps most pathological is that machines were required to bring immigrants into the society as fast as they were (Sharpe, 1973).

7.9 Conclusions

The existing systems of resource allocation in the United States and the United Kingdom have a number of pathological features which they would share with the majority of budgetary systems in the world. These deficiencies have not gone unnoticed and any number of attempts have been made to eliminate or reduce the pathologies. For example, in the United States, both program budgeting and zero-base budgeting have been tried—with equal lack of success. In the United Kingdom the PESC (Public Expenditure Survey Committees) system produced some apparent improvements, as did the associated PAR (Programme Analysis and Review) system. PESC has persisted in modified form after increased pressure on public expenditure in the late 1960s through the 1980s; first cash limits and then 'hiccup money' were used as a means of 'solving' the problems created by the volume budgeting in PESC (Copeman, 1981). Any number of other budgetary reforms have been tried in any number of other countries (Peters, 1984, ch. 8), but all have been less successful than anticipated and none has been the magic solution for problems of resource allocation in government. Further, many if not most had pathological results of their own which were at least as great as those of the budgetary systems they supplanted. Again, as with Simon's (1957) proverbs, pathologies tend to come in pairs. For example, those working with the PESC system found that they could either control the volume of public services (the original idea) or they could control the amount of cash being spent (cash limits); they could not control both, and the lack of control of either produced problems for government. The traditional means of allocating resources in the public sector, despite their well-known problems, do tend to persist.

Wildavsky (1979a), in his discussion of why traditional budgeting systems persist, argues that although traditional budgeting does nothing well, it does nothing totally badly either, while most reform proposals had more extreme pathological features. In addition, most problems we have been discussing here cannot be solved by gimmickry as readily as by the willingness of those in government to take the, at times politically difficult, steps necessary to solve (or ameliorate) the problems. The political process does not make it easy for those constructing the public budget to take revenue and expenditure decisions simultaneously, but there is little to prevent them from doing so. Likewise, it may be convenient to allow a problem to continue to 'bleed' rather than to spend the money to address the root causes of the problem, but there is little to prevent those in government from making the more difficult choices. Reforming the machinery of resource allocation is no substitute for making the right decisions about resource allocation.

8
Terminal Illnesses: An Autopsy

8.1 Change through death

Death might seem to be the ultimate pathological consequence, a definite sign of failure. Yet just as a developing society will undergo a process of change over time through some members of the population dying and others being born, so too might we expect some no longer useful policy organizations to die and other more relevant ones to be established. Kaufman (1984) likens this process to the biological process of natural selection in which some organizations find stable environmental 'niches' while others are not so fortunate and die off early.

Science fiction has warned of the pathological consequences of immortality compared to natural death (see the entry on immortality in Nicholls, 1979). While reincarnation in humans is speculative, the spirit of terminated organizations may be reborn Dalai-Lama-like in 'new' organizations established at the moment of death of the old. As we and others have noted, the difficulty of termination of programs and organizations can have pathological consequences (Hogwood and Peters, 1983; see also e.g. deLeon, 1978). However, circumstances under which policies and organizations are terminated can have pathological features, especially from the perspective of those engaged in delivering the policy. The pathological feature of a terminal illness may not be death itself but the fact of 'a long time adying'.

In the health care area the major reason to be concerned about the excessive prolonging of life is the cost of treatment. The same is to some extent true of public policies, with the additional problem that an obsolete program may actually be causing harm. We should be careful to differentiate between changes—or failure to make changes—which are done purely for the sake of saving money and those which are done with good intentions for the clients, albeit misguided.

In any given society, there will be more or less subjective assessments of 'natural' and 'unnatural' deaths, of 'avoidable' and 'inevitable' or 'will-of' God' deaths. Similarly, in public policy there may be general recognition that some policies are no longer functioning usefully and that their life-support system should be switched off. In other cases where a deliberate act terminates an organization there may be dispute about whether a program was 'executed' for producing adverse policy outputs or 'murdered' to prevent it doing good.

The image of bureaucracy as a collection of officials mindlessly pursuing their tasks while paying no attention to developments in the outside world is an inaccurate one (see chapter 3). Organizations are highly adaptive, especially if their own survival is at risk:

Should discrepancies arise between the organization's objective and its environment, the organization is designed to recognize, act upon, and reduce the problem before the threat can attain a magnitude that would endanger the institution's very existence, or at least its nominal jurisdiction in dealing with such problems (deLeon, 1978, 288).

An organization may use its strengths by resisting change, but if its own existence comes under threat it may be willing to allow one of its programs to be terminated if offset by other advantages.

8.2 Problem death

One of the remarkable features of public policy is the ability of organizations or professional or occupational groupings to survive even after the problem they were engaged in dealing with has disappeared or their original skills or functions have become obsolescent. DeLeon (1978, 286) notes that while Federal agents from the US Treasury are no longer needed to enforce Prohibition, they now enforce firearm, drug, and tobacco laws. Problem death can arise in a variety of ways, including the evaporation or depletion of the problem as a result of exogenous forces and the disappearance of the problem because public policy has been so successful that the problem has been completely cured.

8.2.1 Problem depletion

Problems which are the target of public policy may disappear or decline in scale as a consequence of developments which have nothing to do with the effect of public policy. For example, there may be problem depletion as a result of demographic factors, such as a decline in the number of children of school age. Rather than adjust automatically to such changes in the scale of the target problem, the recipients of the policy and, above all, the staff involved in delivering it, may seek in the first place to resist cutbacks in the program, and then when such cutbacks are perceived as inevitable to adopt a series of short-term measures. Among the tactics to resist decline resulting from problem depletion are arguments for improved standards, new tasks (such as 'community education' by school teachers), the highlighting of the short-term costs of rundown and an emphasis on the possibility of future upturns in the size of the target clientele (see CPRS, 1977; Levine, 1978).

When cutbacks seem inevitable, there may be a series of short-term tactics to attempt to ward off the most damaging consequences (to the existing permanent delivery staff). Thus, there may be a hiring freeze, temporary or part-time staff may be dismissed, and early retirement, perhaps with a raid on the pension fund, will be encouraged. (Almost invariably these will result in a skewed career structure.) There may be cuts in maintenance and supplies. Accounts may be 'massaged', for example, by greater use of leasing as opposed to purchase. However, if problem depletion is accompanied by long-run cutbacks in expenditure there may eventually be planned redundancies and closure of facilities.

What may appear to be pathological from a model of rapid adjustment to problem depletion may appear entirely functional from the perspective of delivery staff or advocates of an expanded role for an existing service (see Glennerster, 1980). Ideally, we should distinguish between a healthy and a pathological continuation of an organization in the face of problem exhaustion. The March of Dimes, a US charity, did not conclude its operations with the discovery of the Salk polio vaccine, but appears to have made what, in a commonsense definition, was a very functional transition from aiding the victims of polio to aiding the victims of other crippling diseases, especially birth defects. Other organizations appear to have persisted without need. For example, the Renegotiation Board of US federal government, established to ensure that companies did not make excessive profits from contracts in World War II was not terminated until 1973.

8.2.2 The pining widower: problem decoupling

We have so far assumed that each program was directly targeted at a single problem. Where such a problem disappeared the program also terminated or the organization found a new 'problem' to service. However, many programs are advanced as solutions to several problems simultaneously. Where such a treatment genuinely tackles all the specified problems it is a politician's—and a policy analyst's—dream. However, where a program attempts to tackle one or more problems and is unable to tackle any or all of them effectively as a result, it is suffering from 'overtargeting' (see also 9.4).

One such set of 'dream' programs would appear to the British regional policy as developed in the 1960s. Regional incentives to encourage industrialists to invest in areas of high unemployment were alleged both to serve a social justice purpose by ensuring that no region suffered unduly and a national growth-maximizing goal by ensuring that expansion did not have to be reined back when certain regions became 'overheated' and led to national inflationary problems (see McCrone, 1969). However, when from 1975 onwards all regions of Britain had increasingly high levels of unemployment, the national growth maximizing justification for regional programs evaporated. As a consequence, regional programs were terminated or cut back. Regional Employment Premium was abolished in 1977 by a Labour government, and a series of reviews under the Conservative government from 1979 onwards led to reductions in geographical coverage and rates of subsidy.

Leaving aside the possible ineffective impact of overtargeted programs, the marketing of a program as solving a set of closely coupled problems can backfire. If the disappearance or transmogrification of one problem leads to a reappraisal of priorities in terms of how the program continues to meet the remaining goal, then such a reappraisal is far from being pathological. Where, however, a program was seen as substantively meeting one goal with the other goals being added as part of a 'selling' operation, such political oversell may boomerang if the problems previously linked together are now seen to have become decoupled. Both analytically and politically, there is a need to beware of selling as coupled problems what are temporarily coincident rather than intrinsically interlinked problems.

8.3 Dying from success

'The successful completion of a policy objective is scarcely sufficient grounds for disbanding the organization. New objectives can be defined within the organization that require its continued existence' (deLeon, 1978, 289). Switching to a new objective to ensure continuation of activity following successful accomplishment of the initial objective can have pathological consequences if the initial success leads to overambition and the new objective is beyond the organization's capacity. DeLeon (1978, 289) cites the example of the UN operation in Korea in the early 1950s which successfully achieved its initial objective of driving the invading forces out of South Korea, but became bogged down when that objective was replaced by an expanded set of objectives.

'The contrary case—the inability of an organization to resolve a problem in its domain—is similarly unlikely to result in its termination' (deLeon, 1978, 289). The problem still remains and requires treatment. Of course, failure to meet an objective will increase the chances of termination, but only relatively so. From the perspective of an organization wishing to avoid the threat of termination altogether, the ideal type of problem is one where the objective is not to remove the problem but merely to cope with a problem that is recognized as permanent and inevitable, and where there is a lack of clarity about what would constitute effective treatment. Where such a task, such as looking after the elderly, is also viewed with social approbation, institutional permanence is assured. The care of the soon-to-die is a guarantee against termination, since although such individual client inevitably dies, there is a perpetual turnover because of the inevitability of death, an inevitability which does not apply to organizations in the way it does to individual humans.

8.4 Death from a thousand cuts?: resource change

Until the mid 1970s, public policy was largely based on an assumption of continuing growth of the resources able to fund it. Considerable intellectual endeavor went into seeking to explain why governments throughout the world were growing: less thought was devoted to considering whether such growth was contingent (see Larkey, Stolp and Winer, 1981). Such assumptions have been shattered both by economic setbacks since 1973 and by a political perception of the limitations to taxpayer tolerance. At the level of individual local governments in the United States more acute problems have arisen as the effects of previous policies have led to fiscal crisis. Thus cutbacks and even complete terminations have been under active consideration. Even within a growing total of public expenditure (as in Britain under the Thatcher government) cutbacks of some programs receive active consideration for both ideological and cost-saving reasons.

Renewed growth will not necessarily remove the need for considering cutbacks and terminations for resource constraint reasons (see Tarschys, 1982). Rose and Peters (1978) point out that because the costs of public policy represent a greater proportion of the national product than they did thirty years ago, a much higher rate of growth of the national product would be required to sustain the historical rates of growth of public policy without cutting into the real take-home pay of citizens. The latitude for avoiding the problems of policy termination by instituting a new program without cutting the old is considerably reduced.

Governments responding to fiscal pressure will rarely take from the very start a long-run perspective. Their most immediate response is likely to be to 'buy time', for example by drawing down existing surpluses (Wolman, 1983, 249–51). Other short-term devices include 'borrowing' from other funds, 'creative bookkeeping', selling off assets, and short-term borrowing. While such devices may give a government time to consider longer-term action, they can themselves contribute to or precipitate major fiscal crises. Once it becomes clear that longer-term cutbacks cannot be avoided, for example by increased intergovernmental grants or by shuffling costs or services off to other governmental agencies or the private sector, expenditure is likely to be cut in a way which minimizes *visible* service reductions and impact on employees (Wolman, 1983, 256). Thus maintenance and capital budgets will tend to be cut most. To avoid industrial relations problems, reductions in employment are likely to be through attrition or voluntary redundancies, which may result in an employee profile which is not the optimal for long-run service delivery.

Where cuts for reasons of fiscal stress do occur they will tend to be on a pro rata basis between programs and between individual facilities rather than targeted in terms of policy priorities (though there may be some safeguarding of pet programs or demand-led entitlement programs). This reflects fundamental features of organizational behavior relating to resource allocation (see chapter 7 and Wildavsky, 1975).

Thus, while fiscal stress may precipitate the termination of a program or a project if the closure of the program was already under consideration, it is unlikely in its early stages to lead to targeted terminations as a result of a reappraisal of policy priorities in the light of reduced resources. This strategy may appear to spread the pain evenly, but may lead to such budgetary pathologies as 'malnutrition' and 'bleeding' described in 7.5 and 7.6.

8.5 Homicide

There can be a variety of motives for wanting to kill off a program. Behn (1978, 409) distinguishes among 'Opponents', who seek to terminate a policy because they consider it to be wrong, 'Economizers', who seek to terminate a policy because it is inefficient, ineffective, or expensive, and 'Reformers' who seek to terminate a program as a prerequisite to the introduction of a better, replacement policy. As we have argued elsewhere, the 'reformer' type of advocate is concerned not so much with termination as with policy succession (Hogwood and Peters, 1983). Whether would-be terminators are 'opponents' or 'economizers' will affect the focus of their attack and their willingness to compromise. Opponents may settle for the elimination of a largely symbolic element of a policy, even if it saves little or no money; on the other hand, they are unlikely to be willing to compromise on what they regard as a point of principle. Economizers may be willing to settle for a reorganization or modification of the existing policy if that saves money. Money is an infinitely subdividable commodity, well adapted to being the subject of compromise. Policy homicides or amputations are therefore more likely to arise from political opposition than cut-back management (see also 8.4).

For the would-be policy terminator it is also important to be clear what level of policy, program or organizational termination is being aimed it. Termination can be considered under the heading of the number of different aspects of organization and policy, though in practice they may be intertwined (see deLeon, 1978, 283-5; Bothun and Comer, 1979):

1. *Functional*. A function is a service such as 'health care' which transcends individual organizations and policies; a number of

agencies and policies can all serve the same policy function. Cases of functional termination in modern Western states are almost unheard-of (the termination of the colonial function is an exception), and a huge political effort would appear to be necessary to achieve success.

2. Organization. Organization termination could be easier to achieve than functional termination, but as we have already noted, organizations are designed to last, and evidence from both the United States and Britain suggests that most of them do just that (albeit undergoing considerable transformations in many cases). Organizations may survive the termination or replacement of policies and programs they were responsible for delivering.

3. Policy. Policies are generalized approaches or strategies for solving a particular problem. We would expect that policies would be easier to terminate than the sponsoring organization for a number of reasons: (a) an organization will prefer to forsake some of its policies or programs rather than have the organization itself terminated; (b) policies as such will have fewer political allies than organizations as such; (c) policies are easier to evaluate relative to a given objective than organizations with multiple objectives; (d) most policies will have critics. Policies are most vulnerable to termination if their underlying theory or approach is no longer considered legitimate (see below). A policy can survive the termination of programs designed to pursue the policy if they are replaced by an alternative program.

4. Program. Program here refers to the specific measures designed to carry out a policy (e.g. either tax allowances or investment grants can be used for a policy of encouraging industrial investment through financial incentives). Arguably, programs are the most vulnerable aspect of policy liable to termination. On the one hand, they are closest to the problem and therefore their impact can be most directly measured and, if found inadequate, blame most easily affixed. Against that, there may be close client identification with the program. Program termination is, of course, likely to be much easier if an alternative program is initiated at the same time.

5. Facility. We use the term 'cutback' to refer to reductions in scale, for example, reduction in numbers of a given category of clients or level of benefit, and 'termination' to refer to the elimination of complete programs or program elements. Of course, the distinction may often be difficult to maintain, and will be partly dependent on the level of aggregation at which a program is observed. What is merely a cutback in school enrollment at county level may entail the complete closure of a school in a small community. Thus cutbacks in programs delivered through a large number of community-based facilities will typically generate more widespread political controversy and have 'termination' features, contrasted with programs delivered through large-scale units with only indirect contact with clients.

Governments coming into office are particularly likely to seek to kill off programs, normally but not always those introduced by their political opponents. The extent to which party governments seek to overturn the political work of their predecessors has been exaggerated (Rose, 1984), but the early months of office provide both a motivation and a recognizably legitimate opportunity to cancel programs. Thus, in the United States President Carter killed off the production of the B-1 bomber, having no vested interest in the program in terms of political support or personal prestige. In Britain, Conservative governments have undone some, but far from all, of the programs introduced by predecessor Labour governments. For example, the 1979 Conservative government abolished the Prices Commission (and unlike the Conservative government of 1970 did not subsequently set up a similar body to the one it abolished).

The special feature of the Conservative government of 1979 is the sustained attempt, well beyond the initial months in office, to reduce in whole or in part state ownership of selected nationalized industries. This strategy has not been without its setbacks and delays and the major utility and heavy industries will remain fully in public ownership. Hogwood (1983) has also suggested that selling off shares does not necessarily diminish effective government involvement. A much-heralded 'cull' of government appointed agencies (Pliatzky, 1980) produced few casualties (Hood, 1981). Nevertheless, the Thatcher government does indicate the possibilities not merely of a few initial selected homicides, but of a sustained campaign of assassination. Similarly, President Reagan continued his efforts at regulatory reform and deregulation in the face of mounting political and legal concern.

It was only in the mid-1970s, in the context of fiscal strains and increased political interest, that the policy analysis literature began to concern itself with termination issues, but that literature has now generated a number of hints about how policies are most easily terminated or replaced. They do not quite amount to a Do-It-Yourself Murder Kit for the advocate of termination. For the defender of the existing policy who would regard its demise or alteration as pathological they provide a list of the tactics they may have to counter (Hogwood and Peters, 1982, 13–14).

1. Attention should be paid to the 'political context' and 'natural points' for succession and termination (e.g. a change of administration or an economic crisis) (see deLeon, 1978, 295).

2. Thought should be given to the time horizon of succession and termination and whether the change should be a gradual process or an immediate and total action (see deLeon, 1978, 295). The first is more likely to be successful in minimizing opposition to the decision, but is also more vulnerable to procrastination and deflection.

3. If agencies were allowed to retain some or all of the money saved from terminating or cutting a policy or program or even carry it over to the following financial year, they would have a greater incentive to cancel or change questionable programs (see Biller, 1976, 144–5). This would, of course, reduce the savings from termination or succession.

4. Arrangements could be made to ease adverse transitional or distributional impacts of succession or termination among staff, clients and the localities of any facilities (Behn, 1978, 407–8). Such arrangements might include redundancy payments or guaranteed redeployment for employees, alternative uses of facilities so that closure would not have an adverse impact on the locality, or help to localities where facilities are phased out (see Tarschys, 1982, 220).

5. An important, perhaps necessary, strategy for policy succession or termination is the *delegitimation* of the theory or assumptions underlying the existing policy (e.g. the institutionalization of the mentally ill, pupil selection at 11 +) (see also 9.6).

While the principle of seeking the termination of policies would seem to be beyond reproach, whatever the controversy surrounding individual proposals, there can be ethical problems arising from being engaged in a termination effort. Because it can be so difficult to achieve termination, there may be the temptation to go beyond what is regarded as traditional and legitimate political activity (Behn, 1978, 411–12). For example, potential legislative opposition may be sidestepped by not seeking legislative approval and attempting to eliminate the program by executive action. Such tactics may, of course, be thwarted by judicial or legislative action.

Opponents of the existing program may deliberately seek to polarize debate to eliminate the chances of achieving a compromise. Given the inevitable controversy surrounding termination, agreement on all aspects of procedure cannot be expected. However, the termination process does raise a set of ethical issues at least as difficult to resolve as those surrounding the debate about the appropriate circumstances under which doctors can cease to provide medical care or even cooperate with terminally ill patients who wish to end their existence.

Where the concern is not with termination or replacement but with cutback, perhaps involving the closure of individual facilities, a central executive or budgetary agency or division faces a dilemma in seeking to ensure that other agencies or levels of government accept the cuts that the center wants:

(1) The more locally based the decision about the fate of individual facilities, particularly when any budgetary allocations from above are related to the volume of provision rather than the level of demand, then the less chance of the total number of closures corresponding to the overall decline the center wants.

(2) On the other hand, a more centralized decision-making structure may become overwhelmed with the volume of representations relating to individual facilities.

The advantages and possible pathological consequences (from the perspective of the center) of different approaches can be seen if we look at three main strategies:

(1) Where it has the legal or executive authority to do so, the agency can issue direct commands. However, even where the intent of an instruction may be perfectly clear, the wording of the instruction, i.e. the 'information' actually conveyed, may lead to the intent of the instruction being deliberately ignored or thwarted (see 4.4). In a context of recalcitrance, watertight correctness is required. DeLeon (1978, 290) refers to an extreme example: in November 1969 President Nixon ordered that all stocks of biological weapons should be destroyed. The CIA ignored the order on the grounds that shellfish toxin was a chemical, not biological toxin. In February 1970 the President issued a second, clarificatory order that all chemical and biological toxins were to be destroyed. The CIA ignored this order too, on the grounds that the second order had been directed to the Defense Department and the CIA was not part of the Defense Department. The moral would appear to be that even after initial

authoritative intentions have been made clear there may still be recalcitrance. If the direct command strategy is to be used orders must be specified clearly and precisely—and followed up.

(2) Where a service facing decline in demand is delivered through a local government or other grant-aided agency, some aspects of the adjustment may be dealt with automatically; for example, where a grant is allocated on the basis of, say, school enrollments. The snag with this strategy is that it is only applicable in cases of clearly defined demand and that cuts in grants may be offset by other funds.

(3) In both the previous two strategies the blame for cuts in services can clearly be attributed to the center. Astute central bodies seeking to implement cuts may therefore seek to delegate responsibility for decisions about closure of individual facilities to a lower level, but will seek to set budgetary constraints that will make termination decisions inevitable. An example would be in the Reagan strategy of merging existing specific grants and cutting the overall total. Thus at one and the same time the federal government can secure cuts and claim that it is allowing the states more freedom. This particular strategy will be effective if the primary aim is to secure specified global levels of cuts. It is not a very effective mechanism for targeting cuts on specific programs which are disliked for political reasons.

The comments above indicate that analysis can provide insights into both the consequences of termination and political strategies for promoting or hindering it. To date, policy analysts have not been trained in murder, but to many in government they have been perceived as *outsiders* who were all too willing to come in and advocate the elimination of programs. The implications of who carries out the analysis underpinning proposals for treating public policy pathologies is the subject of chapter 10.

8.6 Coming back from the dead: the Lazarus strategem

Programs slated for termination can show a remarkable resilience, not only surviving a death sentence but bouncing back to life with renewed vigor. In Nebraska state legislation passed in 1974 had the implication, albeit deliberately ambiguous to minimize political opposition, that traditional state mental hospitals would be run down and in some cases closed while additional resources would be devoted to community mental health care (Bothun and Comer, 1979). After an abortive attempt at a closure program, what actually happened was that while the number of inpatient treatment days declined by 7 percent, the amount of state funds appropriated to the hospitals grew by 21 percent. The argument used to produce this result was that the hospitals were providing more intensive and costly services for the severely disturbed. At the same time, hospitals sought out patients around the state and expanded the types of services they provided.

Even where the core element of a program is terminated, policy termination frequently results in 'policy residues', that is, elements of a terminated program which are maintained either to meet existing commitments under the program or to cope with future contingencies (Hogwood and Peters, 1983, 81–3). Some policy residues may either by design or the turn of events or political fashion serve as a base for reactivating the original policy (see Biller, 1976, 147). An example of a residue deliberately maintained to meet a contingency is the retention of Selective Service Boards in the United States after the introduction of the policy of an all-volunteer army in 1971; these were able to participate in registration of potential conscripts when a policy of registration was reintroduced by President Carter in 1980. Thus while the failure to design programs with the possibility of termination or replacement in mind can require the continuation of outdated programs for residual clients or functions, it is important to distinguish contingency residues which facilitate policy reactivation.

It is the failure to recognize that death is frequently not permanent that leads to the 'comet phenomenon'. Bodies may be set up on a more or less regular cycle, blazing into activity for a period, and then disappear after a 'policy hiatus' (Hogwood and Peters, 1983, 65–6). For example, there has been a series of abolitions followed by subsequent reappearances of machinery for administering pay policy in Britain.

Another manifestation of the Lazarus phenomenon occurs when there is a temporary absence of a policy which will soon be replaced by another program. This may result from the action of the courts, which may rule invalid or unconstitutional the programs adopted by government. Anti-pornography policy in the United States has frequently been subject to such hiatuses as the courts rule a particular set of criteria for deciding on obscenity invalid. In the United States the courts have a unique role as 'licensed assasins' of public policy.

8.7 The ultimate pathology

One explanation offered for the relatively rare occurence of the complete termination of policies is that the reluctance that most people have concerning death carries over to an intellectual reluctance to consider policy termination: 'Cognitive reluctance to realize policy shortcomings is reinforced for the analyst because policies are typically designed to solve or at least reduce a specified problem; the options proposed and the programs chosen are not selected with the expectation that they will prove deficient' (deLeon, 1978, 287). While policy analysts do not take a Hippocratic Oath to maintain policy life (contrary to popular wisdom, doctors do not swear to the Hippocratic Oath anyway), the intellectual origins of policy analysis lay in greater activism by government and even the idea of 'mercy killing' of ineffective policies was not one that was clearly faced up to. The implication was that earlier analysis had been deficient. However, recent developments on the political side, principally fiscal stress, have been accompanied by a greater interest in termination among writers on policy analysis (see deLeon, 1978; Biller, 1976; Behn, 1978).

Despite this recent interest in the policy analysis literature, the termination of policies raises a set of issues which analysts and decision-makers are reluctant to confront. Termination is regarded as an unfortunate, unusual and traumatic event. Like those engaged in the illness industry, policy practitioners like to project a caring, activist and supportive role. This imagery is supported by the direct copying of terms such as 'treatment' and 'client' and their application to policy programs. Terms such as 'hatchetman', 'hired gun', and 'program assassin' are invoked (deLeon, 1978, 294), as though the proponent of policy termination were the equivalent of a doctor who deliberately switched off a life-support machine.

It is not death that is the ultimate pathology, but a fear of it which prevents a balanced approach to policy change. This may point to one of the dangers of the analogy we have been making. Those who may be affected by a policy termination can use the biological language about death to invoke from those making the decision a response which is inappropriate for the actual human consequences of the termination.

9
Treatment

9.1 Treatment versus cure

This chapter is deliberately entitled 'Treatment' rather than 'Cure'. This reflects two assumptions: first, that a complete cure may not be practicable, and, second, that attempting a complete cure may not be cost-effective or desirable.

A treatment may result in the elimination of the immediate causes of a disease, but even by intention it may not seek to do so. Other objectives of treatment include:

—Suppression of symptoms while at the same time seeking to treat the underlying disease.
—Suppression of symptoms while allowing the body's natural defenses to deal with the disease.
—Alleviation of suffering while allowing death or injury to take its course.
—The facade of treatment with no intention of substantive physiological effect either as
    (a) a placebo (see 9.7) or
    (b) to avoid a sense of hopelessness on the part of patients (or friends or relatives of the patient) especially in terminal illnesses or
    (c) to avoid the sense or appearance of helplessness on the part of the physician.
—Treatment may be designed to deal with the effects of other treatment rather than the original disease, either
    (a) the necessary side effects of treatment (e.g. pain or bleeding associated with operations) or
    (b) Unforeseen adverse consequences of treatment.

All these treatment forms can be seen to have parallel manifestations in public policy, and we should not expect that any policy instrument or set of instruments will necessarily eliminate all the causes or even manifestations of a problem.

Some diseases should not be treated even where it is technically feasible to do so. This may seem to be a brutally inhumane statement, but it is based on a recognition that the pain, suffering or inconvenience caused by an illness may be slight compared to the cost of treatment. Further, the resources which can be devoted to health care are finite, and resources committed to treating some ailments prevent the treatment of others. In other words, cost-benefit comparisons can be made between treatment of different diseases and different treatments of the same disease. In practice, doctors have mostly evaded making such calculations through their exercise of 'clinical judgement', which sounds less inspiring when it is translated as a doctor making up his mind about each patient as he goes along.

Politicians also typically make up their minds about each problem as they go along, though without the scientific underpinning and extensive training which informs the judgement of doctors. Thus, while the opportunity cost of alternative treatments for a given problem may be considered, the wider cost-benefit implications rarely are. For both medical and policy problems the current state of the methodology of cost-benefit analysis is unable to handle all the technical and ethical problems which broad allocations to treatments or categories of patients would pose. A recognition that treatments devised for one patient/problem have wider implications for the treatments that can be given to others should be an objective of the training of both medical practitioners and policy analysts.

There are also trade-offs between the costs and benefits of treating the symptoms only or attempting to cure the underlying disease. The balance will not always obviously lie in favor of attempting to deal only with the symptoms: treatment of symptoms may be a continuing process, while removing the underlying causes of the problem maybe a one-off, albeit expensive, operation. Judgement about whether to treat symptoms or underlying causes will depend also on whether the political problem is defined as the symptoms or the underlying problem. If symptoms can be suppressed the problem can be said to be 'cured' politically, even if in terms of a causal understanding of the issue only the effects of a process are being tackled.

In talking of cures as removal of underlying causes, we should avoid falling into the 'miracle cure' analogy, that is the assumption that a one-off application of a treatment will permanently resolve a problem. Permanent treatment may be required, or where the problem recurs, perhaps triggered by other problems, occasional reapplication of treatment may be necessary. Treatment may even create dependency which necessitates continuation of the treatment (see 7.3).

To focus on treatment rather than cure reminds us that both medical and policy decisions are often dilemmas, that is choices among alternatives all of which have undesirable consequences. There can be dilemmas between treatments both of which have adverse side effects and dilemmas between pathological features of disease and of treatment. While both medical and policy decisions face cost constraints, policy decisions may be more difficult because of multiple and often competing objectives.

9.2 Prevention is better than cure

Just as in medicine, far more resources are poured into dealing with the consequences of public policy pathologies than their prevention, despite the fact that after the event treatment will often be more resource-hungry than prevention (bearing in mind the costs of the pathology as well as of its treatment). Crisis-oriented demands are more likely to be successful than those directed at longer-term avoidance: arguments about the need for resources to treat heart patients, who are specifically identifiable and in clear and immediate need, are likely to win out over less dramatic and, at the individual level, more hypothetical and probabilistic, 'needs'. In addition, prevention may be seen as the responsibility of the individual in a way that treatment of diseases once manifest is not. In the study of public policymaking, the crisis-oriented and reactive nature of most decision-making is a largely accurate cliché.

Total prevention of the emergence of public policy pathologies is impossible. It may be logically or practically impossible to take a policy decision which did not involve some pathological features. However, even where some pathological features are inevitable, there may be scope for containing them through preventive measures built into the program from the start.

Limitations in our causal knowledge of social processes or the impact of policies may also preclude a focus on prevention. We may know how to treat symptoms but not underlying causes and therefore have to wait for symptoms to emerge in order to treat them. Also, pathologies may be easier to classify in terms of their treatment requirements or part of the body in which symptoms manifest themselves than in terms of their underlying causes. In public policy terms, it is easier to classify 'policy problems' by policy area than by type of pathology or underlying causes. Ability to classify assists the formation of sub-professions and bureaucratic bases for budget allocation.

Some of the factors advantaging treatment rather than prevention can themselves be regarded as pathological, but they are difficult pathologies to treat, since they are ingrained in approaches to decision-making and attitudes to the role of policy analysis. Thus, the promotion of a more prevention-oriented approach would have to aim at tackling such attitudes and the political rewards and penalties of such a style of decision-making.

The training of medical practitioners is treatment rather than prevention-oriented. The whole process is more under the control of the medical professions in a treatment-oriented approach than in prevention. Similarly, we would argue that much of the training of policy analysts is 'solutionist'-oriented, that is problems are selected and defined according to their susceptibility to analysis by one of a set of maximization techniques which will point to a particular form of public policy treatment. An awareness of policy-caused pathologies is essential both to ensure that potentially pathological features of options are identified, and, more problematically, to promote a focus on pathologies and their avoidance rather than on given problems and related specific decisions.

9.3 The need for timely treatment

Delayed or inappropriate timing may mean than treatment is ineffective or irrelevant or more costly, and may actually produce reverse effects. Unfortunately, a number of factors can delay a timely response to a policy problem.

The first type of delay is in recognizing that there is a problem which might need to be tackled (see 4.1). When there is recognition of the need for information there will almost inevitably be delays in collecting it. Even where routine statistical collection procedures have been established, as in the case of economic indicators, the information collected may be a month to a year out of date, and subject to subsequent sizeable revisions. The problem may have been reinforced or have disappeared in the interim.

There are often delays in information getting to the right decision-makers in useful form, and the danger of difficult issues being shunted among various agencies without a clear decision being taken (see 4.2 and 4.3). By the time a decision emerges, the optimum time for action may have passed.

Few of the treatments necessary to remedy public policy pathologies are likely to involve instantaneous implementation. An organizational structure may have to be established or adapted. Particular delays are likely if capital facilities have to be constructed or staff newly trained. There can be problems in getting everything organized at the right time and the right sequence.

The impact of a decision will often be the result of decisions and actions by a large number of private (and public) actors in response to the government policy or its announcement. There will be considerable variation in the timing of any response, as well as uncertainty about what the aggregate effect of those responses might be.

These various delays may have the effect of precluding some kinds of policy treatment. Delays in recognizing the emergence of problem will reduce the scope for preventive measures.

Cyclical problems pose special problems in obtaining up-to-date information and judging the time when the effects of a response will actually be manifested. The most obvious examples are from economic cycles, where a set of government reactions to the unemployment implications of recession may come into effect at a time when the cycle is already on the upturn and hence reinforce the inflationary pressures associated with it (see Brittan, 1971).

The spread of the policy response over time once commenced is also important. Too concentrated a response, perhaps in an attempt to make up for lost time in arriving at a decision, can lead to 'choking': too spread out a response can lead to 'bleeding', that is, too low a level of policy output to achieve a sustainable impact (see 7.6).

The design of policy treatments is therefore not only about the selection of particular instruments but about the timing of their impact and their spread over time. We would think it a strange doctor who simply specified a drug, perhaps also quoting the total amount to be used over the course of the treatment as a whole. We would hope that the nurse would ask when the treatment should commence (assuming of course that the hospital had that drug in stock), how frequently the treatment should be given and at what dosage. Similarly, we should regard any decision about a program which simply specified the method to be used and the total appropriation to be sought as only partially specified.

9.4 Targeting

It may appear self-evident that the greatest precision practicable in identifying the target individuals or organizations of a program is desirable. Only in that way can we be sure that resources are aimed at all the potential targets and that resources are not wasted in delivering the program to those who do not have the relevant characteristics. However, there are trade-offs between the costs of targeting and the benefits gained by precision (Rossi, Freeman, and Wright, 1979, 116). Such costs and benefits may often be subjective, of the nature of 'it is better that nine guilty men go free than that one innocent man be convicted'. In other cases, such as whether it is better than those not entitled should receive benefit relative to those entitled who do not, the political assessment may be different. In cases involving the delivery of benefits the choice is fairly simple as the cost of identifying targets approaches or exceeds the cost of providing the benefit.

Use of a broader definition of target beneficiaries than those the program is really aimed at may have other benefits. To label clients as being 'remedial' may be stigmatizing and may have broader consequences for how they are treated both by public employees and others (see Rossi *et al.*, 1979; Dexter, 1981; Sieber, 1981).

The most usual pathology is lack of sufficient thought in identifying target populations in an operationalizable form, that is, using a means by which the policy can actually be delivered to them and by which those who have authorized the program can identify whether the program has actually reached its intended beneficiaries. Where a method of 'proxy targets' is used there is even less chance of accurate targeting. For example, teachers in areas with large concentrations of disadvantaged ethnic groups may be paid a supplement, but this may merely compensate them for working in a depressed area and may of itself do nothing to improve the education going to disadvantaged children. The use of proxy targets is justified when there is a well-understood 'pathway' between the proxy target and the target which is the actual aim of the programme (Rossi *et al.*, 1979).

The level of aggregation of targeting is therefore crucial. Treatment at the level of the individual or the local community may be irrelevant if problems are caused by changes to the national or international economy (though it may be possible to alleviate symptoms). Causal analysis and its significance for targeting policies may be controversial, as in case of Community Development Projects (CDPs) in Britain (McKay and Cox, 1979, 238–48; Edwards and Batley, 1978, 225–34).

One of the pathological features of public policy is the use of broad categories whereby any potential recipient who fell within a particular category would receive policy outputs in a more or less standardized form (see 4.4, 4.5). It might seem obviously desirable that treatment should be designed so that each individual, area or manifestation of a problem, as appropriate, received treatment specifically related to individual requirements. This would ensure that the program was delivered in the correct amount and form to those for whom it was intended, and that resources would not be wasted on delivering inappropriate or perhaps even counter-productive amounts or types of treatment.

However, the apparent desirability of customized treatment is offset by the costs of identifying the special needs of each target (whether an individual, area or particular manifestation of a problem) and of administering the treatment. These will invariably be higher than for programs where standardized forms of policy outputs are delivered to broad categories. Costs of administering policies tailored to individual targets will be lower where the tailoring is quantitative only, as where the amount of social security paid to a family is related to family size and means. Even here, the administrative costs of calculating benefit are not trivial, but will, in a well designed system, be small in relation to the danger of some families starving if a standard amount was set too low and much larger financial cost if a higher standard amount was set too high.

Even with such quantitative tailoring there can be disadvantages, including possible long-term disincentives to making own provision for difficult times and the greater difficulty of understanding eligibility and consequent lower take-up rates. A further danger arises from viewing target-specific programs in isolation from each other. There is a danger of 'over-tailoring' where several programs all use similar criteria in delivering output, as when a number of income-maintenance programs all attempt to relate benefit to financial means, thus resulting in a very high overall rate of withdrawal of benefit when gross earned income increases.

In making qualitative judgements discretion will have to be given to service-delivery staff and there is a danger that in making case-by-case judgements the overall pattern of delivery may not be what was originally intended. Staff made responsible for such judgements may claim professional status and a right to influence policy beyond their individual casework decisions. The consequence of a policy design meant to maximize individual flexibility may be to induce long-term policy rigidity.

The case for target-specific treatment is therefore not universally self-evident. Such an approach will be desirable where delivery in standardized amounts to all targets would produce severe pathological consequences because the standardized amount was set too low or too high. In many other cases, the costs of administering a target-specific system of delivery will outweigh any benefits to be gained over standardized delivery.

Policy is rarely concerned with attaining only one target at a time (see 2.1.1 and 3.2). It has been shown by economists that it is not normally possible to pursue a set of objectives unless there are at least as many policy instruments as there are objectives. This general condition is often ignored both in economic and other policies because of the temptation of forming coalitions of supporters each of whom look to a particular instrument to achieve a different objective and because the additional instruments necessary to ensure movement towards all targets may be politically unpalatable. The attribution of multiple objectives can also have the political advantage that only those objectives which are successfully achieved need be retrospectively stressed.

The use of at least as many instruments as there are objectives does not, of course, ensure that any chosen target level can be achieved: intrinsic constraints and trade-offs between objectives will limit the levels of achievement attainable by any given mix of commitments to each instrument.

As we noted in 8.2.2, there are occasions when a single instrument can fulfill more than one objective, but such occasions may be only a temporary coincidence, and when the program ceases to fulfill one objective its continuing existence and its ability to handle the remaining objective may come under threat.

The opposite of such 'overtargeting' is 'overinstrumenting', by which many instruments all target at the same client group or objective. This can be wasteful of effort and resources and may lead to the kinds of interorganizational problems discussed in 3.2. When it comes to evaluating the success of policy instruments it may be difficult to work out which is producing the effect, though a beneficial impact may arise only as the result of the interaction of two or more programs. Casual use of instruments all aimed at the same target may therefore hinder long-term learning. However, in case of an urgent problem and poor understanding, throwing everything at a problem may be justified.

Unfortunately, the very act of selecting a precise target variable may become self-defeating. Any target variable which is selected for the purposes of control may become unreliable for the purpose. This proposition as applied to British monetary policy became known as 'Goodhart's Law' after the Bank of England official who formulated it. In monetary policy there is a wide range of interchangeable forms of money and degrees of liquidity as well as considerable inventiveness in devising new ones, but in principle 'Goodhart's Law' applies to a wider set of problems. The labelling of certain activities as taxable or certain family circumstances as rendering the family eligible for benefit will lead to a switch out of such activities and into such family circumstances respectively (see 4.5).

Such behavioral responses to the specificiation of policy control variables suggests that we should be cautious in using the imagery of targetry in public policy. The target is not merely moving but ducking and weaving in response to being aimed at. Few programs have adequate initial policy design and built-in feedback to enable swift response to changes in the target. In the case of monetary policy, the response to the phenomenon encapsulated in Goodhart's Law was to abandon the use of M3 as the sole target variable and attempt to control a wider range of monetary measures and keep track of an even larger number. However, monetary policy is unusual in being a discretionary policy operated by central banks, and the bureaucratic delivery apparatus and considerations of due process present in most policy programs limit the scope for multiple and changing target variables and put a special premium on an initial policy design which minimizes 'leakage'.

The slipperiness of defining targets is further emphasized when we consider the phenomenon known as 'creaming', by which the apparent success of a program is improved by program staff selecting for treatment under a program only those potential clients from within a large target group who will score highly on the measures of success set for the program (see Rossi *et al.*, 1979, 124–5). Indeed, such clients might well have been successful even without the intervention of the program. Creaming may also result deliberately or inadvertently from self-selection by clients rather than active search by program staff, since the very act of self-presentation may indicate a higher than average degree of personal initiative.

Creaming is not intrinsically pathological where the whole point of a program is to concentrate limited resources on those who with a small amount of assistance can improve their chances, as with some training programs. However, where the program is aimed at a broad range of clients or indeed at the most disadvantaged then creaming represents target displacement, and indicates that the target was not adequately defined in the first place. In the absence of careful definition of targets, creaming can be expected, both because it makes life easier and perhaps more personally fulfilling for program staff, and because it will have the effect of improving the apparent success of the program.

9.5 Treatment through structural or process change

Just as a doctor can choose between surgical or drug-based treatments, so policymakers seeking to remedy public policy pathologies can choose varying combinations of organizational restructuring and attempts to adapt processes. Where a previous policy has had pathological features, one obvious option is to abolish the existing organization and establish a new organization. However, a more common pattern is likely to be the adaptation of existing organizations to administer a replacement policy, in part because the undoubted dangers of a continuation of the original pathology may be outweighed by the disruption which attempting to start from scratch may entail (Hogwood and Peters, 1983, 138–42). In such circumstances, organizational restructuring will inevitably entail changes in internal organizational processes by accident or design.

Two broad guidelines can be offered about the circumstances in which organizational change should accompany an attempt at removing a public policy pathology (Hogwood and Peters, 1983, 140). First, the greater the extent of change involved in the treatment, both in terms of the changes in targets set for the policy and the instruments used, the greater the need for organizational change to be part of the treatment. This can arise because of a lack of commitment to the new approach by the existing organizational personnel or because of their lack of expertise in implementing a program using the new methodology. Of course, organizational change in such circumstances may appear to existing staff to have the attributes of termination with the consequences and possible tactics to cope with them described in chapter 8.

Second, the characteristics of the policy succession associated with removing a pathology will be relevant: policy splitting and policy consolidation imply that 'new' organizations would be required for adequate administration of the new approach.

However, the policy process in practice often involves a network of relations among a number of organizations. Formal allocations of organizational remit do not totally determine the pattern of inter-organizational interaction in arriving at decisions, a pattern which also reflects characteristics of the issues surrounding those decisions. Designing for effective decision-making *processes* is even more difficult than the problem of determining the allocation of jurisdiction to individual organizations and the well-known dilemmas that occur (Peters, 1984).

There are a number of reasons why organizational responses have been used rather than confronting policy problems directly. First, the organization is a visible manifestation of the problem, and it is politically easier to restructure or abolish the organization than to attempt the more difficult task of redesigning policy to eliminate its pathological features.

Second, the structure of organizations is often procedurally easier to modify than are substantive polices. Presidents and Prime Ministers are given considerable latitude in changing the organization of the executive branch, and consequently they can make a response to a perceived pathology without having to become involved with the legislature, clients and service providers associated with the existing policy (Mansfield, 1970; Pollitt, 1984).

Finally, it has to be remembered that some politicians and top officials believe in the organizational response. This was the case with President Carter, and to some extent was true of Harold Wilson and Edward Heath (Johnson, 1976; Pollitt, 1984). This may be associated with a distaste for the messier aspects of political conflict and a belief in mechanistic organizational engineering.

Despite developments in organizational theory and public administration there is no academic theory or set of working guidelines which can relate organizational changes to other changes necessary to treat public policy pathologies. Organizational change may be a necessary but not a sufficient condition for effective treatment. Changing the organization does not of itself produce any real changes in the policies being implemented, although it can facilitate making those policy changes.

9.6 Changes in acceptable treatment

A program may be severely cut back or even totally terminated if its underlying approach is shown to be ineffective or no longer conforms to the types of standards acceptable in public policy. The delegitimation of the theory or ideology underlying a program is one of the most effective ways of facilitating a policy termination. One of the major recent examples of such a process is the running down of mental hospitals in both Britain and the United States (Cameron, 1978). The institutions were shown not merely to be ineffective in curing some types of mental illness or mental handicap but to have pathological effects in reinforcing dependence through institutionalization and therefore rendering patients less rather than more able to cope with a normal life. This formed part of a broader anti-institutional movement which applied also to other programs such as institutions for juvenile offenders and provided an impetus to terminating such programs (Behn, 1978, 400).

However, the manner in which deinstitutionalization has taken place in many cases has itself had pathological consequences for the expatients, since they have been decanted into the community without adequate preparation—and many cases would never be adequately prepared—and without continuing adequate support. This illustrates the sad truth that the fact that an existing program is clearly ineffective and has pathological consequences does not ensure that its termination or replacement will necessarily resolve those problems or will be free of its own pathological consequences. The idea underlying the new policy may in its turn continue to be considered valid well after its pathological consequences have become apparent (Cameron, 1978, 306). Above all, this example illustrates the importance of paying attention to the process of *transition* between one program, however bad, and another, however good (Hogwood and Peters, 1983, ch. 7).

Changes in prevailing wisdom about acceptable forms of public policy do not inevitably lead to the termination of programs embodying previous ideas. Would-be terminators have to take advantage of changes in attitude, or even play a direct part in shifting them (Behn, 1978, 400).

9.7 Ineffective treatments

Some treatments may be designed from the start to be ineffective in producing substantive impact—though it will be unusual to get decision-makers to admit that at the time. The ineffectiveness of the treatment may take the form of treating only superficial manifestations of the problem ('cosmetic' treatment) or largely symbolic policies or other acts, which are not designed to produce substantive outputs ('placebos').

One literally cosmetic public policy is where, faced with a severely run down inner city area, the government embarks on a scheme of environmental improvements such as demolishing derelict buildings, sowing grass, planting trees, and putting nice railings round car parks, all accompanied by a proliferation of signboards announcing that this is part of a scheme organized by the agency. However, dereliction is only a manifestation of economic decline, and not necessarily the manifestation most important to the remaining inhabitants, though it is the manifestation most physically visible to outsiders.

Cosmetic treatments can make a patient feel better and this may actually produce substantive results. Thus environmental improvements may assist in the rehabilitation of an area in terms of attracting new jobs, but it will be relatively rare that such treatments alone will have sufficient leverage to remove social and economic malaise.

Placebo policies are designed to produce the impression of action with little or no substance in order to placate those demanding action (*placebo* is Latin for 'I shall please'). Thus a doctor pestered by a patient might prescribe for a hypochondriac patient tablets that had no physiological effects. Placebo policies are part of a range of placebo actions which government can take, including making declarations of intent and setting up 'independent' commissions of inquiry (see 10.4). Placebo policies can involve restructing existing organizations, though this might turn out to have substantive results after all (Hogwood and Peters, 1983, 137–8).

A policy may appear at first sight to be a vigorous expression of government action, with a new regulatory organization being set up with new staff and apparently extensive regulatory powers. However, if through lack of funding, lack of commitment by staff, or a 'sweetheart' relationship with the regulatory targets, little restriction results, then the policy could be argued to be a placebo or 'symbolic' one (Edelman, 1964, 1971). Another type of symbolic policy would be where one program was designed to appear to meet the demands or needs of a particular section of the population by visible means such as welfare payments, while the effects of this were being offset by other programs, or greater benefits went to other sections of the population by less visible means such as tax reliefs.

Placebo actions do not merely have a nil effect. The removal of an issue from the political agenda by the announcement of a placebo policy makes it difficult to get attention paid to arguments for more substantive policies. Further, the 'lulling effect' produced by the belief that a problem is being dealt with might enable the problem to deteriorate drastically in the meantime (Sieber, 1981, 166–72). In the long run, symbolic gestures may be worse than nothing. They may cause disappointment and alienation, and this may cause more damage than ignoring the problem entirely (Midlarsky, 1961).

Academic and political critics of apparently placebo treatments should be cautious in assuming that their criticism is valid under all likely present-day circumstances. Edelman (1964; 1971) is probably the foremost academic analyst of the symbolic uses of politics. However, his argument that regulatory policies were of only symbolic significance and were designed to ensure political quiescence looks less plausible with the upsurge of social and environmental regulation and the subsequent interest in deregulation than it did in the late 1950s and early 1960s. Political quiescence does not necessarily imply lack of substantive policy impact.

There is also a tendency to label a policy as being 'symbolic' when it has turned out to be partly ineffective or exhibits some pathology. While recognizing the difficulty of untangling the complex motives and components of programs, and the importance of understanding why programs known to be ineffective or pathological are allowed to continue, we do consider it worthwhile to attempt to distinguish analytically between policies which had from the start a major placebo function and those which have, with the benefit of hindsight, turned out to be ineffective.

9.8 Making sure the patient takes the treatment

However good a proposed treatment, it can do no good if a patient refuses to take the treatment, or fails to persist in a course of treatment. In public policy terms we can divide consideration of treatment into an initial decision to make use of policy-relevant analysis and whether or not a proposed treatment is followed through in practice.

The literature on the use of the social sciences and that on evaluation research in policymaking provide an overwhelming consensus that individual pieces of analysis are very rarely used in a direct way to influence specific identifiable decisions, but that such analysis does get 'utilized' in a more diffuse way, in part by altering decision-makers' perceptions of the nature of problems and possibilities for dealing with them (see e.g. Weiss, 1977, 16; Rich, 1977; Weiss and Bucuvalas, 1977; Kogan and Henkel, 1983).

There are a number of ways in which government agencies do utilize analysis which they have commissioned:

Research makes the client group think. As they absorb research it influences them, if unobtrusively, and cumulatively. Research can help them in discussions with pressure groups. Research both raises questions and reinforces the questions that customers formulate. Even when research does not confirm policy-makers expectations it makes them ask why they do not agree with the research (Kogan and Henkel, 1983, 147).

Administrators may even welcome findings which challenge the conventional wisdom, but only if they do not raise questions about basic institutions of the society or challenge fundamental economic arrangements, and only where ideas have already been in circulation and are therefore not totally unexpected (Weiss and Bucuvalas, 1977, 277).

Kogan and Henkel (1983, 148) note that there are several different ways in which a research program may bear fruit: 'through individual projects; by the accumulation of a "critical mass"; by providing information which enabled providers to have an increasing understanding of the basis of their work; and by reflecting the general climate in which the Department's work was carried out'. There is often a need to relate findings from commissioned research to other data, including developing practice in the field (Kogan and Henkel, 1983, 156).

Clearly we should be extremely cautious about pursuing a public policy analogy of the relationship between diagnosis of a specific health problem and a specific course of treatment. Similarly, the analogy of a patient taking a decision to accept prescribed treatment breaks down for public policy, given that a decision may require assent from a number of different policy actors. The chances of proposed treatments being questioned and of a veto on treatment are much higher than is the case in medicine.

Failure to follow through the implementation of an authorized course of treatment can arise in two different ways. First, there can be active refusal to continue treatment because of the unpleasant nature of treatment or side-effects. Refusal can occur even when the pathology is life-threatening. For example, the drug cisplatin has been used since 1979 to combat certain cancers, but the side-effects of vomiting and kidney poisoning can be so horrible that many patients refuse to continue with the drug (*The Economist*, 14 Apr. 1984, 94). Second, through inadvertence or absentmindedness there may be a failure to stick strictly to prescribed dosage, etc.

Courses of treatment to remedy public policy pathologies will normally involve implementing change to *existing* programs and organizations. Not all treatments will involve policy changes; some may only involve changes in internal operation of organizations, but this in itself is non-trivial. We have argued elsewhere that implementation of changes to existing activities has problems distinct from implementation of a completely new program (Hogwood and Peters, 1983).

The treatment prescribed for public policy pathologies is unlikely to involve only the leadership of an agency. Here the analogy with a patient breaks down; there is not a single public policy agency which has to keep 'taking the pills', but frequently a large number of workers in the field. Indeed not all the delivery staff who are expected to take the treatment may be in the same agency.

Where clients are expected to alter their behavior as part of the remedy for a public policy pathology, the ability to control their actions will be even weaker. In such cases it may be better to move away from the medical metaphor of a doctor treating a patient to an environmental health metaphor, where adjustments are aimed at general environmental influences rather than at the individual ill person. There is no guarantee that all target clients would respond to changes (such as adjustments to market prices), but there is no certainty either that treatments directly aimed at clients would produce desired responses (see 9.4).

The problem is not simply to initiate a course of treatment but to maintain it. To pursue an analogy, it is not enough to ensure that repeat prescriptions are dispensed but that they are actually being used by the correct patient for the purposes intended. For example, a specific grant may have been devised to remedy some identified deficiency in previous provision, but the fact that checks are collected and cashed is no guarantee that the entire sum of money has been used for its remedial purpose (see 9.4).

Equally important is ensuring that the treatment is terminated or modified when it is no longer required or may actually become harmful. Unfortunately, some members of the medical profession are prone to issuing repeat prescriptions without seeing the patient. By analogy, while the importance of evaluating public policy programs which are themselves intended to overcome the pathological features of public policy is recognized in principle, the methodology and practice of public policy evaluation still allows and 'repeat prescription' of no longer appropriate public policy remedies.

Arguably both medicine and public policy have tended to focus on dramatic moments of decision rather than the less glamorous process of ensuring that prescribed treatment is followed through in practice and continues to be delivered in that form only as long as required.

9.9 Iatrogenic illnesses

Many of the pathologies listed in this book have been the consequence of government attempts to treat some social or economic problem. It is worth distinguishing between (a) undesirable side effects of a program which is having some beneficial impact (or at worst no impact) in terms of its major objective and (b) actual reverse effects where, far from ameliorating a condition, government intervention actually makes it worse (Sieber, 1981). We should therefore be cautious in considering possible treatments for pathologies that similar adverse side effects or reverse effects do not occur. Since we are dealing with second-order pathologies, it is worth considering all the possibilities (see table 9.1). A treatment for a pathology can remove that pathology while causing new perverse effects, or may even make the original pathology worse. While focusing on the removal of reverse effects, a treatment may introduce unwanted new side effects.

Table 9.1
Possible outcomes of treatment of policy pathologies

	Original side effects			Original reverse effects	
	Yes	No		Yes	No
New side effects	New side effects plus original side eff: better/ same/ worse	Side effects where none before	New reverse effects	Reverse effects worse	Reverse effects where none before
No new side effects	Original side effects: better/ same/ worse	Nil side effects	No new reverse effects	Reverse effects: same/ better	Nil Reverse effects

Just as a doctor may find it difficult to disentangle the effects of a drug from symptoms of the original disease, so too a policy analyst may find it difficult to identify pathological features of policy and their linkages, if any, to the developing problem which the policy was designed to tackle. If both problems and pathologies had the decency to appear singly the task would be a tractable one, but while for purposes of exposition we have for the most part dealt with pathological features one at a time, really problematic programs are likely to have a number of pathological features, and attempts to reduce one pathology may increase the effect of another.

9.10 Is the treatment worse than the disease?

It is not always obvious that a pathological feature of public policy should be treated or that when it is what the best method of treatment or prevention should be. As we have shown in this chapter, each mode of treatment has its own costs and benefits, both in resource terms and in degree of precision in tackling a pathology. The removal of a pathology may be at the expense of reducing the effectiveness of a program in meeting its original objectives.

If analysis which produces a policy leads to pathological features, then we should expect the analysis surrounding the disentangling of such pathologies while still promoting the original policy objectives to be even more complex, difficult and uncertain. The design of policy instruments and strategies for using them is in a surprisingly underdeveloped state in policy analysis (see Peters and Linder, 1984). The design of treatments for public policy pathologies is an almost non-existent topic (but see Sieber, 1981). This may seem a cause for pessimism, but it should instead be seen as an indication of the scope for development of the analysis of policy instruments and their consequences.

10

Is There a Doctor in the House?

Physician, heal thyself
Luke 4:23.

A number of institutions have the potential for diagnosing and proposing treatment for policy pathologies. Just as some writers have identified doctors as themselves a source of health problems, so too such institutions may cause further problems for public policy. This can occur in a number of ways:

1. The ways in which these institutions go about their tasks may actually exacerbate the policy problem.
2. The process of considering public problems may itself have pathological features which hinder its effectiveness.
3. By failing to take a 'whole body' perspective, that is by failing to consider how a specified treatment would interact with the operation of an organization as a whole, the treatment may be rendered ineffective.

10.1 Self-diagnosis

Ill persons rarely require a doctor to tell them that they are ill—after all the very act of self-presentation for anything other than a routine check-up implies a preliminary diagnosis on the part of a patient. The self-designation of being ill does not necessarily imply that the person will seek professional medical advice. There is a 'hierarchy of resort' through which people try less extreme (and expensive) options before seeking professional advice. Many minor ailments are self-treated, sometimes with advice from a friendly neighborhood pharmacist; in Britain 90 percent of perceived episodes of illness are dealt with by the ill persons themselves (*The Economist*, 28 Apr. 1984, 28).

In other cases the disease may be recognized as self-limiting, and any treatment taken is solely to suppress some of the symptoms. Except for hypocondriacs, for whom there appears to be no public policy parallel (unless we inlude the perennial cries of the 'death of local government' in Britain and of states' rights in the US), many people with ailments they consider to be relatively minor will take the attitude that it is bad enough being ill without having to go to a doctor as well. Even when a patient does present himself to a doctor, he may convey his own self-diagnosis. It would be a foolish doctor who simply accepted such a diagnosis, but it does inevitably provide him with cues.

Similarly we would expect that public policy organizations, far from calling in outside help whenever they felt there was a problem, would normally seek to deal with such a problem themselves, even if only by treating some of its more obvious symptoms and suffering (or allowing its staff or clients to suffer) in silence. In some ways the ideal might seem to be the self-diagnosing, self-treating organization. Wildavsky (1972) sets up such a model of 'evaluative man' only to emphasize how rare he is. In practice policy reviews, whether of the effectiveness of goals or the efficiency with they are discharged, are often seen as a threat to policy values—and jobs. This may be true even when there is general recognition that some pathological. features of policy delivery exist.

Wildavsky (1972, 509) stresses the threat which evaluation reviews pose in stating the problem to be: 'How to convince administrators to collect information that might help others but can only harm them?' This is only one side of the coin, however. Analysis of pathological features of an organization's activities may show a case for expanding them where the problem is diagnosed as 'malnutrition' (see 7.5). In other cases, formal diagnosis may confirm the existing view of the organization's leadership about lines for future development. Indeed, particularly given the subjective nature of determining whether a pathological feature exists, there may be a danger that internal reviews may withingly or unwittingly be biased to produce uncritical results (for example, by selecting for appraisal the objective which the organization is currently fullfilling best).

A big advantage of insider reviews is that insiders will have the detailed knowledge of what is involved in delivering the program and of any points not foreseen at the policy design stage. However, this understanding can also be achieved by an outsider if he has access to information and the cooperation of staff. Indeed, as we saw in chapter 4, one of the major problems of information flow is *within* an organization, a problem faced by both insiders and outsiders.

Operating divisions within a public policy agency may lack the specialized skills for formal policy analysis (though there is a shortage of such skills all round, in Britain much more so than in the United States). This is at least as much an argument for having people with policy analysis training in operating divisions rather than confining them to the ghettos of policy analysis units. However, it has to be recognized that the shortage of formal policy analysis skills and a possible intermittent workload militate against relying on self-diagnosis of all pathologies.

Another disadvantage of relying solely on analysis within the operating division is that a number of different organizations may be involved in policy delivery (and indeed we noted in 3.2 that this may have pathological consequences) so that a fully rounded diagnosis cannot be obtained by looking at the activities of one organization.

If the results of any analysis identifying pathological features are to be utilized then changes in the existing program or organizational structure or procedures will have to be carried out by the operating staff. If these staff have been actively involved in the evaluation effort, the chances of willing implementation of the changes are increased. Against that, insider analysis may be less likely to imply threatening changes in the first place. Where an outside analyst is employed the chances of subsequent implementation of changes may be improved if the analyst has involved the operating staff in discussions about objectives, criteria, etc. Here one can draw a parallel with the doctor-patient relationship, where there has been an increased recognition, in theory if not in practice, of the desirability of the doctor discussing diagnosis and treatment with the patient.

10.2 In-house efficiency and evaluation experts

Analysis of pathologies can be carried out by a separate unit specifically concerned with policy analysis or organizational methods, though still within the organization responsible for delivery. Particularly where such staff are concerned with a number of different activities within the organization, they do not have the same vested interests in the continuation of any given program in the same way. The link is even weaker if staff are specially hired temporarily to carry out the analysis.

While the relationship between analysts and operating staff should not be seen as necessarily a clash, given the potential unpredictability of analysis and its results there is bound to be tension. Since both delivery and analysis staff have resources, the identification of pathologies and the implementation of treatments will involve a process of bargaining. The operating staff will often be the ones collecting the information to be used in the analysis, and while unlikely to refuse outright to pass the information on, they may be uncooperative in providing it in the form required for analysis. Special analysis staff have their own advantages, however: 'They are experts in manipulating data and models to justify existing policies or denigrate them' (Wildavsky, 1972, 513). Where analytical staff have the support of the leadership of the organization—which cannot be taken for granted —they will also have the ability to lay down procedures. Further, if there is a lack of clarity among those involved in delivery, this may give wide room for maneuver on the part of analytical staff.

Even where there is a good in-house staff, the question arises of whether it is proper for an organization to be solely responsible for diagnosing and treating its own problems. As Wildavsky (1972, 518) puts it: 'No matter how good its internal analysis, or how persuasively an organization justifies its programs to itself, there is something unsatisfactory about allowing it to judge its own case.' Periodically, therefore, even a self-diagnosing organization should be subject to audits of the methods used in its analysis or to independently conducted reviews of its programs.

Organizations directly involved in policy delivery are far from being the only bodies potentially interested in identifying public policy pathologies and, indeed, we suggested above that they might have some cause to fear it. Legislatures (considered below in 10.5) and executive bodies which originally authorized the policy are likely to be concerned with identifying and if possible eliminating pathological features of those policies. This concern could be with substantive policy effectiveness or the more negative reason of avoiding the political embarrassment of pathological features of government policy being revealed by others.

Central staffing and budgetary agencies, such as OMB in the US federal government and the Management and Personnel Office and HM Treasury in Britain have a special interest in rooting out resource-consuming pathologies, though their concern and expertise are less prominent in the case of pathologies the elimination of which would not produce manpower or budgetary savings. Indeed, a focus on cost-cutting from a narrow perspective can itself have pathological consequences.

The fact that analysis is conducted by another agency within the government might appear to imply greater detachment, but, as we have already hinted, central executive or legislative agencies may have their own axes to grind. For example, delivery organizations may find themselves being evaluated on the basis of objectives and criteria other than those they were originally asked to implement. This emphasizes the subjective and sometimes partisan nature of defining whether a public policy pathology exists in a particular program. What may from the perspective of one agency be considered to be good health might be diagnosed as illness by another. While clearly stated criteria for evaluation established at policy design stage may pose a threat if the program turns out to unsuccessful, they can also provide a protection against the 'retrofitting' of quite different criteria.

Given that analysis by a central agency will still have to rely heavily on information provided by the delivery organization, it obviously makes sense to secure its cooperation. For example, the delivery organization can be involved in the selection of programs to be analyzed and the objectives and criteria for examination. However, as the fate of Programme Analysis and Review within British central government indicates, the adoption of an overly consensual style may lead to the selection of relatively anodyne topics for analysis (see Gray and Jenkins, 1982). The relatively successful 'Rayner exercises' in the period 1979–83 in Britain, which were mostly focused on cost-cutting, suggests that a regular system of reviews requires: a standard procedure for selection of topics and timetable for completion; active involvement of staff from the delivery organization; a central unit or clearing-house; a clearly identified individual responsible for each specific review; strong and continuing support from politicians (in this case Mrs Thatcher) both for carrying out the review and for implementing their results (see Beesley, 1983).

10.3 Consultant pathologists

A blend of technical and political considerations may favor

contracting out policy analysis rather than conducting it in house—
or favor engaging in policy analysis rather than action. Such outside
analysts, who may be academics, not-for-profit organizations, or
commercial firms, may have an opportunity to negotiate the
purpose and focus of the study, but it should always be remembered
that the commissioned analyst is responsible to the organization
(and the level within the organization) which commissioned the
study in a way in which doctors are not responsible to their patients.

Government agencies recognize that they may lack specific expertise relevant to a policy issue (Kogan and Henkel, 1983, 141). Even
'experts' in government departments are often technical rather than
policy analysis experts. Commissioning policy analysis may also get
round the problem, referred to in 10.1, of the scattering of expertise
through departments so that a concentration of group effort on a
particular issue may not be practicable. The uneven timing of the
requirement for policy analysis resources may indicate the
desirability of buying it in when required rather than building up an
internal team which would be underemployed for part of the time.
However, academics may also find it difficult to make themselves
available at short notice, which may help to account for the use of
management consultants as contractors for policy analysis.

It may be not so much expertise that is lacking within government
as a perspective other than that of civil servants. Public officials may
see a need for a 'non-civil service kind of look at something' and
therefore look for help outside the department (Kogan and Henkel,
1983, 141). A role may be seen for outside analysis as promoting
diversity—an addition to rather than a substitute for existing ways
of looking at an issue. Kogan and Henkel (1983, 171, 175) argue that
a 'wise government provides succour for those who test its actions
and provide its counter-analysis' and that government has no
monopoly of wisdom and should foster critics and counter-analysis.

Such a role is both more potentially significant and more problematic in Britain, where central executive departments dominate
the market for commissioning policy analysis to a greater extent
than in the USA. At the same time, British central government is
much less interested in a policy analysis or social science approach
(Kogan and Henkel, 1983, 157; Sharpe, 1977).

Policy analysis can also have more obviously political roles,
where contracting out the analysis may assist the chances of political
success (see Weiss, 1977, 14–15). First, policy analysis can be used to

legitimate a decision already taken on other grounds (Knorr, 1977, 171–3). The availability of an externally prepared report (which may have been prepared to tight terms of reference) will assist this legitimating role. Relatedly, research may be commissioned to make out a case for continuing or terminating an existing policy. The concern may, of course, not be with the policy as such, but with using a report on it as means of attacking a political opponent. Finally, there is the danger of the political non-use of research which contradicts the government's position, and where the research results are made available only to the government department.

Policy analysis may also be seen as a substitute for policy action. 'By initiating, distributing, and publishing a research report, the government official in this case tries to signal to those concerned that something is being done about the problem, while proper decisions and measures that should be taken are postponed or neglected altogether' (Knorr, 1977, 171). Contracting out policy research to consultants or establishing a commission (see 10.4) enables postponement for a minimum time period, while enabling temporary hand-washing about delays in the interim.

Members of a government agency may actually prefer analysis to be commissioned from outsiders because of greater confidence in the credentials of academics or consultants (perhaps overrating the skills of such outsiders and underrating the skills of those who are already on the staff or could be hired). An outside organization may be commissioned to ensure greater public confidence in the published analysis, either for reasons of expertise or because a report from outsiders may appear more objective.

However, there are a number of reasons for questioning whether commissioned analysis of policy problems is necessarily 'objective'. Weiss (1972, 20) suggests that 'It even happens that an outside research firm will sweeten the interpretation of program results (by choice of respondents, by types of statistical tests applied) in order to ingratiate itself with a program and get further contracts.'

Second, the commissioning organization may specify a set of guidelines to be used in an analysis which will tend to predetermine the conclusion. For example, in an evaluation of the effectiveness of a policy program the objectives to be assessed, the criteria to be used, the levels to be judged as 'success' may all be specified. The resulting analysis may then be used as an apparently external legitimation of the agency's viewpoint. Management consultants may be particularly useful for carrying out this sort of legitimation exercise.

However, it would be a mistake to assume that administrators who are interested in a piece of policy analysis being conducted are clear in their own minds about why they want the analysis conducted or how they would use it, or that they would necessarily communicate the purpose of the research clearly to whoever was to carry it out. Caplan (1977) found that nine out of ten respondents in the US federal government thought that a social indicator index was a good idea and could name measures they would like to see included in it. However, 'when asked what use they would make of such data, the responses were so rambling and diverse that it was impossible to derive empirically based coding categories for purposes of quantification' (Caplan, 1977, 189).

Evaluation studies, even when methodologically sound, might be judged useless by policymakers because the researcher's understanding of what was to be evaluated was not what the customer had in mind. Often, the customer has been unclear about what was wanted or was deliberately not explicit because the evaluation was designed to serve political functions. This communication gap will obviously cause problems (see e.g. Kogan and Henkel, 1983, 142). As Caplan (1977, 189) notes:

without knowledge of the policymakers' difficulties, the researcher is unlikely to provide the policymaker with relevant and useful information. In the absence of a clear definition of the purposes to which the research will be addressed, the researcher creates his own objectives, if for no other reason to carry on within a framework in which he can operate.

Vagueness in goals or concentration on immediate operational goals can be a consequence of divergence in views about program goals—often support from many quarters is necessary to get a program off the ground and this may be better met by vague statements on which all can agree (see 2.1.2 and 3.2.2). Even where a statement of clear, specific and reasonable goals is attained, there are still a number of problems. For example, how important relative to each other are goals where more than one is specified? The evaluator may run into difficulty if he relies on program staff to state priorities since they may emphasize innocuous goals or those on which the organization scores highly. How far should the evaluator go in explicitly assigning weights to goals?

Even when what is required of analysis is made clear, improvement in analysis, particularly where social science based, may produce a divergent rather than convergent picture (Sharpe, 1977, 46). The outcome may 'mean *less* clear-cut answers, more complex results and a greater effort needed to interpret those results' (Bulmer, 1982, 122). The twenty-year development of research on schools and race in the USA served not to clarify policy choice but to complicate it (Cohen and Weiss, 1977).

Firms of management consultants are frequently used by governments to advise them in diagnosing problems and proposed treatments. However, the public policy expertise of some firms can be questioned, though many do employ people with policy analysis training. The main concern is the appropriateness of their methodological approach and their standard repertoire of often organizational 'solutions'. While many of the pathologies identified in this book are of an organizational or managerial nature and may well be susceptible to treatments similar to those tried in the private sector, other pathologies are specific to public policy and may relate to special features of the way policy decisions are taken and implemented. To assume that 'management' is the problem and call in management consultants is to risk misdiagnosis and the definition of a problem in terms of how it can be treated by one of a standard list of nostrums.

There have been some expressions of concern that carrying out research for government, including contracted policy analysis, has some dangers, particularly for higher education institutions. The control over the distribution of reports of work supported by government funds, and the barriers that this constitutes to academic dissemination of knowledge, have caused concern on both sides of the Atlantic (Wolfe, 1975, 123; SRA, 1980, 27–30). Most British government departments appear to favor publication of the results of social research which they have commissioned, but retain copyright and the right to approve drafts. In the USA, some agencies have sought to restrict the distribution of reports, while other project directors have complained of pressure to distribute reports before the research was fully developed. Charges of bureaucratic interference seemed more likely to be lodged against agencies which (in the early 1970s) had less experience in dealing with universities and against those who worked in education, urban affairs, or other social science areas rather than the physical sciences. However, there was a lot of variation within these categories.

A further accusation is that contracted or other forms of government-funded research is said to have 'distorted university programs and to have robbed universities of the normal balance among their several activities' (Wolfe, 1975, 126; see also Weiss, 1977, 2). However, Wolfe (1975, 126–9) notes that there is a lack of detailed, objective evidence of the amount and specific nature of any distortion and that it would be difficult to determine the baseline of 'normal', especially in the absence of any clear statements of universities' objectives and priorities.

10.4 Commissions and committees

In both Britain and the United States government-sponsored committees of inquiry are one of the ways in which governments seek to collect information about policy problems, though as will quickly become clear, these inquiries are not solely to do with the collection of information. (In this section we will use the term 'commissions' to refer to departmental committees of inquiry as well as Royal and Presidential Commissions.)

American commentators have tended to consider British Royal Commissions as being more significant bodies than US Presidential Commissions, but in so doing they have exaggerated the differences between them (see Bulmer, 1982, 85–6). Britain has also made extensive use of departmental committees of inquiry, and the distinction between subjects covered by Royal Commissions and those considered by departmental committees is not always easy to discern. In any case, recent British governments have made less use of Royal Commissions since their heyday in the mid 1960s. An interesting innovation in Britain was the establishment in 1983/4 of four committees to consider related issues of income support, chaired directly by government ministers.

In the US, there is a tendency to think that any commission composed of private sector representatives will be inherently superior to one formed from within the public sector, e.g. the Grace Commission on Cost Control and analogues at the state level. This may well not be the case as private sector folk may not understand government and the particular problems of the public sector, and may come into government with preconceptions about waste in government.

Commissions can fulfil a number of purposes, including the collection of information, making broad or specific recommendations about policy, postponing decisions on embarrassing questions, the appreciation of a situation, and an educational role in bringing to the attention of the public some of the issues involved in a particular policy area (see Chapman, 1973, 194; Cartwright, 1974, 101–4). In both the US and the UK much of the information collected by commissions actually comes from government departments.

In his classification Rhodes (1975) links the reason for the use of the commission with the probable consequences in terms of the ways in which governments react to their reports:

Committees set up reluctantly by a government under pressure, with the object of staving off that pressure; likely to be accepted to the extent that they recommend no action or only minor action . . .
Committees set up to postpone an awkward issue; reports likely to be accepted to the extent that they indicate a solution not likely to be too troublesome . . .
Committees set up because the government is in doubt about how an issue should be resolved; reports likely to be accepted to the extent that an acceptable solution is possible . . .
Committees set up where government is fairly clear what course to adopt but needs independent backing before doing so; reports likely to be accepted to the extent that committee provides this backing.

Thus commissions can take a variety of forms and be expected to fulfil a variety of purposes. They have a number of features which give them advantages over other methods of considering public policy problems, but they have come under criticism both from outside commentators and those who have participated in them (see Bulmer, 1980; 1983).

Because commissions are normally independent of government (though with their membership and terms of reference set by the government of the day) they have the potential for taking a fresh look at problems and attempting to build a consensus in a way that may not be possible for partisan political figures. Unfortunately, this freshness to a problem may also be associated with little previous knowledge of it, and one of the criticisms made of commissions by past members is that they were only just coming to grips with the issues when they had to report and were disbanded.

A plus point for use of commissions, especially in the UK, is that they generally enable more open debate about an issue. However, those making representations to a commissions are often the same groups as would have made private representations to government departments—and, indeed, do so after the report of the commission is published. The extensive use of oral evidence by commissions has come under criticism for taking up considerable time but adding little to what could be more quickly obtained by other methods (Bulmer, 1982, 106–7).

Commissions in the US make more extensive use of a social science input than is the case in the UK, but in both countries there are difficulties in meshing the time scale of conducting social science research with the time by which a final report has to be completed (see Bulmer, 1982, ch. 5). Inadequate resources may be provide to conduct appropriate research either by the commission's own staff or contracted out. The predominance of lawyers on the staff of especially US commissions may lead to difficulty in getting accepted solutions which do not involve law enforcement. There are also the usual problems, noted in the context of analysis commissioned directly by government, of communicating what is required to social scientists and of social scientists presenting ideas and findings to commission members (see also Prest, 1980).

From the point of view of commission members, one of the main areas of concern is the way in which action by government on recommendations is delayed or recommendations are ignored or rejected (see Bulmer, 1982, 124–5). However, even when recommendations are not directly acted on, commission reports may have a broader effect on the way in which an issue is perceived by those interested in it (Vickers, 1965).

The work of commissions has to be seen in the context of a continuing pattern of information collection and policymaking. Commissions are not normally used as a systematic method of collecting and appraising information relevant to policymaking (Hogwood, 1979, 219–24). They are ad hoc arrangements with no continuing responsibility for reviewing their conclusions. The information contained in a report may quickly become outdated. Insofar as the initial inquiry was a genuine exercise in collecting and analyzing facts in a way not otherwise possible, this problem could only be resolved by setting up a further inquiry.

Where a rapidly changing economic or social environment is

combined, as it often is, with an institutional separation between policy recommendation, policy decision, and policy implementation, even the best report is likely to be left behind. Ad hoc inquiries by 'apolitical' bodies unaware of the political and administrative problems of implementation cannot be a substitute for continuous review. Edmund Dell (1973, 170), who was for a while a junior Labour Minister at the Ministry of Technology in Britain, later said of the Geddes Report (1966) on the shipbuilding industry:

Fed into a continuously learning administrative machine it would have done some good. It would have alerted officials to important aspects of the industry. It would have improved the government's performance as a 'sponsor' of the industry. But it become a bible, a substitute for thought, a point of continuing reference when changed circumstances had made its recommendations much less relevant. In short, instead of an aid to learning it become a block in the way of learning. The way to learn is to be involved in day-to-day administration.

If the value of information and advice is reduced when it is not related to knowledge of what is involved in implementing proposals, then so is the value of information about the detailed application of a policy if it is not fed back in a systematic way to those responsible for reappraising policy (see also 4.6).

The setting up of commissions is generally a reactive rather than an anticipatory act. Such an inquiry may be a reaction to political embarrassment or to a clearly difficult situation where the government is unsure of what action to take. The role of commissions can be seen not so much as one of providing information for policy planning as of the presentation of information and ideas which improve the chances of mobilizing political support for policy proposals.

10.5 Legislatures

It may appear somewhat odd to consider legislatures as a possible curative agent for the pathologies we have been discussing. After all, much of chapters 2 and 7 dealt with the role which legislatures had in creating pathologies. Despite that, legislatures can play an important role in attempting to correct existing pathologies and prevent the creation of new ones. In many ways legislatures are a crucial component of the treatment process because of their roles in legitimating the actions of government and passing the budget.

Legislatures have a number of instruments and institutions which can be used to exercise 'oversight' (Ogul, 1981). The two which appear most important are committees and specialized policy-analytic organizations. Committees are usually discussed as the central element of legislative control over specific policies and programs. In the United States Congress, the committee structure is fully ramified so that any organization in government will have at least four committees looking over its shoulders (substantive and budget committees in both houses plus special subcommittees investigating specific problems). The committee structure in the House of Commons has not been organized until recently to provide any form of continuous oversight. With the formation in 1979 of Select Committees covering every government department there is a greater opportunity for Parliament to exercise continuing supervision of policy (Hill, 1984).

Even if the committee structure of the legislature is well organized and well staffed as in the United States, there are still a number of barriers to acting as effective 'policy doctors'. Simply being a member of a committee does not remove from the legislator the political pressures at the heart of so many pathologies. On the contrary, it may merely make him a more visible target for pressure. In addition, Congressmen in the United States attempt to be assigned to committees on which they can help their constituents—representatives of farming areas on agriculture committees, etc.—and this may well mean that their oversight is far from neutral and may contain a vision of the public interest not very different from the organizations and programs they are attempting to control.

Specialized analytic bodies offer somewhat greater hope for effective policy analysis and oversight. The best example of such a body is the General Accounting Office in the United States (Mosher, 1980). This organization began simply as the organization responsible for auditing the government's books and reporting any misappropriation to Congress. During the 1970's however, it was transformed into an active policy-analytic organization which told Congress not only if its money was being spent legally, but also if it was being spent in the most effective and efficient manner. It issues thousands of reports annually detailing how government could better utilize its scarce resources. Of course, its advice is not always heeded, but Congress does have a valuable—if *post hoc*— assessment of policy. This, combined with the more prospective work of the Congressional Reference Service, puts legislators in an excellent position to make better policies and eliminate pathologies; all they have to do is to want to do that.

Individual legislators may also have a role to play in rectifying policy pathologies. They receive numerous complaints about the effects of government programs on their constituents; these are the policy equivalent of 'Doctor, I have pain in my knee.' Indeed, a British Member of Parliament's sessions in his constituency to hear such complaints are referred to as his 'surgery'. These individual complaints are a valuable source of information for the legislator, but there is a problem in moving from the particular to the general and in developing recommendations for policy change from the grievances of citizens. Tending to constituents' grievances may be appropriate where the problem is individual to the citizen concerned, but most public policy pathologies are akin to environmental health problems rather than health problems specific to individuals. Rather perversely, legislators may have little incentive to make that inferential leap. It appears that legislators make a great deal of electoral hay from assisting their constituents with problems (Fiorina, 1977; Mayhew, 1974). If they have found out how to deal with a routine problem, their electoral chances may be enhanced by allowing it to persist, thus turning the old political adage 'If it ain't broke, don't fix it' on its head.

10.6 Media

The media have been offered as another possible doctor for the diseases which beset government. They have the distinct advantage of being outside government and hence with little or nothing to gain by supporting unpopular or pathological policies. The role of the media in both the Vietnam war and Watergate in the United States have been cited as examples of the possible beneficial role of active media in exposing and helping to correct government pathologies. The role of the *Sunday Times* in the United Kingdom in placing the issues of thalidomide and contempt of court on the public agenda is an example of how the media can force government to take account of issues which otherwise might have been ignored. The opening of some legislatures and courts to the media—even to the allowing of the televising of sessions—makes it that much more difficult for governments to operate in secret.

However, the media operate with a number of handicaps as the source of correction in policy-making. First, a problem, by no means of their making, is that their audience may not be as interested in the complexity of many issues as is necessary for the media to be effective. This is especially true of broadcast journalism in the United States, which appears more concerned about ratings than dealing with difficult or complex issues. Media coverage will be affected by the extent to which an issue can be portrayed in terms of particular incidents or human interest. For example, the thalidomide campaign by the *Sunday Times* in Britain could be illustrated by pictures of crippled children. The threat of oil pollution on the coasts only became a political issue picked up by the media with the Torrey Canyon being stranded on the Cornish coast (Solesbury, 1976). Thus issues of a complex and relatively abstract nature are more likely to be neglected by the media—the very issues which political institutions are themselves deficient in handling. The media in this matter as in others tend to mirror the advantages and the deficiences of the society in which they operate.

Another problem not of the media's own making is that governments obviously do not want to have an excess of journalistic zeal at their expense and try to control the flow of information by official press releases and, especially in the United Kingdom, secrecy. Even the most dedicated journalist may find it difficult to penetrate government if government does not want to be penetrated. Journalists also tend to work under time pressures—the Six O'Clock News can not wait until seven o'clock—so they may be forced to go with what they have rather than waiting for a more definitive story; space restrictions in print media may have similar effects. Finally, there is a danger that journalists will become too much a part of the system to be able to criticize it effectively (Cockerell, Hennessy, and Walker, 1984). Journalists depend upon access in order to do their job effectively so they cannot always expose everything they know for fear of losing future access.

The media are not, however, neutral in the political battle about public policies. The political line taken by proprietors or editors may inhibit them from criticizing incumbents of their party. Similarly, considerations of party advantage rather than policy improvement as an end in itself may lead proprietors or editors to attack opponents in office. In the United Kingdom, the journalists' and printers' trade unions exercise a potential and on occasionally actually exercised inhibiting influence on comment and coverage.

The media are really middlemen in the policy process, one of the links between government and the public, though also on occasion seeking to act as policy actors in their own right. The only weapons they have are information and the capacity of political leaders to be embarrassed. In that position, they can dependent upon the willingness of government to provide information and the willingness of the public to listen. Thus, even if the press are able and committed to improving the outputs of government, they cannot be successful by themselves.

10.7 Quacks and nostrums

If everyone knew the truth about what can go wrong in hospitals and the damage which can result from treatment by doctors then there would be considerable reluctance on the part of patients to undergo medical 'care'. Yet people's lives are saved and the quality of many others improved as a result of medical intervention. It is only the exaggerated and self-reinforcing myth of the combined scientific and magical skills of doctors which results in expectations higher than those which can reasonably be achieved and in a defensive attitude on the part of doctors when the myth and associated myths such as the sanctity of 'clinical judgement' are challenged.

In this chapter and in the book as a whole we have been at pains to point out that attempts at removing pathological features of public policy may themselves contain flaws. Yet it is possible to improve or even remove problems. Our purpose in pointing to difficulties in doing so is to emphasize that policy analysis has to be about more than the application of standard analytical techniques to standardized problems. Compared to medicine, policy analysis is at a very primitive stage in developing skills in diagnosis and devising treatments.

Doctors in industrialized countries have largely been successful in denouncing unqualified 'quacks' and their 'nostrums', yet they have attempted to retain their scientific respect by ignoring the quackish and nostrum-like nature of the activities of all too much modern medicine. Policy analysis, too, must avoid a nostrum-like response to problems, for example by proposing reorganization as the solution to a wide range of inadequately conceptualized problems with existing policies. We hope that in this book we have made a start to offering some help in the diagnosis of public policy pathologies. We have tried to avoid suggesting nostrum-like cures. In comparing policy analysts with doctors we want to emphasize the features of the medical professions which policy analysts should avoid as well as some they might aspire to.

References

Aaron, H. (1978). *Politics and the Professors*. Washington DC: The Brookings Institution.

Aberbach, J.D., R.D. Putnam, and B.A. Rockman (1981). *Bureaucrats and Politicians in Western Democracies*. Cambridge, Mass.: Harvard University Press.

Aberbach, J.D., and B.A. Rockman (1976). Clashing within the executive branch: the Nixon administration bureaucracy, *American Political Science Review*, 70, 456–68.

Abrahamson, B. (1967). *The Professional in Organizations*. Chicago: Rand McNally.

Agyris, C. (1964). *Integrating the Individual and the Organization*. New York: John Wiley.

Allison, G. (1971). *Essence of Decision*. Boston: Little, Brown.

Ansoff, H.I. (1975). Managing strategic surprise of response to weak signals, *California Management Review*, 18(2), 21–33.

Aranson, P.H., and P.C. Ordeshook (1980). Alternative theories of the growth of government and their implications for constitutional tax and spending limits. Unpublished manuscript.

Arnold, R.D. (1979). *Congress and the Bureaucracy*. New Haven: Yale University Press.

Ascher, W. (1978). *Forecasting*. Baltimore: Johns Hopkins University Press.

Ashford, D.E. (1981). *Policy and Politics in Britain: The Limits of Consensus*. Philadelphia: Temple University Press.

Axelrod, R. (1977). The medical metaphor, *American Journal of Political Science*, 22, 430–2.

Bardach, E. (1978). Subformal warning systems in the species *homo politicus, Policy Sciences*, 9, 415–39.

Bardach, E., and R.A. Kagan (1981). *Going by the Book*. Philadelphia: Temple University Press.

Baumol, W.J. (1967). The macroeconomics of unbalanced growth, *American Economic Review*, 57, 415–26.

Beesley, I. (1983). The Rayner scrutinies. In A. Gray and B. Jenkins (eds.), *Policy Analysis and Evaluation in British Government*, London: Royal Institute of Public Administration, 31–6.

Behn, R.D. (1978). How to terminate a public policy: a dozen hints for the would-be terminator, *Policy Analysis*, 4, 393–413.

Bennett, J.T., and T.J. DiLorenzo (1983). *Underground Government: The Off-Budget Public Sector*. Washington DC: The Cato Institute.

Biller, R.P. (1976). On tolerating policy and organizational termination: Some design considerations, *Policy Sciences*, 7, 13–49.

Blau, P. (1956). *The Dynamics of Bureaucracy*. Chicago: University of Chicago Press.

Blaug, M. (1980). *On the Methodology of Economics*. Cambridge: CUP.

Booth, S.A.S., D.C. Pitt, and W.J. Money (1982). 'Organizational redundancy?: a critical appraisal of the GEAR project', *Public Administration*, 60, 56–72.

Borcherding, T.E. (1977). The sources of growth of public expenditures in the United States, 1902–70. In T.E. Borcherding (ed.), *Budgets and Bureaucrats*, Durham, N. Carolina: Duke University Press.

Boskin, M.D. (1982). *The Crisis in Social Security*, 2nd edn. San Fransisco: Institute of Contemporary Studies.

Bothun, D., and Comer, J.C. (1979). The politics of termination: concepts and process, *Policy Studies Journal*, 7, 540–53.

Boulding, K. (1982). Pathologies of the public grants economy. In R.C.O. Matthews and G.B. Stafford (eds.), *The Grants Economy and Collective Consumption*, London: Macmillan, 3–19.

Bowen, E. (1982). The Pressman-Wildavsky paradox: four addenda or why models based on probability theory can predict implementation success and suggest useful tactical advice for implementers, *Journal of Public Policy*, 2, 1–22.

Bowman, L., E.C. Main, and B.G. Peters (1970). Clients in the model cities program. Mimeo. Atlanta: Emory University.

Bozeman, B., and J.L. Bozeman (1981). Technical information and policy choice: the case of the resource recovery 'nondecision', *Journal of Public Policy*, 1, 251–67.

Breton, A., and R. Wintrobe (1975). The equilibrium size of a budget-maximizing bureau, *Journal of Political Economy*, 83, 195–207.

Brittan, S. (1971). *Steering the Economy: The Role of the Treasury*, revised ed. Harmondsworth, Middlesex: Penguin.

Buchanan, J., and R.E. Wagner (1977). *Democracy in Deficit: The Political Legacy of Lord Keynes*. New York: Academic Press.

Buchholz, R.A. (1979). *Corporate Cost for Compliance with Federal Government Regulation of Information*. St Louis, Missouri: Center for the Study of American Business, Washington University.

Bulmer, M. (ed.) (1980). *Social Research and Royal Commissions*. London: Allen and Unwin.

Bulmer, M. (1982). *The Uses of Social Research: Social Investigation in Public Policy-Making*. London: Allen and Unwin.

Bulmer, M. (1983). *Royal Commissions and Departmental Committees of Inquiry*. London: Royal Institute of Public Administration.

Cameron, D. (1982). On the limits of the political economy, *Annals*, 459, 46–62.

Cameron, J.M. (1978). Ideology and policy termination: restructuring California's mental health system. In J.V. May and A.B. Wildavsky (eds.), *The Policy Cycle*, Beverly Hills, Calif.: Sage.

Campbell, C., and G.J. Szlablowski (1979). *The Superbureaucrats*. Toronto: Macmillan of Canada.

Caplan, N. (1977). A minimal set of conditions necessary for the utilization of social science knowledge in policy formulation at the national level. In C.H. Weiss (ed.), *Using Social Research in Public Policy Making*, Lexington, Mass.: Lexington Books.

Carley, M. (1981). *Social Measurement and Social Indicators: Issues of Policy and Theory*. London: Allen and Unwin.

Cartwright, T.J. (1974). *Royal Commissions and Departmental Committees in Britain*. London: University of London Press.

Chapman, R.A. (ed.) (1973). *The Role of Commissions in Policy-Making*. London: Allen and Unwin.

Cmnd 9143 (1984). *The Government's Expenditure Plans 1984-85 to 1986-87*. London: HMSO.

Cockerell, M.,P. Hennessy, and D. Walker (1984). *Sources Close to the Prime Minister*: London: Macmillan.

Cohen, D.K., and J.A. Weiss (1977). Social science and social policy: schools and race. In C.H. Weiss (ed.), *Using Social Research in Public Policy Making*, Lexington, Mass.: Lexington Books.

Cohen, M.D., J.G. March, and J.P Olsen (1972). A garbage can model of organizational choice, *Administrative Science Quarterly*, 17, 1–25.

Cohen, S.S. (1971). Cancer research and the scientific community, *Science*, 172 (18 June), 1212–14.

Copeman, H. (1981). Analysing public expenditure: (1) planning, control and price, *Journal of Public Policy*, 1, 289–306.

Coughlin, R.M. (1979). Social policy and ideology: public opinion in eight rich countries. In R.F. Tomasson (ed.), *Comparative Social Research*, vol. 2, Greenwich, Conn.: JAI, 1–40.

Cousins, N. (1979). *Anatomy of an Illness*. New York: Norton.

CPRS (1977). Central Policy Review Staff, *Population and the Social Services*. London: HMSO.

Crozier, M. (1964). *The Bureaucratic Phenomenon*. Chicago: University of Chicago Press.

Davis, D.H. (1973). Consensus or conflict: alternative strategies for a bureaucratic bargainer, *Public Choice*, 13, 21–9.

Davis, O.A., M.A.H. Dempster, and A. Wildavsky (1966). A theory of the budgetary process, *American Political Science Review*, 60, 529–47.

Davis, O. A., M.A.H. Dempster, and A. Wildavsky (1974). Toward a predictive theory of government expenditure in US domestic appropriations, *British Journal of Political Science*, 4, 419–52.

Davis, S., and P. Lawrence (1977). *Matrix*. Reading, Mass.: Addison-Wesley.

DeLeon, P. (1978). A theory of policy termination. In J.V. May and A. Wildavsky (eds.), *The Policy Cycle*, Beverly Hills, Calif.: Sage, 279–300.

Dell, E. (1973). *Political Responsibility and Industry*. London: Allen and Unwin.

Deutsch, K.W. (1963). *The Nerves of Government*. New York: Free Press.

Dexter, L.A. (1981). Undesigned consequences of purposive legislative action: alternatives to implementation, *Journal of Public Policy*, 1, 413–31.

Dickinson, J. (tr.) (1927). *The Statesman's Book*. New York: Appleton-Century-Crafts.

Donnison, D. (1982). *The Politics of Poverty*. Oxford: Martin Robertson.

Dornbusch, R., and S. Finster (1982). *Macroeconomics*, 2nd edn. New York: McGraw Hill.

Downs, A. (1960). Why the public budget is too small in a democracy, *World Politics*, 20, 541–63.

Downs, A. (1967). *Inside Bureaucracy*. Boston: Little, Brown.

Downs, A. (1972). Up and down with ecology—the issue attention cycle, *The Public Interest*, 28, 38–50.

Edelman, M. (1964). *The Symbolic Uses of Politics*. Urbana. Illinois: University of Illinois Press.

Edelman, M. (1971). *Politics as Symbolic Action*. Chicago: Markham.

Edwards, G.C. (1980). *Implementing Public Policy*. Washington DC: Congressional Quarterly Press.

Edwards, J., and R. Batley (1978). *The Politics of Positive Discrimination: An Evaluation of the Urban Programs 1967-77*. London: Tavistock.

Etzioni, A. (1976). *Social Problems*. Englewood Cliffs, NJ: Prentice-Hall.

Feyerabend, P.K. (1978). *Against Method: Outline of an Anarchistic Theory of Knowledge*. London: New Left Books.

Fidel, K. (1980). The dynamics of military conspiracy. In S.K. Tefft (ed.), *Secrecy: A Cross-Cultural Perspective*, New York: Human Sciences Press.

Field, F., M. Meacher, and C. Pond (1977). *To Him Who Hath: A Study of Poverty and Taxation*. Harmondsworth, Middlesex: Penguin.

Fiorina, M. (1977). *Congress: Keystone of the Washington Establishment*. New Haven: Yale University Press.

Foley, H.A. (1975). *Community Mental Health Programs: The Formative Process*. Lexington, Mass.: Lexington Books.

Free, L., and H. Cantril (1968). *The Political Beliefs of Americans*. New York: Simon and Schuster.

Freidson, E. (1970). *Professional Dominance: The Social Structure of Medical Care*. New York: Atherton.

Gallup (1983). [Poll results cited in] Opinion roundup, *Public Opinion*, 6, 27.

Geddes Report (1966). *Shipbuilding Inquiry Committee 1965-1966. Report*, Cmnd. 2937. London: HMSO.

Gerth, H.H., and C. Wright Mills (1946). *From Max Weber: Essays in Sociology*. New York: OUP.

Glennerster, H. (1980). Prime cuts: public expenditure and social services planning in a hostile environment, *Policy and Politics*, 8, 367-82.

Glover, J. (1977). *Causing Death and Saving Lives*. Baltimore: Penguin.

Gonzales, J., and J. Rothchild (1979). The Shriver prescription: how the government can find out what it is doing. In C. Peters and M. Nelson (eds.), *The Culture of Bureaucracy*, New York: Holt, Rinehart and Winston, 118-27.

Good, D.A. (1978). *The Politics of Anticipation*. Ottawa: Carleton University, School of Public Administration.

Goodin, R.E. (1975). The logic of bureaucratic backscratching, *Public Choice*, 21, 53-68.

Goodin, R.E. (1982). *Political Theory and Public Policy*. Chicago: University of Chicago Press.

Goodsell, C. (1982). *The Case for Bureaucracy*. Chatham, NJ: Chatham House.

Gough, I. (1979). *The Political Economy of the Welfare State*. London: Macmillan.

Graham, J.D., and J.W. Vaupel (1983). The value of life: what difference does it make? In R.J. Zeckhauser and D. Leebart (eds.), *What Role for Government?*, Durham, NC: Duke University Press.

Gray, A., and B. Jenkins (1982). Policy analysis in British central government: the experience of PAR, *Public Administration*, 60, 429-50.

Hall, P. (1980). *Great Planning Disasters*. London: Weidenfeld and Nicholson.

Hanf, K., and F.W. Scharpf (eds.) (1978). *Interorganizational Policy Making*. London and Beverly Hills, Calif.: Sage.

Hansen, S.B. (1983). *The Politics of Taxation*. New York: Praeger.

Hardin, G. (1968). The tragedy of the commons, *Science*, 162, 1243-8.

Heclo, H. (1977). *A Government of Strangers*. Washington DC: The Brookings Institution.

Heclo, H. (1978). Issue networks and the executive establishment. In A. King (ed.), *The New American Political System*, Washington DC: American Enterprise Institute.

Heclo, H., and A. Wildavsky (1974). *The Private Government of Public Money*. London: Macmillan.

Heidenheimer, A.J. (1973). *Political Corruption*. Englewood Cliffs, NJ: Prentice-Hall.

Hellriegel, D., and J. Slocum (1974). *Management: A Contingency Approach*. Addison-Wesley.

Hill, D. (ed.) (1984). Parliamentary select committees in action, *Strathclyde Papers on Government and Politics*, no. 24. Glasgow: Department of Politics, University of Strathclyde.

Hirsch, F. (1977). *The Social Limits to Growth*. London: Routledge and Kegan Paul.

Hirschman, A.D. (1970). *Exit, Voice and Loyalty*. Cambridge, Mass.: Harvard University Press.

Hjern, B., and C. Hull (1982). Implementation research as empirical constitutionalism, *European Journal of Political Research*, 10, 105–15.

Hofstader, R. (1968). *The Paranoid Style in American Politics*. Bloomington, Indiana: University of Indiana Press.

Hogwood, B.W. (1978). Perspectives on public policy: the case for an eclectic approach. Paper presented to the Workshop on Social Policy, European Consortium for Political Research Joint Sessions, Grenoble, 6–12 Apr.

Hogwood, B.W. (1979). *Government and Shipbuilding: the Politics of Industrial Change*. Farnborough, Hants.: Saxon House.

Hogwood, B.W. (1983). The instruments of desire: how British government attempts to regulate and influence industry, *Public Administration Bulletin*, 42, 5–25.

Hogwood, B.W. (1984). Policy analysis: the dangers of oversophistication, *Public Administration Bulletin*, 44, 19–28.

Hogwood, B.W., and L.A. Gunn (1984). *Policy Analysis for the Real World*. Oxford: OUP.

Hogwood, B.W., and B.G. Peters (1982). *Policy Succession and Policy Termination*, Policy Analysis Teaching (PAT) Module 10.0. Glasgow: University of Strathclyde.

Hogwood, B.W., and B.G. Peters (1983). *Policy Dynamics*. New York: St Martin's Press and Brighton: Wheatsheaf.

Hood, C.C. (1976). *The Limits of Administration*. London: Wiley.

Hood, C.C. (1981). Axeperson, spare that quango. . . . In C. Hood and M. Wright (eds.), *Big Government in Hard Times*, Oxford: Martin Robertson, 199–22.

Hood, C.C. (1983). *The Tools of Government*. London: Macmillan.

Huntington, S.P. (1952). The management of the ICC, *Yale Law Review*, June, 467–509.

Illich, I. (1976). *The Medical Nemesis*. New York: Pantheon.

James, D.B. (1975). *Analyzing Poverty Policy*. Lexington, Mass.: Lexington Books.

Jenkins, R. (1971). On being a minister, *Sunday Times*, 17 January 1971. Reprinted in V. Herman and J. Alt (eds.), *Cabinet Studies: A Reader*, London: Macmillan.

Johnson, N. (1976). Recent administrative reform in Britain. In A. Leemans (ed.), *The Management of Change in Government*, The Hague: Martinus Nijhoff.

Jordan, A.G. (1981). Iron triangles, woolly corporatism, or elastic nets: images of the policy process, *Journal of Public Policy*, 1, 95–123.

Kahn, A.J., and S.B. Kamerman (1984). *Income Transfers for Families with Children: An Eight Country Study*. Philadelphia: Temple University Press.

Kaufman, H. (1960). *Forest Ranger: A Study in Administrative Behavior*. Baltimore: Johns Hopkins.

Kaufman, H. (1974). *Red Tape*. University, Alabama: University of Alabama Press.

Kaufman, H. (1984). *The Life Cycle of Organizations*. Chatham, NJ: Chatham House.

Kellner, P., and Lord Crowther-Hunt (1980). *The Civil Servants: An Inquiry into Britain's Ruling Class*. London: Macdonald.

Kelman, S. (1981). Cost benefit analysis: an ethical critique, *Regulation*, 4, 33–40.

Klein, R., and J. Lewis (1977). Advice and dissent in British government: the case of special advisers, *Policy and Politics*, 6, 1–25.

Knorr, K.D. (1977). Policymakers' use of social science knowledge. In C.H. Weiss (ed.), *Using Social Research in Public Policy Making*, Lexington, Mass.: Lexington Books.

Knowles, J.H. (1978). The responsibility of the individual. In J.H. Knowles (ed.), *Doing Better and Feeling Worse*. New York: Norton.

Kogan, M. and M. Henkel (1983). *Government and Research: The Rothschild Experiment in a Government Department*. London: Heinemann.

Kristensen, O.P. (1980). The logic of political bureaucratic decision-making as a cause of government growth, *European Journal of Political Research*, 8, 249–64.

Kuhn, T. (1970). *The Structure of Scientific Revolutions*. Chicago: University of Chicago Press.

Landau, M. (1969). The rationality of redundancy, *Public Administration Review*, 29, 346–58.

Larkey, P.D., C. Stolp, and M. Winer (1981). Theorizing about the growth of government: a research assessment, *Journal of Public Policy*, 1, 157–220.

Leigh, D. (1982). *The Frontiers of Secrecy*. Frederick, Maryland: University Publications of America.

Le Loup, L.T. (1975). Discretion in national budgeting: controlling the controllables, *Policy Analysis*, 4, 455–75.

Levine, C. (1978). Organization decline and cutback management, *Public Administration Review*, 38, 316–25.

Lewis, A. (1980). Attitudes to public expenditure and their relationship to voting preference, *Political Studies*, 28, 284–92.

Lindblom, C.E.(1959). The science of 'muddling through', *Public Administration Review*, 19, 79–88.

Lynn, L.E. (1981). *Managing the Public's Business*. New York: Basic Books.

McCrone, G. (1969). *Regional Policy in Britain*. London: Allen and Unwin.

McGuire, M.C. (1965). *Secrecy and the Arms Race*. Cambridge, Mass: Harvard University Press.

McKay, D.H., and A.W. Cox (1979). *The Politics of Urban Change*. London: Croom Helm.

Mackie, T. T., and B.W. Hogwood (1984). Decision arenas in executive decision-making: cabinet committees in comparative perspective, *British Journal of Political Science*, 14, 333–62.

McNeill, W.H. (1976). *Plagues and People*. New York: Anchor.

MacRae, D. (1976). *The Social Function of the Social Sciences*. New Haven: Yale University Press.

MacRae, D, and J.A. Wilde (1979). *Policy Analysis for Public Decisions*. North Scituate, Mass.: Duxbury.

Mansfield, H.C. (1970). Reorganizing the federal executive branch: the limits of institutionalization, *Law and Contemporary Problems*, 64, 461–95.

March, J.G., and H.A. Simon (1958). *Organizations*. New York: John Wiley.

Mayhew, D.R. (1974). *Congress: The Electoral Connection*. New Haven: Yale University Press.

Mazmanian, D.A., and J. Nienaber (1979). *Can Organizations Change?* Washington DC: The Brookings Institution.

Mead, M. (1955). *Cultural Patterns and Technical Change*. New York: Mentor.

Merton, R.K. (1940). Bureaucratic structure and personality, *Social Forces*, 18, 560–8.

Merton, R.K. (1964). The latent functions of the machine. In R.K. Merton (ed.), *Social Theory and Social Structure*, New York: Free Press.

Midlarsky, M. (1961). A theory of revolution, *Journal of Conflict Resolution*, 11, 264–80.

Miles, R.E. (1977). Considerations for a President bent on reorganization, *Public Administration Review*, 37, 155–9.

Mishan, E.J. (1973). *Economics of Social Decisions*. New York: Praeger.

Mosher, F. (1980). *The GAO*. Boulder, Colorado: Westview.

Moynihan, D.P. (1967). *Maximum Feasible Misunderstanding*. New York: Vintage.

Moynihan, D.P. (1973). *The Politics of Guaranteed Income*. New York: Vintage.

Natchez, P.B., and J.C. Bupp (1973). Policy and priority in the budgetary process, *American Political Science Review*, 67, 951–63.

Nicholls, P. (1979). *The Encyclopedia of Science Fiction*. London: Granada.

Niskanen, W.A.(1971). *Bureaucracy and Representative Government*. Chicago: Aldine-Atherton.

Nozick, R. (1974). *Anarchy, State, and Utopia*. New York: Basic Books.

O'Connor, J. (1973). *The Fiscal Crisis of the State*. New York: St Martins Press.

Office of Management and Budget (1983). *The Budget of the United States. 1984*. Washington DC: Government Printing Office.

Ogul, M.S. (1981). Congressional oversight: structures and incentives. In L.C. Dodd and B.I. Oppenheim (eds.), *Congress Reconsidered*, 2nd edn, Washington DC: Congressional Quarterly.

Olson, M. (1965). *The Logic of Collective Action*. Cambridge: Havard University Press.

Olson, M. (1969). The plan and purpose of a social report, *The Public Interest*, 15, 86.

Ott, D.J., and A.F. Ott (1977). *Federal Budget Policy*, 3rd edn. Washington DC: The Brookings Institution.

Page, B. (1983). *Who Gets What from Government*. Berkeley: University of California Press.

Peacock, A.T. (1983). Public X-inefficiency: information and institutional constraints. In H. Hanusch (ed.), *Anatomy of Government Deficiences*, Berlin: Springer, 125–38.

Peacock, A.T., and J. Wiseman (1967). *The Growth of Public Expenditure in the United Kingdom*. London: Allen and Unwin.

Penner, R.G. (1982). Forecasting budget totals: why can't we get it right? In M.J. Boskin and A. Wildavsky (eds.), *The Federal Budget*, San

Fransisco: Institute for Contemporary Studies.

Perrow, C. (1961). The analysis of goals in complex organizations, *American Sociological Review*, 26, 854–66.

Peters, B.G. (1982). The problem of bureaucratic government, *Journal of Politics*, 43, 56–82.

Peters, B.G. (1984). *The Politics of Bureaucracy*, 2nd edn. New York: Longmans.

Peters, B.G., and M.O. Heisler (1984). Thinking about public sector growth: conceptual, operational, theoretical and policy considerations. In C.L. Taylor (ed.), *Why Governments Grow*, Beverly Hills, Calif.: Sage.

Peters, B.G., and S.H. Linder (1984). Out of the garbage can and into the fire: the relevance of theory for policy design. Paper presented at Midwest Political Science Association Annual Meeting, Chicago, 12 Apr. 1984.

Piachaud, D. (1980). Taxation and social security. In C. Sandford, C. Pond and R. Walker (eds.), *Taxation & Social Policy*, London, Heinemann, 68–83.

Pliatzky, L. (1980). *Report on Non-Departmental Public Bodies*, Cmnd. 7797. London: HMSO.

Pliatzky, L. (1982). *Getting and Spending*. Oxford: Basil Blackwell.

Pollitt, C. (1984). *Manipulating the Machine: Changing the Pattern of Ministerial Departments 1960–83*. London: Allen and Unwin.

Porter, D.O., and Hjern, B. (1978). Implementation structures: A new unit of analysis. Paper presented to 1978 Meeting of the American Political Science Association.

Porter, R. B. (1980). *Presidential Decision-Making: The Economic Policy Board*. Cambridge: CUP.

Pressman, J., and A.B. Wildavsky (1973). *Implementation*. Berkeley: University of California Press.

Prest, A.R. (1980). Royal Commission reporting. In M. Bulmer (ed.), *Social Research and Royal Commissions*, London: Allen and Unwin, 180–8.

Rawls, J.A. (1971). *A Theory of Justice*. Cambridge: Harvard University Press.

Rees, T.B. (1981). Research, statistics and policy making. Paper to the Royal Institute of Public Administration Conference on Public Influence and Public Policy, 10–11 Apr. 1981.

Reiss, A.J. (1971). *The Police and the Public*. New Haven: Yale University Press.

Rettig, R.A. (1977). *Cancer Crusade: The Story of the National Cancer Act of 1971*. Princeton: Princeton University Press.

Rhodes, G. (1975). *Committees of Inquiry*. London: Allen and Unwin.

Rice, D. (1966). *Estimating the Cost of Illness*. Washington DC: US Public Health Service.

Rich, R.F. (1977). Uses of social science information by federal bureaucrats: knowledge for action versus knowledge for understanding. In C.H. Weiss (ed.), *Using Social Research in Public Policy Making*, Lexington, Mass.: Lexington Books.

Rose, R. (1970). *People in Politics: Observations across the Atlantic*. London: Faber.

Rose, R. (1976). Disciplined research and undisciplined problems, *International Social Science Journal*, 28, 99–121.

Rose, R. (1984). *Do Parties Make a Difference?*, 2nd edn. London: Macmillan.

Rose, R., and G. Peters (1978). *Can Government Go Bankrupt?* New York: Basic Books.

Rossi, P.H., H.E. Freeman, and S.R. Wright (1979). *Evaluation: A Systematic Approach*. Beverly Hills: Calif.: Sage.

Royko, M. (1971). *The Boss*. New York: Dutton.

Rutman, L. (1980). *Planning Useful Evaluations*. Beverly Hills, Calif.: Sage.

Sandford, C. (1980). Taxation and social policy: an overview. In C. Sandford, C. Pond, and R. Walker (eds.), *Taxation & Social Policy*, London: Heinemann, 1–2.

Schick, A. (1966). The road to PPB: the stages of budget reform, *Public Administration Review*, 26, 243–58.

Schon, D. (1972). *Beyond the Stable State*. New York: Norton.

Schulman, P.R. (1980). *Large-Scale Policy Making*. New York: Elsevier.

Sears, D.O., and J. Citrin (1982). *Tax Revolt: Something for Nothing in California*. Cambridge, Mass.: Harvard University Press.

Seidman, H. (1980). *Politics, Position and Power: The Dynamics of Federal Organization*, 3rd edn. New York: OUP.

Self, P. (1975). *Econocrats and the Policy Process*. London: Macmillan.

Sharkansky, I. (1979). *Wither the State?*. Chatham, NJ: Chatham House.

Sharpe, L.J. (1973). American democracy reconsidered, *British Journal of Political Science*, 3, 1–38, 129–67.

Sharpe, L.J. (1977). Social scientists and policymaking: some cautionary thoughts and transatlantic reflections. In C.H. Weiss (ed.), *Using Social Research in Public Policy Making*, Lexington, Mass.: Lexington Books.

Shils, E.A. (1956). *The Torment of Secrecy*. New York: Free Press.

Sieber, S.D. (1981). *Fatal Remedies*. New York: Plenum.

Simon, H.A. (1957). *Administrative Behavior*, 2nd edn. New York: Free Press.

Simon, H.A. (1976). *Administrative Behavior*, 3rd edn. New York: Free Press.

Smith, D. (1975). Public consumption and economic performance, *National Westminster Bank Review*, 13, 17–30.

Solesbury, W. (1976). The environmental agenda, *Public Administration*, 54, 379–97.

SRA (1980). *Terms and Conditions of Social Research Funding in Britain*. London: Social Research Association.

Stringer, J.K., and J.J. Richardson (1980). Managing the political agenda: problem definition and policy making in Britain, *Parliamentary Affairs*, 23, 23–39.

Surrey, S. (1969). *Pathways to Tax Reform*. Cambridge, Mass.: Harvard University Press.

Szanton, P. (1980). *Federal Reorganization: What Have we Learned?* Chatham, NJ: Chatham House.

Tarschys, D. (1977). The problem of pre-planned society. Paper presented to 1977 Annual Meeting of American Political Science Association.

Tarschys, D. (1982). The scissors crisis in public finance, *Policy Sciences*, 15, 205–24.

Taylor-Gooby, P. (1982). Two cheers for the welfare state: public opinion and private welfare, *Journal of Public Policy*, 2, 319–46.

Tropman, J.E. (1981). The constant crisis: social welfare and the American cultural structure. In J.E. Tropman, M.J. Dkuhy and R.M. Lind (eds.), *New Strategic Perspectives on Social Policy*, New York: Pergamon.

Tullock, G. (1965). *The Politics of Bureaucracy*. Washington DC: Public Affairs Press.

Vickers, G. (1965). *The Art of Judgement*. London: Chapman and Hall.

Wagner, R.E. (1976). Revenue structure, fiscal illusion, and budgetary choice, *Public Choice*, 25, 45–61.

Walker, G., and H. Krist (1980). Regional incentives and the investment decision of the firm: a comparative study of Britain and Germany, *Studies in Public Policy*, no. 57. Glasgow: Centre for the Study of Public Policy, University of Strathclyde.

Wanat, J. (1975). Bureaucratic politics in the budget formulation arena, *Administration and Society*, 7, 191–212.

Weidenbaum, M., and R. Defina (1978). *The Cost of Federal Government Regulation of Economic Activity*. Washington DC: American Enterprise Institute.

Weiss, C.H. (1972). *Evaluation Research*. Englewood Cliffs, NJ: Prentice-Hall.

Weiss, C.H. (ed.) (1977). *Using Social Research in Public Policy Making*. Lexington, Mass.: Lexington Books.

Weiss, C.H., and M.J. Bucuvalas (1977). The challenge of social research to decision-making. In C.H. Weiss (ed.), *Using Social Research in Public Policy Making*, Lexington, Mass.: Lexington Books.

White, D. (1979). How polluted are we—and how polluted do we want to be?, *New Society*, 11 Jan. 1979, 63–6.

Wildavsky, A. (1972). The self-evaluating organization, *Public Administration Review*, 32, 509–20.

Wildavsky, A. (1979). *Speaking Truth to Power: The Art and Craft of Policy Analysis*. Boston: Little, Brown. (Published in Britain in 1980 as *The Art and Craft of Policy Analysis*, London: Macmillan.)

Wildavsky, A. (1979a). A budget for all seasons?: why the traditional budget lasts, *Public Administration Review*, 33, 501–9.

Wildavsky, A. (1980). *How to Limit Government Spending*. Berkeley: University of California Press.

Wildavsky, A. (1984). *The Politics of the Budgetary Process*, 4th edn. Boston: Little, Brown.

Wilensky, H.L. (1967). *Organizational Intelligence: Knowledge and Policy in Government and Industry*. New York: Basic Books.

Williams, W. (1983). British policy analysis: some preliminary observations from the United States. In A. Grey and B. Jenkins (eds.), *Policy Analysis and Evaluation in British Government*, London: Royal Institution of Public Administration.

Williamson, O.E. (1967). Hierarchical control and optimal firm size, *Journal of Political Economy*, 75, 123–38.

Wiseman, C. (1978). Selection of major planning issues, *Policy Sciences*, 9, 71–86.

Wolf, C. Jr. (1979). A theory of non-market failure: framework for implementation analysis, *Journal of Law and Economics*, 22, 107–40.

Wolfe, D. (1975). The university's compact with society. In B.L.R. Smith (ed.), *The New Political Economy: The Public Use of the Private Sector*, New York: Halsted and London: Macmillan, 109–48.

Wolman, H. (1981). The determinants of program success and failure, *Journal of Public Policy*, 1, 433–64.

Wolman, H. (1983). Understanding local government responses to fiscal pressure: a cross national analysis, *Journal of Pubic Policy*, 3, 245–64.

Wright, D.S. (1983). *Understanding Intergovernmental Relations*. Monterey, Calif.: Brooks/Cole.

Wright, M. (1980). From planning to control: PESC in the 1970s. In M. Wright (ed.), *Public Spending Decisions: Growth and Restraint in the 1970s*, London: Allen and Unwin.

Zald, M. (1970). *Organizational Change: The Political Economy of the YMCA*. Chicago: University of Chicago Press.

Zuncker, A. (1969). Consequences of the federal system for parliamentary control of the budget in the Federal Republic of Germany. In D. Coombes (ed.), *The Power of the Purse*, London: Allen and Unwin.

Index